ADOBE®
Dreamweaver® CS3
Introductory Concepts and Techniques

Gary B. Shelly
Thomas J. Cashman
Dolores J. Wells
Steven M. Freund

THOMSON
COURSE TECHNOLOGY

COURSE TECHNOLOGY
25 THOMSON PLACE
BOSTON, MA 02210

SHELLY
CASHMAN
SERIES®

Australia • Canada • Denmark • Japan • Mexico • New Zealand • Philippines • Puerto Rico • Singapore
South Africa • Spain • United Kingdom • United States

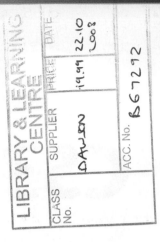
THOMSON

COURSE TECHNOLOGY™

Adobe Dreamweaver CS3:
Introductory Concepts and Techniques

Gary B. Shelly

Thomas J. Cashman

Dolores J. Wells

Steven M. Freund

Executive Editor
Alexandra Arnold

Senior Product Manager
Mali Jones

Associate Product Manager
Klenda Martinez

Editorial Assistant
Jon Farnham

Print Buyer
Julio Esperas

Content Project Manager
Matt Hutchinson

Marketing Manager
Tristan Kendall

Marketing Coordinator
Julie Schuster

QA Manuscript Reviewers
Susan Whalen, Danielle Shaw,
John Freitas

Art Director
Bruce Bond

Cover Design
Joel Sadagursky

Cover Photo
Jon Chomitz

Composition
GEX Publishing Services

Printer
RRD Menasha

ADOBE®

Dreamweaver® CS3

Introductory Concepts and Techniques

Contents

Preface

The Shelly Cashman Series® offers the finest textbooks in computer education. We are proud of the fact that our textbook series has been the most widely used books in education. With each new edition of our Dreamweaver books, we have made significant improvements based on the software and comments made by the instructors, reviewers, and students. *Adobe® Dreamweaver® CS3: Introductory Concepts and Techniques* continues with the innovation, quality, and reliability that you have come to expect from the Shelly Cashman Series.

Adobe Dreamweaver is known as the standard in visual authoring. Adobe Dreamweaver CS3 enhances the work experience for users in the following ways: simplified XML integration; unified CSS panel and new layout visualizer; style rendering toolbar and CSS rendering improvements; and an updated accessibility evaluation tool.

In this *Adobe Dreamweaver CS3* book, you will find an educationally sound and easy-to-follow pedagogy that combines a step-by-step approach with corresponding screens. All projects and exercises in this book are designed to take full advantage of the Dreamweaver CS3 enhancements. The Other Ways and More About features offer in-depth knowledge of Dreamweaver CS3. The popular Q&A feature provides answers to common questions students have about the Web design process. The Learn It Online page presents a wealth of additional exercises to ensure your students have all the reinforcement they need. The project material is developed carefully to ensure that students will see the importance of learning Dreamweaver for future coursework.

Objectives of This Textbook

Adobe Dreamweaver CS3: Introductory Concepts and Techniques is intended for a course that offers an introduction to Dreamweaver CS3 and creation of Web sites. No experience with a computer is assumed, and no mathematics beyond the high school freshman level is required. The objectives of this book are:

- To teach the fundamentals of Dreamweaver CS3
- To expose students to proper Web site design and management techniques
- To acquaint students with the proper procedures to create Web sites suitable for coursework, professional purposes, and personal use
- To develop an exercise-oriented approach that allows learning by doing
- To introduce students to new input technologies
- To encourage independent study and help those who are working alone

The Shelly Cashman Approach

Features of the Shelly Cashman Series *Adobe Dreamweaver CS3* books include:

- **Project Orientation** Each chapter in the book presents a practical problem and complete solution using an easy-to-understand approach.
- **Step-by-Step, Screen-by-Screen Instructions** Each of the tasks required to complete a project is identified throughout the chapter. Full-color screens with callouts accompany the steps.
- **Thoroughly Tested Projects** Unparalleled quality is ensured because every screen in the book is produced by the author only after performing a step, and then each project must pass Thomson Course Technology's Quality Assurance program.
- **Other Ways Boxes and Quick Reference** The Other Ways boxes displayed at the end of many of the step-by-step sequences specify the other ways to do the task completed in the steps. Thus, the steps and the Other Ways box make a comprehensive reference unit. The Quick Reference at the back of the book provides a quick reference to common keyboard shortcuts.
- **More About and Q&A Features** These marginal annotations provide background information, tips, and answers to common questions that complement the topics covered, adding depth and perspective to the learning process.

- **Integration of the World Wide Web** The World Wide Web is integrated into the Dreamweaver CS3 learning experience by (1) More About annotations that send students to Web sites for up-to-date information and alternative approaches to tasks; and (2) the Learn It Online page at the end of each chapter, which has chapter reinforcement exercises, learning games, and other types of student activities.

Organization of This Textbook

Adobe Dreamweaver CS3: Introductory Concepts and Techniques provides detailed instruction on how to use Dreamweaver CS3. The material is divided into an introduction chapter, three chapters that build on a common Web site, three appendices, and a quick reference summary.

End-of-Chapter Student Activities

A notable strength of the Shelly Cashman Series *Adobe Dreamweaver CS3* books is the extensive student activities at the end of each chapter. Well-structured student activities can make the difference between students merely participating in a class and students retaining the information they learn. The activities in the Shelly Cashman Series *Adobe Dreamweaver CS3* books include the following:

- **What You Should Know** A listing of the tasks completed within a chapter together with the pages on which the step-by-step, screen-by-screen explanations appear.
- **Learn It Online** Every chapter features a Learn It Online page comprising ten exercises. These exercises include True/False, Multiple Choice, Short Answer, Flash Cards, Practice Test, Learning Games, Tips and Tricks, Newsgroup usage, Expanding Your Horizons, and Search Sleuth.
- **Apply Your Knowledge** This exercise usually requires students to open and manipulate a file that is provided in the Data Files for Students. To obtain a copy of the Data Files for Students, follow the instructions on the inside back cover of this textbook.
- **In the Lab** Three in-depth assignments per chapter require students to utilize the chapter concepts and techniques to create additional Web sites.
- **Cases and Places** Five unique real-world case-study situations, including one small-group activity.

Shelly Cashman Series Instructor Resources

The Shelly Cashman Series is dedicated to providing you with all of the tools you need to make your class a success. Information on all supplementary materials is available through your Thomson Course Technology representative or by calling one of the following telephone numbers: Colleges, Universities, Continuing Education Departments, and Post-Secondary Vocational Schools: 800-648-7450; Career Colleges, Business, Industry, Government, Trade, Retailer, Wholesaler, Library, and Resellers: 800-477-3692; K-12, Secondary Vocational Schools, Adult Education, and School Districts: 800-824-5179.

The Instructor Resources for this textbook include both teaching and testing aids. The contents of each item on the Instructor Resources CD-ROM (ISBN 1-4239-1243-8) are described below.

INSTRUCTOR'S MANUAL The Instructor's Manual is made up of Microsoft Word files, which include detailed lesson plans with page number references, lecture notes, teaching tips, classroom activities, discussion topics, projects to assign, and transparency references. The transparencies are available through the Figure Files described below.

LECTURE SUCCESS SYSTEM The Lecture Success System consists of intermediate files that correspond to certain figures in the book, allowing you to step through the creation of an application in a chapter during a lecture without entering large amounts of data.

SYLLABUS Sample syllabi, which can be customized easily to a course, are included. The syllabi cover policies, class and lab assignments and exams, and procedural information.

FIGURE FILES Illustrations for every figure in the textbook are available in electronic form. Use this ancillary to present a slide show in lecture or to print transparencies for use in lecture with an overhead projector. If you have a personal computer and LCD device, this ancillary can be an effective tool for presenting lectures.

POWERPOINT PRESENTATIONS PowerPoint Presentations is a multimedia lecture presentation system that provides slides for each chapter. Presentations are based on chapter objectives. Use this presentation system to present well-organized lectures that are both interesting and knowledge based. PowerPoint Presentations provides consistent coverage at schools that use multiple lecturers.

SOLUTIONS TO EXERCISES Solutions are included for the end-of- chapter exercises, as well as the Chapter Reinforcement exercises.

TEST BANK & TEST ENGINE The ExamView test bank includes 110 questions for every chapter (25 multiple-choice, 50 true/false, and 35 completion) with page number references, and when appropriate, figure references. A version of the test bank you can print also is included. The test bank comes with a copy of the test engine, ExamView, the ultimate tool for your objective-based testing needs. ExamView is a state-of-the-art test builder that is easy to use. ExamView enables you to create paper-, LAN-, or Web-based tests from test banks designed specifically for your Course Technology textbook. Utilize the ultra-efficient QuickTest Wizard to create tests in less than five minutes by taking advantage of Course Technology's question banks, or customize your own exams from scratch.

DATA FILES FOR STUDENTS All the files that are required by students to complete the exercises are included. You can distribute the files on the Instructor Resources CD-ROM to your students over a network, or you can have them follow the instructions on the inside back cover of this book to obtain a copy of the Data Files for Students.

ADDITIONAL ACTIVITIES FOR STUDENTS These additional activities consist of Chapter Reinforcement Exercises, which are true/false, multiple choice, and short answer questions that help students gain confidence in the material learned.

Online Content

Blackboard is the leading distance learning solution provider and class-management platform today. Thomson Course Technology has partnered with Blackboard to bring you premium online content. Instructors: Content for use with *Adobe Dreamweaver CS3: Introductory Concepts and Techniques* is available in a Blackboard Course Cartridge and may include topic reviews, case projects, review questions, test banks, practice tests, custom syllabi, and more.

Thomson Course Technology also has solutions for several other learning management systems. Please visit http://www.course.com today to see what's available for this title.

CourseCasts Learning on the Go. Always Available...Always Relevant.

Want to keep up with the latest technology trends relevant to you? Visit our site to find a library of podcasts, CourseCasts, featuring a "CourseCast of the Week," and download them to your portable media player at http://coursecasts.course.com.

Our fast-paced world is driven by technology. You know because you are an active participant — always on the go, always keeping up with technological trends, and always learning new ways to embrace technology to power your life.

Ken Baldauf, a faculty member of the Florida State University (FSU) Computer Science Department, is responsible for teaching technology classes to thousands of FSU students each year. He knows what you know; he knows what you want to learn. He is also an expert in the latest technology and will sort through and aggregate the most pertinent news and information so you can spend your time enjoying technology, rather than trying to figure it out.

Visit us at http://coursecasts.course.com to learn on the go!

CourseNotes

Course Technology's CourseNotes are six-panel quick reference cards that reinforce the most important and widely used features of a software application in a visual and user-friendly format. CourseNotes will serve as a great reference tool during and after the student completes the course.

About Our New Cover Look

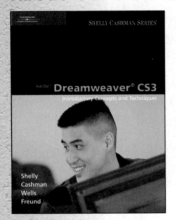

Learning styles of students have changed, but the Shelly Cashman Series' dedication to their success has remained steadfast for over 30 years. We are committed to continually updating our approach and content to reflect the way today's students learn and experience new technology. This focus on the user is reflected in our bold new cover design, which features photographs of real students using the Shelly Cashman Series in their courses. Each book features a different user, reflecting the many ages, experiences, and backgrounds of all of the students learning with our books. When you use the Shelly Cashman Series, you can be assured that you are learning computer skills using the most effective courseware available. We would like to thank the administration and faculty at the participating schools for their help in making our vision a reality. Most of all, we'd like to thank the wonderful students from all over the world who learn from our texts and now appear on our covers.

Adobe Dreamweaver CS3 30-Day Trial Edition

A copy of the Dreamweaver CS3 30-Day trial edition can be downloaded from the Adobe Web site (www. adobe.com). Point to Downloads in the top navigation bar, click Trial Downloads, and then follow the on-screen instructions. When you activate the software, you will receive a license that allows you to use the software for 30 days. Course Technology and Adobe provide no product support for this trial edition. When the trial period ends, you can purchase a copy of Adobe Dreamweaver CS3, or uninstall the trial edition and reinstall your previous version.

The minimum system requirements for the 30-day trial edition is a Intel® Pentium® 4, Intel Centrino®, Intel Xeon®, or Intel Core™ Duo (or compatible) processor; Microsoft® Windows® XP with Service Pack 2 or Windows Vista™ Home Premium, Business, Ultimate, or Enterprise (certified for 32-bit editions); 512 MB RAM; 1024 × 768, 16-bit display (32-bit recommended); and 1 GB available disk space; DVD-ROM drive; Internet or phone connection required for product activation; and Broadband Internet connection required for Adobe Stock Photos and other services.

ADOBE
Dreamweaver CS3

Adobe
DREAMWEAVER CS3

Web Site Development and Adobe Dreamweaver CS3

Objectives

You will have mastered the material in this chapter when you can:

- Describe the significance of the Internet and its associated terms
- Describe the World Wide Web and its associated terms
- Identify the difference between the Internet and the World Wide Web
- Specify the difference between a Web page and a Web site
- Define Web browsers and identify their main features

- Identify the 12 types of Web sites
- Discuss how to plan, design, develop, test, publish, and maintain a Web site
- Identify the various methods and tools used to create a Web page and Web site
- Recognize the basic elements within HTML/XHTML
- Discuss the advantages of using Web page authoring programs such as Dreamweaver

The Internet

The **Internet**, sometimes simply called the **Net**, is a global network connecting millions of computers. Within this network, a user who has permission at any one computer can access and obtain information from any other computer within the network. A **network** is a group of computers and associated devices that are connected by communications facilities. A network can span a global area and involve permanent connections, such as cables, or temporary connections made through telephone or other communications links. Local, regional, national, and international networks constitute a global network. Each of these networks provides communications, services, and access to information.

No one person or organization is responsible for the birth of the Internet. The Internet origin, however, can be traced to the early 1960s when the Advanced Research Projects Agency (ARPA) working under the U.S. Department of Defense began a networking project. The purpose of the project was to create a network that would allow scientists at different locations to share military and scientific information. Today, the Internet is a public, cooperative, and self-sustaining facility that hundreds of millions of people worldwide access.

The World Wide Web and Web Browsers

The **World Wide Web** (**WWW**), also called the **Web**, is one of the more popular services on the Internet. The Web consists of a system of global **network servers**, also known as **Web servers**, that support specially formatted documents and provide a means for sharing these resources with many people at the same time. A network server is known as the **host computer**, and your computer, from which you access the information, is called the **client**. **Hypertext Transfer Protocol** (**HTTP**) enables the transfer of data from the host computer to the client.

Accessing the Web

Users access Web resources, such as text, graphics, sound, video, and multimedia, through a **Web page**. A unique address, or Uniform Resource Locator (URL), identifies every Web page. The URL provides the global address of the location of the Web page. URLs are discussed later in this Introduction. Viewing data contained on a Web page requires a **Web browser,** a software program that requests a Web page, interprets the code contained within the page, and then displays the contents of the Web page on your computer display device.

Web Browsers

Web browsers contain special buttons and other features to help you navigate through Web sites. The more popular Web browser software programs are **Microsoft Internet Explorer, Mozilla Firefox,** and **Netscape Navigator**. This book uses Internet Explorer as the primary browser. When you start Internet Explorer, it opens a Web page that has been set as the start, or home, page (Figure I-1). Using the browser's Tools menu, the user can designate any page on the Web as the home page or start with a blank page. Important features of Internet Explorer are summarized in Table I-1 on the next page.

FIGURE I-1

Table I-1 Internet Explorer Features	
FEATURE	DEFINITION
Title bar	Displays the name of the Web page you are viewing
Search box	Allows Web searches using your favorite search provider
Command bar	Contains buttons, boxes, and menus that allow you to perform tasks quickly
Address bar	Displays the Web site address, or URL, of the Web page you are viewing
Document window	Contains the Web page content
Web page tab	Provides the option to use tabs to switch from one site to another in a single browser window

Nearly all Web pages have unique characteristics, but almost every Web page contains the same basic elements. On most Web pages, you will find headings or titles, text, pictures or images, background enhancements, and hyperlinks. A **hyperlink**, or **link**, can connect to another place in the same Web page or site—or to an entirely different Web page on a server in another city or country. Normally, you click the hyperlink to follow the connected pathway. Figure I-2 contains a variety of link types. Clicking a link causes the Web page associated with the link to be displayed in a browser window. Linked pages can appear in the same browser window or in a separate browser window, depending on the HTML or XHTML code associated with the link. HTML and XHTML are discussed later in this Introduction.

FIGURE I-2

Most Web pages are part of a **Web site,** which is a group of related Web pages that are linked together. Most Web sites contain a home page, which generally is the first Web page visitors see when they enter the site. A **home page** (also called an **index page**) typically provides information about the Web site's purpose and content. Most Web sites also contain additional content and pages. An individual, company, or organization owns and manages each Web site.

Accessing the Web requires a connection through a regional or national Internet service provider (ISP), an online service provider (OSP), or a wireless service provider (WSP). Figure I-3 illustrates ways to access the Internet using these service providers. An **Internet service provider** (**ISP**) provides temporary connections to individuals, companies, or other organizations through its permanent Internet connection. Similar to an ISP, an **online service provider** (**OSP**) provides additional member-only services such as financial data and travel information. America Online and CompuServe are examples of OSPs. A **wireless service provider** (**WSP**) provides Internet access to users with Web-enabled devices or wireless modems. Generally, all of these providers charge a fee for their services.

FIGURE I-3

Types of Web Sites

Web sites are classified as 12 basic types: portal, news, informational, business/ marketing, educational, entertainment, advocacy, blog, wiki, social networks, content aggregator, and personal. A **portal Web site** (Figure I-4a) provides a variety of Internet services from a single, convenient location. Most portals offer free services such as search engines; local, national, and worldwide news; sports; weather; reference tools; maps; stock quotes; newsgroups; chat rooms; and calendars. A **news Web site** (Figure I-4b) contains news articles relating to current events. An **informational Web site** (Figure I-4c) contains factual information, such as research and statistics. Governmental agencies and nonprofit organizations are the primary providers of informational Web pages. A **business/ marketing Web site** (Figure I-4d) contains content that promotes or sells products or services. An **educational Web site** (Figure I-4e) provides exciting, challenging avenues for formal and informal teaching and learning. An **entertainment Web site** (Figure I-4f) offers an interactive and engaging environment and contains music, video, sports, games, and other similar features. Within an **advocacy Web site** (Figure I-4g), you will find content that describes a cause, opinion, question, or idea. A **blog** (Figure I-4h), which is short for Weblog, uses a regularly updated journal format to reflect the interests, opinions, and personality of the author and sometimes of site visitors. A **wiki** is a collaborative Web site that allows users to create, add to, modify, or delete the Web site content via their Web browser. Most wikis are open to modification by the general public (Figure I-4i). A **social network** (Figure I-4j) is an online community that encourages members to share their interests, stories, photos, music, and videos with other members. A **content aggregator** (Figure I-4k) is a business that gathers and organizes Web content and then distributes the content to subscribers free or for a fee. A **personal Web site** (Figure I-4l) is published by an individual or family and generally is not associated with any organization. As you progress through this book, you will have an opportunity to learn more about different types of Web pages.

FIGURE I-4a (portal)

FIGURE I-4b (news)

FIGURE I-4c (informational)

FIGURE I-4

FIGURE I-4d (business/marketing)

FIGURE I-4e (educational)

FIGURE I-4f (entertainment)

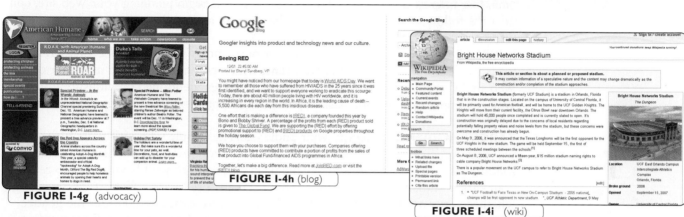

FIGURE I-4g (advocacy)

FIGURE I-4h (blog)

FIGURE I-4i (wiki)

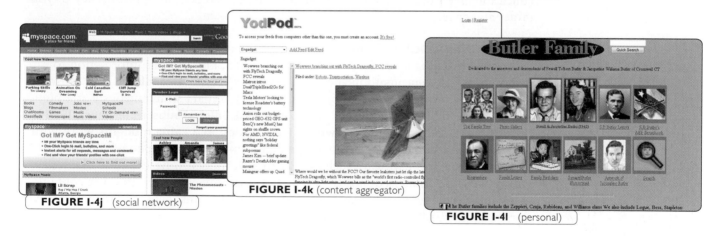

FIGURE I-4j (social network)

FIGURE I-4k (content aggregator)

FIGURE I-4l (personal)

FIGURE I-4 (*continued*)

Planning a Web Site

Thousands of individuals create and publish Web pages every day, some using word-processing software or markup languages, such as XHTML, to create their pages. Others use professional design and management editors such as Dreamweaver. Although publishing a Web page and/or a Web site is easy, advanced planning is paramount in ensuring a successful Web site. Publishing a Web site, which makes it available on the Internet, is discussed later in this Introduction.

Planning Basics — Purpose

Those who rush into the publishing process without proper planning tend to design Web sites that are unorganized and difficult to navigate. Visitors to this type of Web site often lose interest quickly and do not return. As you begin planning your Web site, consider the following guidelines to ensure that you set and attain realistic goals.

PURPOSE AND GOAL Determine the purpose and goal of your Web site. Create a focus by developing a **purpose statement**, which communicates the intention of the Web site. Consider the nine basic types of Web sites mentioned previously. Will your Web site consist of just one basic type or a combination of two or more types?

TARGET AUDIENCE Identify your audience. The people who visit your Web site will determine the success of your site. Although you welcome all visitors, you need to know as much as possible about the primary group of people you wish to reach—your target audience. To learn more about the visitors to your Web site, determine whether you want to attract people with similar interests, and consider the gender, education, age range, income, profession/job field, and computer proficiency of your target audience.

WEB TECHNOLOGIES Evaluate whether your potential visitors have access to high-speed broadband media or to baseband media, and use this information to determine what elements to include within your Web site. **Broadband** can transmit a large number of moving images or a vast quantity of data simultaneously at a high speed. Media and hardware such as **T1 lines**, **DSL (digital subscriber lines)**, **ISDN (Integrated Services Digital Network)**, **fiber optics**, and **cable modems** work with broadband. **Baseband** transmits one signal at a time over a telephone line and includes media and hardware such as 28K to 56K modems. Baseband works well with a Web site composed mostly of text and small images. Web sites that contain many images or multimedia, such as video and animations, generally require that visitors have a broadband connection.

WEB SITE COMPARISON Visit other Web sites that are similar to your proposed site. What do you like about these sites? What do you dislike? Look for inspirational ideas. How can you make your Web site better?

Planning Basics — Content

To ensure a successful Web experience for your visitors, consider the following guidelines to provide appropriate content and other valuable Web page elements.

VALUE-ADDED CONTENT Consider the different types of content you can include within your Web site. Use the following questions as guidelines:

- What topics do you want to cover?
- How much information will you present about each topic?
- What will attract your target audience to your Web site?
- What methods will you use to keep your audience returning to your site?
- What changes will you have to make to keep your site updated?

TEXT Text accounts for the bulk of all content on most Web pages, so be brief and incorporate lists whenever possible. Statistical studies indicate that most people tend to scan the page, picking out individual words and sentences. Use common words and simple language, and check your spelling and grammar. Create your textual content to accomplish your goals effectively by highlighting key words, using bulleted lists, maintaining one idea per paragraph, and including meaningful subheadings.

IMAGES After text, images constitute the next most commonly included content. Ask yourself these questions with respect to your use of images:

- Will you have a common logo and/or theme on all of your Web pages?
- Are these images readily available?
- What images will you have to locate?
- What images will you have to create?
- How many images per page will you have?

COLOR PALETTE The color palette you select for your Web site can enhance or detract from your message or goal. Do not think in terms of your favorite colors. Instead, consider how color can support your goal. Ask yourself the following questions:

- Do your selected colors work well with your goal?
- Are the colors part of the universal 216-color, browser-safe color palette?
- Did you limit the number of colors to a selected few?

MULTIMEDIA Multimedia adds interactivity and action to your Web pages. Animation, audio, and video are types of **multimedia**. If you plan to add multimedia, determine whether the visitor will require plug-ins. A **plug-in** extends the capability of a Web browser. Some of the more commonly used plug-ins are Shockwave Player, Adobe Flash, and Windows Media Player. Most plug-ins are free and can be downloaded from the Web.

Web Site Navigation

Predicting how a visitor will access a Web site or at what point the visitor will enter within the Web site structure is not possible. Visitors can arrive at any page within a Web site by a variety of ways: a hyperlink, a search engine, a directory, typing a Web address directly, and so on. On every page of your Web site, you must provide clear answers to the three basic questions your visitors will ask: Where am I? Where do I go from here? How do I get to the home page? A well-organized Web site provides the answers to these questions. Once the visitor arrives at a Web site, **navigation**, the pathway through your site, must be obvious and intuitive. Individual Web pages cannot be isolated from the rest of the site if you want it to be successful. At all times and on all pages in your site, you must give the visitor a sense of place, of context within the site. Most Web designers use a navigation map to visualize the navigation pathway.

Design Basics — Navigation Map

Q: I want to develop a Web site. What should I do first?

A: Start with and organize your content. Then create your navigation map.

A **navigation map**, or **site map**, outlines the structure of the entire Web site, showing all pages within the site and the connections from one page to the others. The navigation map acts as a road map through the Web site, but does not provide detail of the content of the individual pages. Web site navigation should be consistent from page to page, so your visitors do not have to guess where they are within the site each time they encounter a new page. All pages in the site should contain a link to the home page. Consider the following for site navigation:

STRUCTURE The goal and the type of a Web site often determine the structure selected for a specific Web site. Create a navigation map to serve as a blueprint for your navigational structure. Consider the following navigational structures and determine which one best meets your needs:

- In a **linear structure** (Figure I-5a) the user navigates sequentially, moving from one page to the next. Information that flows as a narrative, as a time-line, or in logical order is ideal for sequential treatment. Simple sequential organization, however, usually works only for smaller sites. Many online tutorials use a linear structure.

- A **hierarchical structure** (Figure I-5b) is one of the better ways to organize complex bodies of information efficiently. Because many visitors are familiar with hierarchical charts, many Web sites employ this structure. Be aware that effective hierarchical structures require thorough organization of the content.

- A **Web structure** (Figure I-5c), which also is called a **random structure**, places few restrictions on organizational patterns. This type of structure is associated with the free flow of ideas and can be confusing to a user. A random structure is better suited for experienced users looking for further educa-tion or enrichment and is not recommended if your goal is to provide a basic understanding of a particular topic. If a Web site is relatively small, however, a random structure could work well.

- Use a **grid structure** if your Web site consists of a number of topics of equal importance (Figure I-5d). Procedural manuals, events, and item lists work well in a grid structure.

- Large Web sites frequently use a **hybrid structure**, a combination of the pre-vious listed structures, to organize information (Figure I-6).

(a) Linear Structure

(b) Hierarchical Structure

(c) Web Structure

(d) Grid Structure

FIGURE I-5

FIGURE I-6

TOOLS Determine the tool necessary to create the navigation map. For small Web sites, consider using the organizational chart included in the Microsoft PowerPoint application, as shown in Figure I-7 on the next page. For larger, more diverse Web sites, you can chart and organize your content using Visio Professional, Flow Charting PDQ, FlowCharter Professional, and SmartDraw. Dreamweaver also provides a site map feature. An ideal tool for laying out and evaluating a site structure, the Dreamweaver site map shows the site structure two levels deep, starting from the home page.

FIGURE I-7

NAVIGATION ELEMENTS The more common types of navigation elements include text, buttons, other images, image maps, a site index, a menu, a search feature, navigation bars, and frames. Depending on the complexity of your Web site, you may want to include some or all of these elements.

Developing a Web Site

Once you have established a structure for your Web site, you can begin developing the site. Make text and images the main focus because they are the more common elements. Then consider page layout and color.

Development Basics — Typography, Images, Page Layout, and Color

Typography, images, page layout, and color are the key design elements that will make up your finished Web site. Correct use of these elements plays an important part in the development process. Consider the following guidelines:

TYPOGRAPHY As in all media, good **typography**, the appearance and arrangement of the characters that make up your text, is vital to the success of your Web page. A **font** consists of all the characters available in a particular style and weight for a specific design. Text should always be easy to read, whether in a book, magazine, Web page, or billboard. Keep readability in mind as you select fonts, especially when you consider that some of your visitors may only be viewing them on screen.

When selecting a font, determine its purpose on your Web page. Is it to be used for a title? For on-screen reading? Is it likely to be printed? Will the font fit in with the theme of the Web site? Is it a Web-safe font, such as Times New Roman, Courier, or Arial? **Web-safe fonts** are the more popular fonts and the ones that most visitors are likely to have installed on their computers. Also, while visitors to your Web page may never consciously notice the design of the text characters, or the **typeface**, it often subconsciously affects their reaction to the page.

IMAGES Images can enhance almost any Web page if used appropriately. Without the visual impact of shape, color, and contrast, Web pages can be visually uninteresting and will not motivate the visitor to investigate their contents. Consider the balance between the number of images and page performance as you develop your site. When adding images, consider your potential audience and the technology they have available. Remember that a background image or a graphical menu increases visitor download time. You may lose visitors who do not have broadband access if your Web page contains an excessive number of graphical items.

PAGE LAYOUT The importance of proper page layout cannot be overemphasized. A suitable design draws visitors to your Web site. Although no single design system is appropriate for all Web pages, establish a consistent, logical layout that allows you to add text and images easily. The Web page layouts shown in Figure I-8 on the next page illustrate two different layouts. The layout on the left (Figure I-8a on the next page) shows a plain page with a heading and text. The page layout on the right (Figure I-8b on the next page) presents strong visual contrast by using a variety of layout elements.

Maintaining consistency and updating changes throughout a site are two of the biggest challenges faced by Web designers. A **template,** a special type of document, can help with these challenges. Dreamweaver provides several page layout templates that can be modified easily. In laying out your Web pages, consider the following guidelines to ensure that visitors have the best viewing experience:

- Include only one topic per page.
- Control the vertical and horizontal size of the page.
- Start text on the left to accommodate the majority of individuals who read from left to right.
- Use concise statements and bulleted points to get your point across; studies indicate most people scan the text.

COLOR When creating a Web page, use color to add interest and vitality to your site. Include color in tables, as backgrounds, and with fonts. Use the right combination of colors to decorate the layout and tie the Web site pages together.

Q&A

Q: Many pages on the Web contain multiple elements and appear very "busy." Is this a good practice?

A: Not necessarily. Simple pages download faster and make an immediate impression on the reader.

(a)   (b)

FIGURE I-8

Reviewing and Testing a Web Site

Some Web site developers argue that reviewing and testing should take place throughout the developmental process. While this may be true, it also is important to review and test the final product. This ongoing process ensures that you identify and correct any problems before publishing to the Web. When reviewing and testing your Web site, ask the following questions:

- Is the Web site free of spelling and/or grammatical errors?
- Is the page layout consistent, and does it generate a sense of balance and order?
- Are any links broken?
- Do multimedia interactivity and forms function correctly?
- Do the more widely used browsers display the Web site properly?
- Does the Web site function properly in different browsers, including older browser versions?
- Have you initiated a **group test**, in which you have asked other individuals to test your Web site and provide feedback?

Publishing a Web Site

After your Web site has been tested thoroughly, it can be published. **Publishing** a Web site, making it available to your visitors, involves the actual uploading of the Web site to a server. After you complete the uploading process, all pages within the Web site should be tested again.

Publishing Basics — Domain Name, Server Space, and Uploading

With your Web site thoroughly tested and any problems corrected, you must make the site available to your audience by obtaining a domain name, acquiring server space, and uploading the site. Consider the following to ensure site availability:

OBTAIN A DOMAIN NAME To allow visitors to access your Web site, you must obtain a domain name. Visitors access Web sites by an IP address or a domain name. An **IP address** (**Internet Protocol address**) is a number that uniquely identifies each computer or device connected to the Internet. A **domain name** is the text version of an IP address. The **Domain Name System** (**DNS**), an Internet service, translates domain names into their corresponding IP addresses. The **Uniform Resource Locator** (**URL**), also called a **Web address**, tells the browser on which server the Web page is located. A URL consists of a communications standard, such as **Hypertext Transfer Protocol** (**HTTP**), the domain name, and sometimes the path to a specific Web page (Figure I-9 on the next page).

Domain names are unique and must be registered. The **Accredited Registrar Directory** provides a listing of **Internet Corporation for Assigned Names and Numbers** (**ICANN**) accredited domain name registrars. Your most difficult task likely will be to find a name that is not already registered. You can locate a name by using a specialized search engine at one of the many accredited domain name registrars listed on the ICANN Web site (icann.org/registrars/accredited-list.html). In addition to registering your business name as a domain name, you may want to register the names of your products, services, and/or other related names. Expect to pay approximately $10 to $35 per year for a domain name.

Consider the following guidelines when selecting a domain name:

- Select a name that is easy to pronounce, spell, and remember.
- Select a name that relates to the Web site content and suggests the nature of your product or service.
- If the Web site is a business, use the business name whenever possible.
- Select a name that is free and clear of trademark issues.
- Purchase variations and the .org and .net versions of your domain name.
- Some ISPs will obtain a domain name for you if you use their service to host your Web site.

ACQUIRE SERVER SPACE Locate an ISP that will host your Web site. Recall that an ISP is a business that has a permanent Internet connection. ISPs offer temporary connections to individuals and companies free or for a fee.

If you select an ISP that provides free server space, most likely your visitors will be subjected to advertisements and pop-up windows. Other options to explore for free or inexpensive server space include the provider from which you obtain your Internet connection; online communities, such as Yahoo! GeoCities (geocities.yahoo.com), Tripod (tripod.lycos.com), and MSN Web Communities (communities.msn.com); and your educational institution's Web server. An **online community** is a group whose members are connected by means of information technologies, typically the Internet.

More About

Domain Name Selection

When selecting a domain name, keep it simple. If possible, avoid hyphens. To learn more about domain name selection, visit the Dreamweaver CS3 More About Web page (scsite.com/dwcs3/more.htm) and then click Domain Name Selection.

FIGURE I-9

If the purpose of your Web site is to sell a product or service or to promote a professional organization, you should consider a fee-based ISP. Use a search engine such as Google (google.com) and search for Web site hosting, or visit the WebSite Hosting Directory (www.websitehostdirectory.com), where you will find thousands of Web hosting plans, as well as reviews and ratings of Web hosting providers. Selecting a reliable provider requires investigation on your part. Many providers offer multiple hosting plans. When selecting an ISP, consider the following questions and how they apply to your particular situation and Web site:

1. What is the monthly fee? Is a discount available for a year-long subscription? Are setup fees charged?

2. How much server space is provided for the monthly fee? Can you purchase additional space? If so, how much does it cost?

3. What is the average server uptime on a monthly basis? What is the average server downtime?

4. What are the server specifications? Can the server handle many users? Does it have battery backup power?

5. Are **server logs**, which keep track of the number of accesses, available?

6. What is the ISP's form of connectivity — that is, how does it connect to the Internet: OC3, T1, T3, or some other way?

7. Is a money-back guarantee offered?

8. What technical support does the ISP provide, and when is it available? Does it have an online knowledge base?

9. Does the server on which the Web site will reside have CGI capabilities and Active Server Page (ASP) support?

10. Does the server on which the Web site will reside support e-commerce, multi-media, and **Secure Sockets Layer (SSL)** for encrypting confidential data such as credit card numbers? Are additional fees required for these capabilities?

11. Does the ISP support Dreamweaver and/or other Web site development software programs?

12. Are mailboxes included in the package? If so, how many?

PUBLISH THE WEB SITE You must publish, or upload, the files from your computer to a server where your Web site will then be accessible to anyone on the Internet. Publishing, or **uploading**, is the process of transmitting all the files that make up your Web site from your computer to the selected server or host computer. The files that make up your Web site can include Web pages, PDF documents, images, audio, video, animation, and others.

A variety of tools and methods exist to manage the upload task. Some of the more popular of these are FTP programs, Windows Web Publishing Wizard, Web Folders, and Web authoring programs such as Dreamweaver. These tools allow you to link to a remote server, enter a password, and then upload your files. Dreamweaver contains a built-in function similar to independent FTP programs. The Dreamweaver FTP function to upload your Web site is covered in Chapter 3 and in Appendix C.

Maintaining a Web Site

Most Web sites require maintenance and updating. Some types of ongoing Web maintenance include the following:

- Changing content, either by adding new text and images or by deleting obsolete material
- Checking for broken links and adding new links
- Documenting the last change date (even when no revisions have been made)

Use the information from the server logs provided by your ISP to determine what needs to be updated or changed. Statistics contained within these logs generally include the number of visitors trying to access your site at one time, what resources they request, how long they stay at the site, at what point they enter the site, what pages they view, and what errors they encounter. Learning to use and apply the information contained within the server log will help you to make your Web site successful.

After you make updates and/or changes to the site, notify your viewers with a What's New announcement.

Methods and Tools Used to Create Web Pages

Web developers have several options for creating Web pages: a text editor, an HTML or XHTML editor, software applications, or a WYSIWYG text editor (discussed in detail on page DW 20). Microsoft Notepad and WordPad are examples of a **text editor**. These simple, easy-to-use programs allow the user to enter, edit, save, and print text. An **HTML** or **XHTML editor** is a more sophisticated version of a text editor. In addition to basic text-editing functions, these programs include more advanced features such as syntax highlighting, color coding, and spell-checking. Software applications such as Microsoft Word, Excel, and Publisher provide a Save as Web Page command on the Office Button or File menu. This feature converts the application document into a file Web browsers are able to display. Examples of a WYSIWYG text editor are programs such as Microsoft FrontPage, Expression Web, and Adobe Dreamweaver. These programs provide an integrated text editor with a graphical user interface that allows the user to view both the code and the document as you create it.

A Web developer can use any of these options to create Web pages. Regardless of the option selected, however, it still is important to understand the specifics of HTML and XHTML.

Web Site Languages

Web pages are written in plain text and saved in the **American Standard Code for Information Interchange**, or **ASCII** (pronounced ASK-ee), format — the most widely used coding system to represent data. Using the ASCII format makes Web pages universally readable by different Web browsers regardless of the computer platform on which they reside.

The language of the Web is not static; it evolves just like most other languages. HTML (Hypertext Markup Language) has been the primary language of the Web and most likely will continue to be so for at least the near future. HTML is useful for creating headings, paragraphs, lists, and so on, but is limited to these general types of formatting. XHTML is a rewritten version of HTML using XML (Extensible Markup Language).

Unlike HTML, **Extensible Hypertext Markup Language** (**XHTML**) is an authoring language that defines the structure and layout of a document so that it displays as a Web page and is compatible with Web browsers such as Microsoft Internet Explorer, Mozilla Firefox, or Netscape Navigator. Browser rules for interpreting HTML are flexible. XHTML, however, requires Web designers to adhere strictly to its markup language rules.

Two components constitute a Web page: source code and document content. The **source code**, which contains elements, acts as the program instructions. The **elements** within the source code control the appearance of the document content. Browsers display the **document content,** or the text and images. The browser interprets the elements contained within the code, and the code instructs the browser how to display the Web page. For instance, if you define a line of text on your Web page as a heading, the browser knows to display this line formatted as a heading.

All XHTML element formats and HTML tags start with a left angle bracket (< or less than symbol), are followed by the name of the element, and end with a right angle bracket (> or greater than symbol). Most elements have a start and an end element and are called **two-sided elements**. End elements are the same as start elements except they are preceded by a forward slash (/). Some XHTML elements, such as the one used to indicate a line break <br />, do not have an end element. Instead, the right angle bracket is preceded by a space and forward slash. These are known as **one-sided elements**, or **self-closing elements**. In some browsers, the end element can be omitted from certain elements, such as the end element for a new paragraph, </p>. Unlike HTML, however, XHTML standards require you to include both the start and end elements for all two-sided elements.

Some elements can contain an **attribute**, or **property**, which is additional information placed within the angle brackets. Attributes are not repeated or contained in the end element. Some attributes are used individually, while other attributes can include a value modifier. A **value modifier** specifies conditions within the element, and should always be enclosed in double quotation marks. For example, you can use a value modifier to specify the font type or size or the placement of text on the page. To create and display a centered heading, for instance, you would use the following code:

```
<h1 style="text-align:center">This is the largest header element and the text will be
centered</h1>
```

In this example, h1 is the XHTML element, align is the attribute, and center is the value modifier. Notice that the attribute does not appear as part of the end element, </h1>.

You can use the Dreamweaver Code window and Microsoft Notepad or Word-Pad (text editors) to create XHTML documents. Place each element in a pair around the text or section that you want to define (**mark up**) with that element. Use lower-case characters when typing XHTML elements.

XHTML elements also format the hyperlinks that connect information on the World Wide Web. While XHTML elements number in the hundreds, some are used more than others. All documents, however, require four basic elements. Figure I-10 illustrates the basic elements required for all XHTML documents. Table I-2 on the next page summarizes the more commonly used XHTML elements.

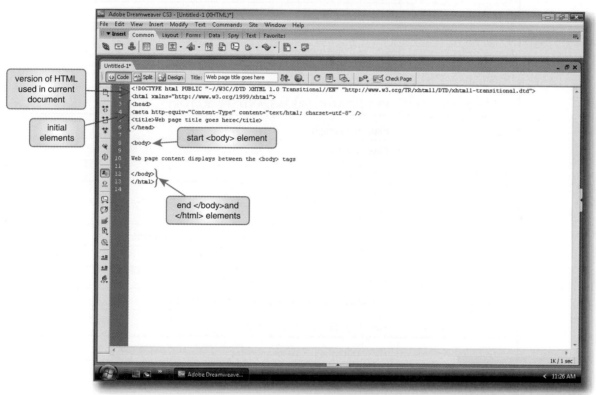

FIGURE I-10

Table I-2 Commonly Used XHTML Elements

ELEMENT (TAGS)	STRUCTURE
\<html>...\</html>	Encloses the entire XHTML document
\<head>...\</head>	Encloses the head of the XHTML document
\<body>...\</body>	Encloses the body of the XHTML document

ELEMENT (TAGS)	TITLE AND HEADINGS
\<title>...\</title>	Indicates the title of the document
\<h1>...\</h1>	Heading level 1
\<h2>...\</h2>	Heading level 2
\<h3>...\</h3>	Heading level 3
\<h4>...\</h4>	Heading level 4
\<h5>...\</h5>	Heading level 5
\<h6>...\</h6>	Heading level 6

ELEMENT (TAGS)	PARAGRAPHS, BREAKS, AND SEPARATORS
\<p>...\</p>	Plain paragraph
\ 	Line break
\<hr />	Horizontal rule line
\<ol>...\</ol>	Ordered, numbered list
\<ul>...\</ul>	Unordered, bulleted list
\<li>...\</li>	List item, used with \<ol>, \<ul>, \<menu>, and \<dir>
\<dl>...\</dl>	Definition of glossary list
\<dt>...\</dt>	Definition term; part of a definition list
\<dd>...\</dd>	Definition corresponding to a definition term

ELEMENT (TAGS)	CHARACTER FORMATTING
\...\	Bold text
\<u>...\</u>	Underlined text
\<i>...\</i>	Italic text

ELEMENT (TAGS)	LINKS
\<a>...\</a>	Combined with the href attribute, creates a link to another document or anchor
\<a>...\</a>	Combined with the name attribute, creates an anchor to which elements can be linked

ELEMENT (TAGS)	IMAGE
\<img />	Inserts an image into the document

Web Page Authoring Programs

Many of today's Web page authoring programs, including Dreamweaver, are What You See Is What You Get (WYSIWYG) text editors. As mentioned earlier, a **WYSIWYG text editor** allows a user to view a document as it will appear in the final product and to edit the text, images, or other elements directly within that view. Before programs such as Dreamweaver existed, Web page designers were required to type, or hand-code, Web pages. Educators and Web designers still debate the issue surrounding the necessity of knowing HTML and XHTML. Technically, you do not need to know either HTML or XHTML to create Web pages in Dreamweaver; however, an understanding of HTML and XHTML will help you if you need to alter Dreamweaver-generated code. If you know HTML and XHTML, then you can make changes to the code and Dreamweaver will accept the changes.

Adobe Dreamweaver CS3

The standard in visual authoring, Adobe Dreamweaver CS3 is part of the Adobe Creative Suite 3, which includes Adobe Flash, ColdFusion, and Fireworks. Dreamweaver provides features that access these separate products. Some of the new features of Dreamweaver CS3 include the following:

- A drag-and-drop workflow
- Visual Cascading Style Sheets (CSS) tools, layouts, and support
- Integration with Adobe PhotoShop CS3 and Adobe Contribute CS3
- New Adobe Device Central CS3 for creating mobile device content
- Increased support for cross-platform development
- Enhanced coding and editing for coding and style rendering
- Extended XML integration using either XSL or the Spry framework for Ajax
- Added support for Flash video

Dreamweaver makes it easy to get started and provides you with helpful tools to enhance your Web design and development experience. Working in a single environment, you create, build, and manage Web sites and Internet applications. In Dreamweaver, you can customize the workspace environment to fit your particular needs.

Dreamweaver contains coding tools and features that include references for HTML, XHTML, XML, CSS, and JavaScript as well as code editors that allow you to edit the code directly. Using **Adobe Roundtrip technology**, Dreamweaver can import Microsoft Office or other software Web pages and delete the unused code. Downloadable extensions from the Adobe Web site make it easy to add functionality to any Web site. Examples of these extensions include shopping carts and online payment features.

Instead of writing individual files for every page, you can use a database to store content and then retrieve the content dynamically in response to a user's request. Implementing and using this feature, you can update the information once, in one place, instead of manually editing many pages. Another key feature is **Cascading Style Sheets styles** (**CSS styles**). CSS styles are collections of formatting definitions that affect the appearance of Web page elements. You can use CSS styles to format text, images, headings, tables, and so forth. Implementing and applying this feature, you can update the formatting one time across many Web pages.

Dreamweaver provides the tools that help you author accessible content. These accessible pages comply with government guidelines and Section 508 of the Federal Rehabilitation Act. Accessibility is discussed in more detail as you progress through the book.

Dreamweaver allows you to publish Web sites with relative ease to a local area network, which connects computers in a limited geographical area, or to the Web, so that anyone with Internet access can see them. The concepts and techniques presented in this book provide the tools you need to plan, develop, and publish professional Web sites, such as those shown in Figures I-11 and I-12.

FIGURE I-11

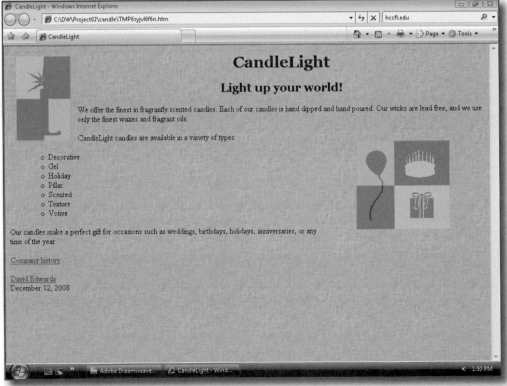

FIGURE I-12

Summary

The Introduction to Web Site Development and Adobe Dreamweaver CS3 provided an overview of the Internet and the World Wide Web and the key terms associated with those technologies. An overview of the 12 basic types of Web pages also was presented. The Introduction furnished information on developing a Web site, including planning basics. The process of designing a Web site and each phase within this process were discussed. Information about testing, publishing, and maintaining a Web site also was presented, including an overview of obtaining a domain name, acquiring server space, and uploading a Web site. Methods and tools used to create Web pages were introduced. A short overview of HTML and XHTML and some of the more commonly used HTML tags and XHTML elements were presented. Finally, the advantages of using Dreamweaver in Web development were discussed. These advantages include a WYSIWYG text editor; a visual, customizable development environment; accessibility compliance; downloadable extensions; database access capabilities; and Cascading Style Sheets.

Learn It Online

For an updated list of links, visit the Dreamweaver companion site at http://scsite.com/dwcs3.

Instructions: To complete the Learn It Online exercises, start your browser, click the Address bar, and then enter the Web address `scsite.com/dwcs3/learn`. When the Dreamweaver CS3 Learn It Online page is displayed, follow the instructions in the exercises below. Each exercise has instructions for printing your results, either for your own records or for submission to your instructor.

1 Chapter Reinforcement TF, MC, and SA

Below Dreamweaver Introduction Chapter, click the Chapter Reinforcement link. Print the quiz by clicking Print on the File menu for each page. Answer each question.

2 Flash Cards

Below Dreamweaver Introduction Chapter, click the Flash Cards link and read the instructions. Type 20 (or a number specified by your instructor) in the Number of playing cards text box, type your name in the Enter your Name text box, and then click the Flip Card button. When the flash card is displayed, read the question and then click the ANSWER box arrow to select an answer. Flip through Flash Cards. If your score is 15 (75%) correct or greater, click Print on the File menu to print your results. If your score is less than 15 (75%) correct, then redo this exercise by clicking the Replay button.

3 Practice Test

Below Dreamweaver Introduction Chapter, click the Practice Test link. Answer each question, enter your first and last name at the bottom of the page, and then click the Grade Test button. When the graded practice test is displayed on your screen, click Print on the File menu to print a hard copy. Continue to take practice tests until you score 80% or better.

4 Who Wants To Be a Computer Genius?

Below Dreamweaver Introduction Chapter, click the Computer Genius link. Read the instructions, enter your first and last name at the bottom of the page, and then click the PLAY button. When your score is displayed, click the PRINT RESULTS link to print a hard copy.

5 Wheel of Terms

Below Dreamweaver Introduction Chapter, click the Wheel of Terms link. Read the instructions, and then enter your first and last name and your school name. Click the PLAY button. When your score is displayed, right-click the score and then click Print on the shortcut menu to print a hard copy.

6 Crossword Puzzle Challenge

Below Dreamweaver Introduction Chapter, click the Crossword Puzzle Challenge link. Read the instructions, and then enter your first and last name. Click the SUBMIT button. Work the crossword puzzle. When you are finished, click the Submit button. When the crossword puzzle is redisplayed, click the Print Puzzle button to print a hard copy.

7 Tips and Tricks

Below Dreamweaver Introduction Chapter, click the Tips and Tricks link. Click a topic that pertains to the Introduction Chapter. Right-click the information and then click Print on the shortcut menu. Construct a brief example of what the information relates to in Dreamweaver to confirm you understand how to use the tip or trick.

8 Newsgroups

Below Dreamweaver Introduction Chapter, click the Newsgroups link. Click a topic that pertains to the Introduction Chapter. Print three comments.

9 Expanding Your Horizons

Below Dreamweaver Introduction Chapter, click the Expanding Your Horizons link. Click a topic that pertains to the Introduction Chapter. Print the information. Construct a brief example of what the information relates to in Dreamweaver to confirm you understand the contents of the article.

10 Search Sleuth

Below Dreamweaver Introduction Chapter, click the Search Sleuth link. To search for a term that pertains to this chapter, select a term below the Introduction Chapter title and then use the Google search engine at google.com (or any major search engine) to display and print two Web pages that present information on the term.

Apply Your Knowledge

1 Web Site Creation

Instructions: As discussed in this Introduction, creating a Web site involves planning, designing, developing, reviewing and testing, publishing, and maintaining the site. Open the Apply I-1 Web Site Creation file in your Dreamweaver data files. See the inside back cover of this book for instructions for downloading the data files or see your instructor for information on accessing the files required for this book. As shown in Table I-3, the Apply I-1 Web Site Creation file contains information about the Web site creation process. Use the information contained in this table to develop a plan for creating a Web site.

Table I-3 Creating a Web Site	
PLANNING	
Web site name	What is your Web site name?
Web site type	What is the Web site type: portal, news, informational, business/marketing, educational, entertainment, advocacy, blog, wiki, social network, content aggregator, or personal?
Web site purpose	What is the purpose of your Web site?
Target audience	How can you identify your target audience?
Web technologies to be used	Will you design for broadband or baseband? Explain your selection.
Content	What topics will you cover? How much information will you present on each topic? How will you attract your audience? What will you do to entice your audience to return to your Web site? How will you keep the Web site updated?
Text, images, and multimedia	Will your site contain text only? What type of images will you include? Where will you obtain your images? Will you have a common logo? Will plug-ins be required?
DESIGNING	
Navigation map	What type of structure will you use? What tools will you use to design your navigation map?
Navigational elements	What navigational elements will you include?
DEVELOPING	
Typography	What font will you use? How many different fonts will you use on your site?
Images	How will you use images to enhance your site? Will you use a background image?
Page layout	What type of layout will you use? How many topics per page? How will text be presented: bulleted or paragraph style? Will the audience need to scroll the page?
Color	What color combinations will you use for your site? To what elements will you apply the color(s) — fonts, background, tables, other elements?

(continued)

Web Site Creation *(continued)*

Table I-3 Creating a Web Site *(continued)*	
REVIEWING AND TESTING	
Review	What elements will you review? Will you use a group review?
Testing	What elements will you test? Will you use self-testing? Will you use group testing?
PUBLISHING	
Domain name	What is your domain name? Have you registered your domain name? What ISP will host your Web site? What criteria did you use to select the ISP?
MAINTAINING	
Ongoing maintenance	How often will you update your Web site? What elements will you update? Will you add additional features? Does your ISP provide server logs? Will you use the server logs for maintenance purposes?

Perform the following steps using your word-processing program and browser.

1. With the Apply I-1 Web Site Creation file open in your word-processing program, select a name for your Web site.
2. Use a specialized search engine at one of the many accredited domain name registrars to verify that your selected Web site name is available.
3. Answer each question in the table. Use complete sentences to answer the questions. Type your answers in column 3.
4. Save the document with the file name Apply I-1 My Web Site Creation.doc or Apply I-1 My Web Site Creation.docx. Submit the document in the format specified by your instructor.

In the Lab

1 Using Internet Explorer

Problem: Microsoft Internet Explorer (IE) has many new features that can make your work on the Internet more efficient. Using the Media feature, for example, you can play music, video, or multimedia files; listen to your favorite Internet radio station; and enhance your browsing experience. You can customize the image toolbar that displays when you point to an image on a Web page. IE also includes other enhancements. Visit the Microsoft Internet Explorer: The Features Web page (Figure I-13) and select three articles concerning topics with which you are not familiar. Read the articles and then create a word-processing document detailing what you learned.

FIGURE I-13

Instructions: Perform the following tasks:

1. Start your browser. Open the Microsoft Internet Explorer: The Features Web page (microsoft.com/windows/products/winfamily/ie/features.mspx).
2. Scroll down the page.
3. Select three of the bulleted items that contain information with which you are not familiar.
4. Click the link for each article and read the article.
5. Start your word-processing program.
6. List three important points that you learned from this Web site.
7. Write a summary of what you learned from each article. Include within your summary your opinion of the article and if you will apply what you learned or use it with your Web browser.

(continued)

In the Lab

Using Internet Explorer *(continued)*

8. Save the document with the file name Lab I-1 IE features.doc or Lab I-1 IE features.docx. Submit the document in the format specified by your instructor.

2 Types of Web Pages

Problem: A Web designer should be familiar with different types of Web pages and the sort of information displayed on these types of Web pages. The Introduction describes 12 types of Web pages. Search the Internet and locate at least one example of each type of Web page.

Instructions: Perform the following tasks:

1. Start your browser. Open the Google (googlc.com) search engine Web page (Figure I-14) and search for an example of each of the following types of Web pages: portal, news, informational, business/marketing, educational, entertainment, advocacy, blog, wiki, social networks, content aggregator, and personal.

FIGURE I-14

2. Start your word-processing program.
3. Copy and paste the link for each of these Web page types into your word-processing document.
4. Identify the type of Web page for each link.
5. Explain why you selected this Web page and how it fits the definition of the specific type.

6. Save the document with the file name Lab I-2 Web Page types.doc or Lab I-2 Web Page types.docx. Print a copy of the document if instructed to do so.

7. Submit the document in the format specified by your instructor.

3 Web Site Hosting

Problem: Selecting the correct host or ISP for your Web site can be a confusing process. Many Web sites offer this service, but determining the best one for your particular needs can be somewhat complicated. Assume your Web site will sell a product. Compare several ISPs and select the one that will best meet your needs.

Instructions: Perform the following tasks:

1. Review the information and questions on pages DW 16–17 discussing the guidelines for acquiring active server space to host your Web site.

2. Start your browser. Open the Web Site Hosting Directory Web page shown in Figure I-15 (www.websitehostdirectory.com).

FIGURE I-15

3. Click the eCommerce Hosting link.

(continued)

Web Site Hosting *(continued)*

4. Click one of the host server links and review the information relating to the services offered by your selected ISP.
5. Start your word-processing program.
6. Read and answer the questions on pages DW 16–17. Use the information provided in the list of services offered by your selected ISP.
7. Write a short summary explaining why you would or would not select this ISP to host your Web site.
8. Save the document with the file name Lab I-3 Web Site Hosting.doc or Lab I-3 Web Site Hosting.docx. Submit the document in the format specified by your instructor.

Cases and Places

The difficulty of these case studies varies:
■ are the least difficult and ■■ are more difficult. The last exercise is a group exercise.

1 ■ Use a search engine such as Google (google.com) and research information about planning a Web site. Use your word-processing program and write a two-page summary of what you learned. Save the document as caseI-1.doc or caseI-1.docx. Submit the document in the format specified by your instructor.

2 ■ Your goal is to create a personal Web site navigation map that contains three pages — the home page, a page about your favorite hobbies, and a page about places you like to visit. On a piece of paper, draw a navigation map for your proposed Web site. Write a sentence or two describing the type of structure you used and why you selected that structure. Save the document as caseI-2.doc or caseI-2.docx. Submit the document in the format specified by your instructor.

3 ■■ Plug-ins are used on many Web sites. Start your browser and search the Web for plug-ins. Prepare a list of the plug-ins you found. Create a summary statement describing how and why you could use each plug-in in a Web site. Include the link where you can download each of the plug-ins. Save the document as caseI-3.doc or caseI-3.docx. Submit the document in the format specified by your instructor.

4 ■■ Typography within a Web page is one of its more important elements. Start your browser and search for examples of Web sites that include what you consider appropriate typography and Web sites with inappropriate typography. Write a short summary of why you consider these to be appropriate and inappropriate. Copy and paste the Web site addresses into your document. Save the document as caseI-4.doc or caseI-4.docx. Submit the document in the format specified by your instructor.

5 ■■ **Working Together** Each team member is to search the Internet for Web sites illustrating each of the Web site structures on pages DW 6–7. Each team member will then use word-processing software to write a minimum of 100 words describing the Web sites and explaining why he or she thinks the structure used is appropriate or inappropriate for that particular Web site. Save the document as caseI-5.doc or caseI-5.docx. Submit the document in the format specified by your instructor.

Creating a Dreamweaver Web Page and Local Site

CHAPTER

CASE PERSPECTIVE

Colorado native David Edwards worked with you last summer at a state environmental agency. Your job at the agency included Internet communications. Because you both love the outdoors, particularly Colorado's national parks and monuments, you became good friends. David visits several parks every year. During each visit, he discovers something new and exciting. David wants to share his knowledge and to provide a way to make Colorado residents and visitors aware of the uniqueness, beauty, and wildlife of the parks.

David knows the far-reaching capabilities of the Internet. He wants to use the Web to communicate to the public about Colorado's parks, but he has limited knowledge about Web design and development. David knows that your interest and experience with the Internet could assist him in this endeavor, and he asks for your help. You like the idea and tell him that you can create a Web site using Dreamweaver. You get together to define the Web site and to plan the index page. When you are finished creating the Colorado National Parks and Monuments Web page, you will show it to David for his feedback.

As you read through this chapter, you will learn how to use Dreamweaver CS3 to define a local site, create a Web page, and display the Web page in a browser.

Creating a Dreamweaver Web Page and Local Site

CHAPTER

Objectives

You will have mastered the material in this chapter when you can:

- Describe Dreamweaver and identify its key features
- Start Dreamweaver
- Describe the Dreamweaver window and workspace
- Define a local site
- Create and save a Web page
- Add a background image
- Open and close panels
- Display and describe the Property inspector
- Format and modify text elements on a Web page

- Define and insert a line break
- Change a Web page title
- Check spelling
- Preview a Web page in a Web browser
- Print a Web page
- Define Dreamweaver Help
- Quit Dreamweaver
- Open a new Web page

What Is Adobe Dreamweaver CS3?

Adobe Dreamweaver CS3 is a powerful Web page authoring and Web site management software program with an HTML editor that is used to design, code, and create professional-looking Web pages, Web sites, and Web applications. The visual-editing features of Dreamweaver allow you to create pages without writing a line of code. Dreamweaver provides many tools and features, including the following:

- **Automatic Web Page Creation** — Dreamweaver provides tools you can use to develop Web pages without having to spend hours writing HTML code. Dreamweaver automatically generates the HTML code necessary to publish your Web pages.

- **Web Site Management** — Dreamweaver enables you to view a site, including all local and remote files associated with the selected site. You can perform standard maintenance operations such as viewing, opening, and moving files; transferring files between local and remote sites; and designing your site navigation with the Site Map.

- **Standard Adobe Web Authoring Tools** — Dreamweaver includes a user interface that is consistent across all Adobe authoring tools. This consistency enables easy integration with other Adobe Web-related programs such as Adobe Flash, Director, Shockwave, and ColdFusion.

Other key features include the integrated user interface, the integrated file explorer, panel management, database integration, and standards and accessibility support. Dreamweaver CS3 is customizable and runs on many operating systems including Windows Vista, Windows XP, Mac OS X, and others.

Chapter One — Colorado Parks

To create documents similar to those you will encounter on the Web and in academic, business, and personal environments, you can use Dreamweaver to produce Web pages such as the Colorado National Parks and Monuments Web page shown in Figure 1-1. This Web page is the index page for the Colorado Parks Web site. This informational page provides interesting facts about Colorado's national parks and monuments. The page begins with a centered main heading, followed by two short informational paragraphs, and then an introductory sentence for a bulleted list. The list contains three bulleted items. A concluding sentence, the author's name, and current date end the page. A background image is applied to the page.

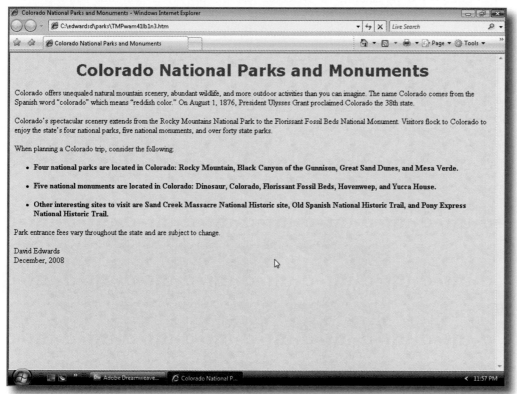

FIGURE 1-1

Starting Dreamweaver

Your **screen resolution** is the number of pixels in the width and height of your screen (width × height). A higher resolution results in a sharper image, but items appear smaller. Having a screen resolution such as 1024 × 768 gives you more space — your computer can display more of a program or a Web page or more icons on your desktop.

If you are stepping through this chapter on a computer and you want your screen to agree with the Dreamweaver figures in this book, you should change your screen's resolution to 1024 × 768. The browser used to display the Web page figures is Internet Explorer. The browser text size is set to Medium.

Getting started in Dreamweaver is as easy as opening an existing HTML document or creating a new document. The Dreamweaver environment consists of toolbars, windows, objects, panels, inspectors, and tools you use to create your Web pages and to manage your Web site, which is a collection of Web pages. It is important to learn the basic concepts behind the Dreamweaver workspace and to understand how to choose options, use inspectors and panels, and set preferences that best fit your work style.

Dreamweaver provides the Web site developer with three workspace layouts: Designer, Coder, and Dual Screen. Programmers who work primarily with HTML and other languages generally select the Coder workspace. The Dual Screen option requires two monitors. In this layout, the Document window and Property inspector are displayed on one monitor and the panels are displayed on a secondary monitor. The Designer workspace contains a visual integrated workspace and is ideal for beginners and nonprogrammers. For the exercises in this book, select the Designer workspace.

The settings on your computer determine what is displayed when the Dreamweaver CS3 program starts. By default, the Welcome screen is displayed each time you start Dreamweaver. The Welcome screen's visual representation is a good tool for beginners, but more proficient Dreamweaver users generally disable this feature. You will disable the Welcome screen at the end of this chapter. If you are opening Dreamweaver from a computer at your school or other location, most likely the program is set up and ready to use.

To start Dreamweaver, Windows must be running. This book uses the Microsoft Windows Vista operating system. If you are using a different operating system, the copying process will be somewhat different. The following steps show how to start Dreamweaver, or you can ask your instructor how to start the program.

More About

Dreamweaver CS3 Features

For more information about Dreamweaver CS3 features, visit the Dreamweaver CS3 More About Web page (scsite.com/dwcs3/more.htm) and then click Dreamweaver CS3 Features.

To Start Dreamweaver

1

• **Click the Start button on the Windows taskbar, point to Adobe Dreamweaver CS3 on the Start menu or point to All Programs on the Start menu, and then point to Adobe Dreamweaver CS3 on the All Programs menu.**

The Start menu is displayed. (Figure 1-2). Your Start menu will display different programs from those in Figure 1-2. Your version of Dreamweaver might start differently. If so, check with your instructor.

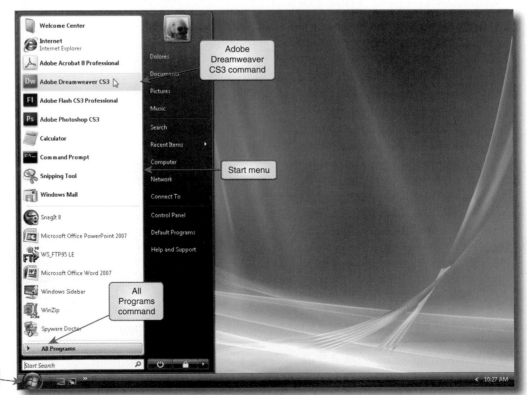

FIGURE 1-2

2

- **Click Adobe Dreamweaver CS3.**

The Welcome screen appears (Figure 1-3). You disable the Welcome screen at the end of this chapter. If a message appears regarding default file types, close it.

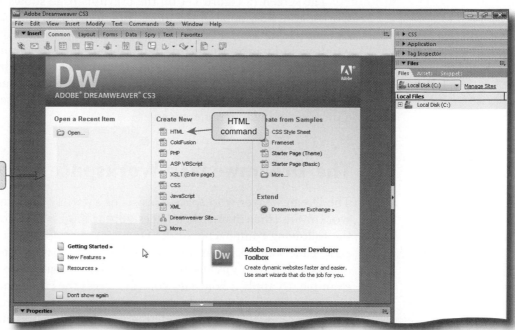

FIGURE 1-3

3

- **Click HTML in the Create New column. If necessary, maximize the Dreamweaver window and the Document window by clicking the Maximize button in the upper-right corner of the windows.**

- **If the Insert bar is not displayed, click Window on the menu bar and then click Insert.**

The Welcome screen closes, and the Dreamweaver workspace is displayed (Figure 1-4). The Dreamweaver workspace contains menu names, toolbars, and panel groups. The Windows taskbar displays the Adobe Dreamweaver CS3 button, indicating that Dreamweaver is running.

FIGURE 1-4

Other Ways

1. Double-click Dreamweaver icon on desktop

The screen in Figure 1-4 on the previous page shows a typical Dreamweaver workspace, with some of the more commonly used components displayed. The **Dreamweaver workspace** is an integrated environment in which the Document window and panels are incorporated into one larger application window. The panel groups are docked, or attached, on the right. The Insert bar is located at the top of the Document window, and the Property inspector is located at the bottom of the Document window. You can move, resize, and/or collapse the panels to accommodate your individual preferences.

The Dreamweaver Workspace

The Dreamweaver workspace consists of a variety of components to make your work more efficient and Web pages appear more professional. This section discusses the following components of the Dreamweaver workspace: title bar, Document window, panels and panel groups, status bar, menu bar, and toolbars.

As you learn to use each of these tools, you will discover some redundancy. For example, to apply a Font tag, you can access the command through the Property inspector, the Text menu, or the context menu. The different options accommodate various user preferences. The chapters in this book present the more commonly used methods. The Other Ways boxes at the end of many of this book's step-by-step sequences describe additional methods to accomplish a task when they are available. As you become proficient working in the Dreamweaver environment, you will develop techniques for using the tools that best suit your personal preferences.

Title Bar

The **title bar** displays the application name, Adobe Dreamweaver CS3, and includes [Untitled-1 (XHTML)] as in Figure 1-4. After you give a Web page a title and save the document, the title bar reflects the changes by displaying the document name and path. When you make changes to the document, Dreamweaver includes an asterisk following the file name. The asterisk is removed after the document is saved.

Document Window

The **Document window** displays the current document, or Web page, including text, tables, graphics, and other items. In Figure 1-4, the Document window is blank. The Document window is similar in appearance to the Internet Explorer or Firefox browser window. You work in the Document window in one of three views: **Design view**, the design environment where you assemble your Web page elements and design your page (Figure 1-4 displays Design view); **Code view**, which is a hand-coding environment for writing and editing code; or **Split view**, which allows you to see both Code view and Design view for the same document in a single window. When you open a new document in Dreamweaver, the default view is Design view. These views are discussed in detail in Chapter 2.

Panels and Panel Groups

Panel groups are sets of related panels docked together below one heading. Panels provide control over a wide range of Dreamweaver commands and functions. Each panel group can be expanded or collapsed, and can be docked or undocked with other panel groups. Panel groups also can be docked to the integrated Document window. This makes it easy to access the panels you need without cluttering your workspace. Panels within a panel group are displayed as tabs. Each panel is explained in detail as it is used in the chapters throughout the book.

Some panels, such as the Insert bar and Property inspector, are stand-alone panels. The **Insert bar** allows quick access for frequently used commands. It contains buttons for creating and inserting various types of objects — images, tables, layers, frames, and tags — into a document. As you insert each object, a piece of source code allows you to set and manipulate various attributes. The buttons on the Insert bar are organized into several categories, which you can access through a tab on the Insert bar. Some categories also have buttons with pop-up menus. When you select an option from a pop-up menu, it becomes the default action for the button. Clicking the Insert bar's Forms tab, for example, provides quick access to the form tool and form objects. The default position for the Insert bar is at the top of the Document window (Figure 1-4 on page DW 37). When you start Dreamweaver, the category in which you last were working is displayed. Click the Insert bar arrow to display/hide the Insert bar tabs.

The **Property inspector** (Figure 1-4) displays settings for the selected object's properties or attributes. This panel is context sensitive, meaning it changes based on the selected object, which can include text, tables, images, and other objects. When Dreamweaver starts, the Property inspector is positioned at the bottom of the Document window and displays text properties if a Document window is open. Otherwise, the Property inspector is blank.

To expand or collapse a panel group, click the expander arrow to the left of the group's name; to undock and move a panel group, drag the gripper at the left edge of the group's title bar (Figure 1-4). To open panels, use the Window menu.

Status Bar

The **tag selector** below the Document window (Figure 1-4) provides additional information about the document you are creating. The status bar presents the following options:

- **Tag:** Click any tag in the hierarchy to select that tag and all its contents.
- **Select tool:** Use the Select tool to return to default editing after using the Zoom or Hand tool.
- **Hand tool:** To pan a page after zooming, use the Hand tool to drag the page.
- **Zoom tool:** Available only in Design view. Use the Zoom tool to zoom in and out from a document to check the pixel accuracy of graphics or to better view the page.
- **Set magnification:** Use the Set magnification pop-up menu to change the view from 6% to 6400%; default is 100%.
- **Window size:** Displays the Window size, which includes the window's current dimensions (in pixels) and the Window size pop-up menu.
- **Estimated document size and download time:** Displays the size and estimated download time of the current page. Dreamweaver CS3 calculates the size based on the entire contents of the page, including all linked objects such as images and plug-ins.

Vertical/Horizontal Bars

A vertical bar separates the panel groups, and a horizontal bar separates the Property inspector from the Document window. Both bars contain an expander arrow. Clicking this arrow hides/displays the panel groups and the Property inspector

More About

Panel Groups

To drag a floating (undocked) panel group without docking it, drag the panel group by the bar above its title bar. The panel group does not dock as long as it is not dragged by its gripper.

(Figure 1-5). If your screen resolution is set to 800 × 600, a portion of the Property inspector may not be displayed when the panel groups are expanded.

Menu Bar

The **menu bar** displays the Dreamweaver menu names (Figure 1-5). Each menu contains a list of commands you can use to perform tasks such as opening, saving, modifying, previewing, and inserting data into your Web page. When you point to a menu name on the menu bar, the area of the menu bar containing the name is selected.

FIGURE 1-5

To display a menu, such as the View menu (Figure 1-5), click the menu name on the menu bar. If you point to a menu command that has an arrow at its right edge, a submenu displays another list of commands. Many menus display some commands that appear gray, or dimmed, instead of black, which indicates they are not available for the current selection.

Toolbars

In Designer mode, Dreamweaver contains four toolbars: Document, Standard, Style Rendering, and Insert. You can choose to display or hide the toolbars by clicking View on the menu bar and then clicking Toolbars. If a toolbar name has a check mark next to it, it is displayed in the window. To hide the toolbar, click the name of the toolbar with the check mark, and it is no longer displayed. The Insert toolbar, more commonly referred to as the Insert bar, was discussed previously in this chapter.

The **Document toolbar** (Figure 1-6) is the default toolbar displayed in the Document window. It contains buttons that provide different views of the Document window (e.g., Code, Split, and Design), the Document title, and some common operations, such as File Management, Preview/Debug in Browser, Refresh Design View, View Options, Visual Aids, Validate Markup, and Check Browser Compatibility.

FIGURE 1-6

The **Standard toolbar** (Figure 1-7) contains buttons for common operations from the File and Edit menus: New, Open, Browse in Bridge, Save, Save All, Print Code, Cut, Copy, Paste, Undo, and Redo. The Standard toolbar is not displayed by default in the Dreamweaver Document window when you first start Dreamweaver. You can display the Standard toolbar through the Toolbars command on the View menu, or by right-clicking a blank area on a toolbar and then clicking Standard on the context menu. Similar to other toolbars and panels, you can dock/undock and move the Standard toolbar, so it may be displayed in a different location on your screen.

FIGURE 1-7

A recent addition to Dreamweaver is the **Style Rendering toolbar**, which provides options for designing for different media types, such as screen, print, handheld, projection, TTY (teletype), television, CSS Styles, and Style Sheets. The CSS (Cascading Style Sheets) Styles button works independently of the other seven buttons and provides the option to disable/enable the displaying of CSS styles.

Opening and Closing Panels

The Dreamweaver workspace accommodates different work styles and levels of expertise. Through the workspace, you can open and close the panel groups and display/hide other Dreamweaver features as needed. To open a panel group, select and then click the name of a panel on the Window menu. Closing unused panels provides an uncluttered workspace in the Document window. To close an individual panel group, click Close panel group on the Options pop-up menu accessed through the panel group's title bar (Figure 1-8). To expand/collapse a panel, click the panel's expander arrow at the left of the group's name.

FIGURE 1-8

Opening and closing each panel individually is a time-consuming task. Dreamweaver provides a shortcut to accomplish this job quickly. The F4 key is a toggle key that opens and/or closes all panels and inspectors at one time. The following steps illustrate how to display the Standard toolbar and close and open the panels.

To Display the Standard Toolbar and to Close and Open Panels

1

• **Click View on the menu bar, point to Toolbars, and then point to Standard on the Toolbars submenu.**

The View menu is displayed and Standard is highlighted on the Toolbars submenu (Figure 1-9).

2

• **Click Standard.**

The Standard toolbar is displayed. Previous settings determine the location of the Standard toolbar. The Standard toolbar on your computer may be displayed below the Document toolbar or in another location.

FIGURE 1-9

3

• **Press the F4 key.**

All the open panels and inspectors close, and the maximum workspace is available in the Document window (Figure 1-10).

4

• **Press the F4 key again to redisplay the panels.**

FIGURE 1-10

Defining a Local Site

Web design and Web site management are two important skills that a builder of Web sites must understand and apply. Dreamweaver CS3 is a site creation and management tool. To use Dreamweaver efficiently, you first must define the local site. After defining the local site, you then publish to a remote site. Publishing to a remote site is discussed in Chapter 3 and Appendix C.

The general definition of a **site**, or Web site, is a set of linked documents with shared attributes, such as related topics, a similar design, or a shared purpose. In Dreamweaver, however, the term site can refer to any of the following:

- **Web site**: A set of pages on a server that are viewed through a Web browser by a visitor to the site.
- **Remote site**: Files on the server that make up a Web site, from the author's point of view rather than a visitor's point of view.
- **Local site**: Files on your local disk that correspond to the files on the remote site. You edit the files on your local disk, and then upload them to the remote site.
- **Dreamweaver site definition**: Set of defining characteristics for a local site, plus information on how the local site corresponds to a remote site.

All Dreamweaver Web sites begin with a local root folder. As you become familiar with Dreamweaver and complete the chapters in this book, you will find references to a **local root folder**, **root folder**, and **root**. These terms are interchangeable. This folder is no different from any other folder on your computer's hard drive or other storage media, except for the way in which Dreamweaver views it. When Dreamweaver looks for Web pages, links, images, and other files, the program defaults to the designated root folder. Any media within the Web site that are outside of the root folder will not display when the Web site is previewed in a Web browser. Within the root folder, you can create additional folders or subfolders to organize images and other objects. A **subfolder** (also called a **nested folder**) is a folder inside another folder.

Dreamweaver provides two options to define a site and create the hierarchy: You can create the root folder and any subfolders, or create the pages and then create the folders when saving the files. In this book, you create the root folder and subfolders and then create the Web pages.

One of Dreamweaver's more prominent organizational tools is the Files panel. Use the **Files panel** for standard file maintenance operations, such as the following:

- Creating files
- Viewing, opening, and moving files
- Creating folders
- Deleting items
- Managing a site

The Files panel enables you to view a site, including local, remote, and testing server files associated with a selected site. In this chapter, you view only the local site.

Creating the Local Root Folder and Subfolders

Several options are available to create and manage your local root folder and subfolders: Dreamweaver's Files panel, Dreamweaver's Site Definition feature, or Windows file management. In this book, you use Dreamweaver's Site Definition feature to create the local root folder and subfolders, the Files panel to manage and edit your files and folders, and Windows file management to download the data files.

To organize and create a Web site and understand how you access Web documents, you need to understand paths and folders. The term, path, sometimes is confusing for new users of the Web. It is, however, a simple concept: A **path** is the succession of folders that must be navigated to get from one folder to another. In the DOS world, folders are referred to as **directories**. These two terms often are used interchangeably.

A typical path structure has a **master folder**, usually called the root and designated by the symbol "\". This root folder contains within it all of the other subfolders or nested folders. Further, each subfolder may contain additional subfolders or nested folders. These folders contain the Web site files. One of the more commonly used subfolders contains the site's images.

Because many files are required for a Dreamweaver Web site, it is advisable to create the projects using another type of media rather than the floppy drive (A:). Steps in this chapter instruct you to create the local site on the C:\ drive, the computer's hard drive. It is suggested, however, that you check with your instructor to verify the location and path you will use to create and save your local Web site. Other options may include a USB drive or a network drive.

For this book, you first create a local root folder using your last name and first initial. Examples in this book use David Edwards as the Web site author. Thus, David's local root folder is edwardsd. Next, for this chapter, you create a subfolder and name it parks. Finally, you create another subfolder within parks and name it images. All Colorado Parks related files and subfolders are stored within the parks folder. When you navigate through this folder hierarchy, you are navigating along the path. The path and folder within the Colorado Parks Web site are C:\edwardsd\parks\. The path to the images folder is C:\edwardsd\parks\images\. In all references to edwardsd, substitute your last name and first initial.

Using Site Definition to Create a Local Site

You create a site definition using Dreamweaver's Site Definition dialog box. Two options are available: Basic or Advanced. The Basic method, or **Site Definition Wizard**, guides you through site setup step by step and takes you through a series of six screens. In the Advanced method, all options are contained on one screen. The Advanced method is more efficient. Using this view, you set all the same basic information that the Site Wizard collects, plus additional options such as the following:

- **Case-sensitive links:** Provide for the use of case-sensitive link checking
- **Cache:** Allocates memory to store frequently used site data; checked by default
- **Default images folder:** An optional feature to specify the location of images in the site
- **HTTP address:** Used to define the URL of a Web site and to verify absolute links

The two main categories in a site definition are **Local Info** (Local Information) and **Remote Info** (Remote Information). In this chapter, you create the local site definition using the Advanced method. The site definition is stored in the Windows registry and is not part of the site. If you use removable media to store your files and move to another computer, you must recreate the local site definition on that computer. Remote site definition is discussed in Chapter 3.

After you have completed the Site definition, the hierarchy structure displays in Dreamweaver's Files panel. This hierarchy structure is similar to the Windows file organization. The Files panel provides a view of the devices and folders on your computer and shows how these devices and folders are organized. A small device icon or folder icon is displayed next to each object in the list. The device icon represents a device such as the Desktop or a disk drive, and the folder icon represents a folder. Many of these icons have a plus or minus sign next to them, which indicates whether the device or folder contains additional folders. The plus and minus signs are controls that you can click to expand or collapse the view of the file hierarchy. In the Files panel, the site folders and files appear in a different color than non-site folders and files so that you easily can distinguish between the two.

You define a local site by telling Dreamweaver where you plan to store local files. Use the Site Definition Advanced approach and the following steps to create a local Web site. The C:\ drive is used in the following exercise. If you are saving your sites at another location or on removable media, substitute that location for Local Disk C:\.

To Use Site Definition to Create a Local Web Site

1

• **Click Site on the menu bar and then point to New Site.**

The Site menu is displayed, and New Site is highlighted (Figure 1-11).

FIGURE 1-11

2

- **Click New Site.**
- **If necessary, click the Advanced tab. Verify that Local Info is selected in the Category column.**

The Site Definition dialog box is displayed, and the Advanced tab is selected. Unnamed Site 2 is selected in the Site name text box (Figure 1-12). Your site number might be different. A default path is displayed in the Local root folder. A different path may be displayed on your computer.

FIGURE 1-12

3

- **Type** Colorado Parks **as the site name.**

This name is for your reference only. It is not part of the path and is not visible to viewers of your site (Figure 1-13).

FIGURE 1-13

4

• **Click the folder icon to the right of the Local root folder text box.**

• **If you are creating and saving your sites at another location or on other media, navigate to that location and substitute the location for Local Disk (C): default path.**

The Choose local root folder for site dialog box is displayed. Local Disk (C): default path is displayed in the Select text box (Figure 1-14). Folders displayed in the Choose Local root folder for site dialog box will be different on your computer.

FIGURE 1-14

5

• **Click the Create New Folder icon.**

The New Folder text box is displayed (Figure 1-15). New Folder is selected.

FIGURE 1-15

6

• **Type your last name and first initial (with no spaces between your last name and initial) in the New Folder text box.**

In Figure 1-16, the author's name, edwardsd, is displayed in the folder's text box. On your computer, you are the author. Your last name and first initial will be displayed in the folder's text box (Figure 1-16).

FIGURE 1-16

7

• **Press the ENTER key to select the folder.**

The author's folder name is displayed in the Select text box (Figure 1-17). In Figure 1-17, edwardsd is displayed as the folder name. Your last name and first initial will be displayed on your computer screen.

FIGURE 1-17

8

• **Click the Create New Folder icon.**

• **Type** parks **as the name of the new folder and then press the ENTER key.**

The parks subfolder is created, and the folder name is displayed in the Select text box (Figure 1-18).

FIGURE 1-18

9

• **Click the Select button.**

The Site Definition dialog box is displayed, the Advanced tab is selected, and the Local root folder text box contains the C:\edwardsd\parks\ path (Figure 1-19). Your name will be displayed instead of edwardsd on your computer screen and the path may be to a different location.

FIGURE 1-19

10

- **Click the folder icon to the right of the Default images folder text box.**
- **If necessary, navigate to the your name\parks folder.**
- **Click the Create New Folder icon.**
- **Type** images **as the name of the new folder and then press the ENTER key.**

An images subfolder is created, and the folder name is displayed in the Select text box (Figure 1-20).

FIGURE 1-20

11

- **Click the Select button.**
- **Verify that the Enable cache check box is selected in the Site Definition dialog box.**

The Site Definition dialog box is displayed, and the path for the default images folder is displayed in the Default images folder text box (Figure 1-21). The folder path displayed on your computer will be different.

FIGURE 1-21

12

• **Click the OK button.**

The Dreamweaver workspace is displayed. The Colorado Parks Web site hierarchy is displayed in the Files panel (Figure 1-22).

Document window

Files panel tab

Colorado Parks path

FIGURE 1-22

Copying Data Files to the Colorado Parks Folder

Your data files contain background images for Chapter 1. You can copy the data files one by one through the Dreamweaver Files panel as you progress through this chapter. Alternatively, using the Windows Computer tool, you can establish the basic framework for the parks Web site by copying all the files and images at one time. Windows provides several ways through the View menu for you to arrange and identify your files when viewing them, including Small Icons, List, Details, and Tiles. The figures in this book use the List view when using the Windows Computer tool to copy the data files. Your computer may use a different view to display the files. The following steps illustrate how to copy data files to the local Web site.

To Copy Data Files to the Local Web Site

1

• **Click the Start button on the Windows taskbar and then click Computer. If necessary, click the Views button arrow on the toolbar and then click List.**

The Computer window is displayed (Figure 1-23). Most likely your computer will display different drives.

FIGURE 1-23

2

• **Double-click Local Disk (C:) and then navigate to the location of the data files for Chapter 1.**

If necessary, check with your instructor to verify the location of the data files. In Figure 1-24, the data files are located on Local Disk (C:). Your computer will display different folders from those in Figure 1-24.

FIGURE 1-24

3

• **Double-click the folder containing your data files, and then double-click the Chap01 folder.**

The Chap01 folder is selected, and the path to Chap01 is displayed in the Address text box (Figure 1-25). Figure 1-25 shows four additional folders. These folders are for the end-of-chapter exercises. You will have an opportunity to create these sites when you complete the exercises at the end of this chapter.

FIGURE 1-25

4

• **Double-click the parks folder and then double-click the images folder.**

The images folder is opened, and the path to the images folder is displayed in the Address text box (Figure 1-26).

FIGURE 1-26

5

• **Right-click the parksbg image file.**

• **Point to the Copy command.**

The context menu is displayed (Figure 1-27). Your context menu most likely will display different commands.

FIGURE 1-27

6

• **Click Copy and then click the Back button the number of times necessary to navigate to the your name folder.**

• **Double-click the your name folder, double-click the parks folder, and then double-click the images folder.**

• **Right-click anywhere in the open window to display the context menu.**

• **Point to the Paste command.**

The context menu is displayed and Paste is highlighted (Figure 1-28).

FIGURE 1-28

7

• **Click the Paste command.**

The parksbg image is pasted into the Colorado Parks Web site images folder (Figure 1-29).

8

• **Click the images window Close button.**

• **Double-click the images folder in the Dreamweaver Files panel.**

The images window closes and Dreamweaver is displayed. The images folder is opened, and the parksbg file name is displayed in Dreamweaver's Files panel.

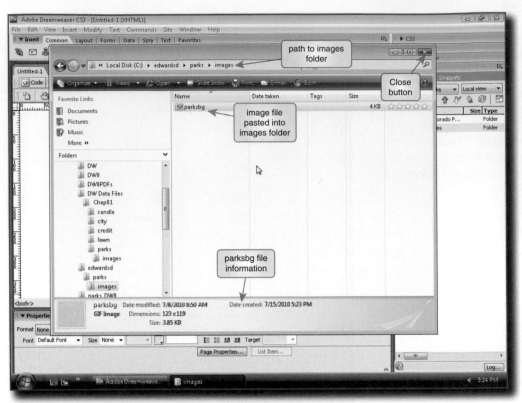

FIGURE 1-29

Your site definition and file hierarchy structure is complete, and your data files are copied into the images folder.

Removing or Editing a Web Site

On occasion, you may need to remove or edit a Web site. To remove or edit a Web site, click Site on the menu bar and then click the Manage Sites command. This displays the Manage Sites dialog box. Select the site name and then click the Remove button to remove the site. Dreamweaver displays a caution box providing you with an opportunity to cancel. Click the No button to cancel. Otherwise, click the Yes button, and Dreamweaver removes the site. Removing a site in Dreamweaver removes the settings for the site. The files and folders remain and must be deleted separately. To edit a site, click the site name and then click the Edit button. Dreamweaver displays the Site Definition dialog box, and from there, you can change any of the options you selected when you first created the site.

Saving a Web Page and Preparing Your Workspace

With the Colorado Parks site defined and the data file copied to the site, the next step is to save the untitled Dreamweaver document. When you defined the site, you designated C:\edwardsd\parks\ as the local root folder. You can copy and paste files into this folder using Windows Vista or XP, or use Dreamweaver's file management tools to copy and paste. You also can save a Dreamweaver document into this folder. Dreamweaver treats any item placed in the folder as part of the site.

When a document is saved as a Web page, the Web page also remains in the computer's memory and is displayed in the Document window. It is a good practice to save when you first open the document and then save regularly while you are working in Dreamweaver. By doing so, you protect yourself from losing all the work you have done since the last time you saved.

Rulers

Rulers help you measure, organize, and plan your layout. By default, they appear on the left and top borders of the page, marked in pixels, inches, or centimeters. They especially are helpful when working with tables or layers. Rulers, however, sometimes can be distracting when first learning how to use Dreamweaver. They easily are turned on and off through the View menu.

The Index Page

The **home page** is the starting point for the rest of your Web site. For most Web sites, the home page is named index. This name has special significance because most Web servers recognize index.htm (or index.html) as the default home page.

Dreamweaver comes with a number of default commands. These defaults are stored in 20 different categories in Dreamweaver's Preferences dialog box. Dreamweaver's default extension for new documents is .html. Although there is some debate about which extension to use — .htm or .html — most Web sites use .htm. You change the default through the Preferences dialog box. Therefore, when you save your document, Dreamweaver automatically appends the extension .htm to the file name. Documents with the .htm extension display in Web browsers.

The home page for your Colorado Parks Web site is named index.htm. The following steps show how to prepare your workspace by turning off the Rulers and changing the .html default extension to .htm. You then save the untitled document as index.htm in the parks local root folder. If the Rulers are not displayed in your Document window, omit Steps 1 and 2 on the next page.

To Hide the Rulers, Change the .html Default, and Save a Document as a Web Page

1

• **Click View on the menu bar, point to Rulers, and then point to Show on the Rulers submenu.**

Dreamweaver displays the View menu and the Rulers submenu. A checkmark is displayed to the right of Show (Figure 1-30).

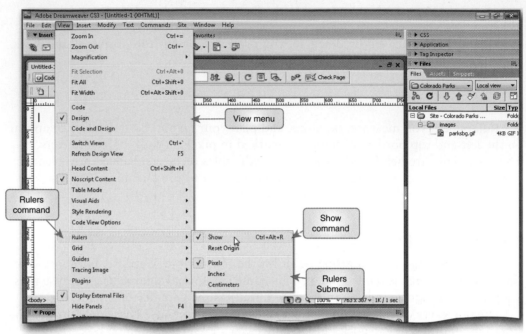

FIGURE 1-30

2

• **Click Show.**

The Rulers are no longer displayed in the Dreamweaver workspace (Figure 1-31).

FIGURE 1-31

3

• **Click Edit on the menu bar and then click Preferences.**

The Preferences dialog box is displayed (Figure 1-32).

FIGURE 1-32

4

• **Click the New Document category, delete .html as the default extension, and then type** `.htm` **as the default.**

The default is changed to .htm (Figure 1-33).

FIGURE 1-33

5

• **Click the OK button.**

The Document window is displayed.

6

• **Click the Save button on the Standard toolbar.**

The Save As dialog box is displayed (Figure 1-34). The parks folder name is displayed in the Save in text box. The default file name, Untitled-1, is selected in the File name text box.

FIGURE 1-34

7

• **Type** index **as the file name.**

The index file name is displayed in the File name text box (Figure 1-35).

FIGURE 1-35

8

• **Click the Save button.**

The parks index page is saved in the parks local folder and is displayed in the Files panel (Figure 1-36). The path and file name (parks\index.htm) are displayed on the Dreamweaver title bar.

FIGURE 1-36

Web Page Backgrounds

Each new Web page you create displays with a default white or gray background and other default properties. You can modify these default properties using the **Page Properties** dialog box. The Page Properties dialog box lets you specify appearance, links, and many other aspects of page design. You can assign new page properties for each new page you create, and modify properties for existing pages. The page properties you select apply only to the active document.

You can change the default background and enhance your Web page, for example, by adding a background image and/or background color. If you use both a background image and a background color, the color appears while the image downloads, and then the image covers the color. In this chapter, you add a background image to the Web page.

Adding a Background Image

When you copied the data files earlier in this chapter, you copied an image file that will be the background for the Colorado Parks Web site pages. You use a background image to add texture and interesting color to a Web page. Use background images cautiously, however. Web page images displayed on top of a busy background image may not mix well, and text may be difficult to read. Images and image formats are discussed in more detail in Chapter 2.

The steps on the next page illustrate how to use the Page Properties dialog box to add a background image to the home page.

To Add a Background Image to the Index Page

1

• **Click Modify on the menu bar and then point to Page Properties (Figure 1-37).**

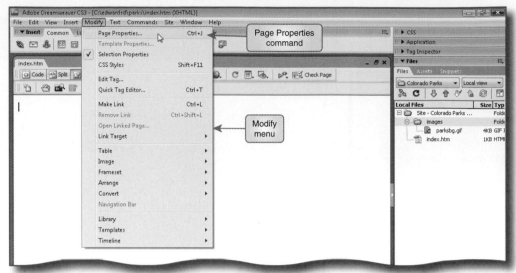

FIGURE 1-37

2

• **Click Page Properties.**

• **Verify that the Appearance category is selected.**

The Page Properties dialog box is displayed, and the Appearance category is selected (Figure 1-38).

FIGURE 1-38

3

• **Click the Browse button and then click the images folder.**

Dreamweaver displays the Select Image Source dialog box (Figure 1-39). The parks folder name is displayed in the Look in text box, and the images folder is selected.

FIGURE 1-39

4

• **Click the OK button.**

• **Click the parksbg file.**

• **If necessary, click the Preview images check box to select it.**

The images folder is opened and displayed in the Look in text box. The file name, parksbg, is displayed in the File name text box. A preview of the image is displayed in the Image preview area. The dimensions of the image, type of image, file size, and download time are listed below the image (Figure 1-40).

FIGURE 1-40

5

• **Click the OK button in the Select Image Source dialog box and then point to the OK button in the Page Properties dialog box.**

The Page Properties dialog box is displayed with the folder and file name in the Background image text box (Figure 1-41).

FIGURE 1-41

6

• **Click the OK button and then click the Save button on the Standard toolbar.**

The background image is applied to the Colorado Parks page, and the updated page is saved (Figure 1-42).

FIGURE 1-42

Other Ways

1. Right-click Document window, click Page Properties on shortcut menu
2. Click Page Properties button on Property inspector

Adding Text to a Web Page

In Dreamweaver, you can create a Web page in several ways: (1) you can type a new document; (2) you can open an existing HTML document, even if it was not created in Dreamweaver; (3) you can copy and paste text; and (4) you can import a Word document.

In this chapter, you create the index page for the Colorado Parks Web page by typing the text in the Document window. Entering text into a Dreamweaver document is similar to typing text in a word-processing document. You can position the insertion point at the top left of the Document window or within another object, such as a table cell. Pressing the ENTER key creates a new paragraph and inserts a blank line. Web browsers automatically insert a blank line of space between paragraphs. To start a new single line without a blank line between lines of text requires a **line break**. You can insert a line break by holding down the SHIFT key and then pressing the ENTER key or by clicking the Line Break command on the Insert HTML Special Characters submenu.

If you type a wrong letter and notice the error before pressing the ENTER key, press the BACKSPACE key to erase all the characters back to and including the one that is incorrect. If you mistakenly press the ENTER key and then discover the error, simply press the BACKSPACE key to return the insertion point to the previous line. Clicking the **Undo** button on the Standard toolbar reverses the most recent actions. The **Redo** button reverses the last undo action. The Undo and Redo commands also are accessible on the Edit menu.

Organizing Your Workspace

To organize your workspace, you can hide the panel groups. This gives you additional workspace in the Dreamweaver Document window. The step on the next page shows how to organize your workspace by hiding the panel groups.

To Hide the Panel Groups

1

• **Click the expander arrow on the panel groups vertical bar.**

• **Click the Property inspector expander arrow.**

The panel group is hidden, and the Property inspector is collapsed (Figure 1-43).

FIGURE 1-43

Adding Text

Table 1-1 includes the text for the Colorado Parks Web page. After typing the sections of the document, you will press the ENTER key to insert a blank line.

Table 1-1	Discovering Scenic Colorado Web Page Text		
SECTION	HEADING, PART 1, AND PART 2	SECTION	PART 3, ITEMS FOR BULLETED LIST, AND CLOSING
Heading	Colorado National Parks and Monuments	Part 3	When planning a Colorado trip, consider the following:
Part 1	Colorado offers unequaled natural mountain scenery, abundant wildlife, and more outdoor activities than you can imagine. The name Colorado comes from the Spanish word "colorado" which means "reddish color." On August 1, 1876, President Ulysses Grant proclaimed Colorado the 38th state.	Items list	Four national parks are located in Colorado: Rocky Mountain, Black Canyon of the Gunnison, Great Sand Dunes, and Mesa Verde. \<enter\> Five national monuments are located in Colorado: Dinosaur, Colorado, Florissant Fossil Beds, Hovenweep, and Yucca House. \<enter\> Other interesting sites to visit are Sand Creek Massacre National Historic site, Old Spanish National Historic Trail, and Pony Express National Historic Trail. \<enter\>
Part 2	Colorado's spectacular scenery extends from the Rocky Mountains National Park to the Florissant Fossil Beds National Monument. Visitors flock to Colorado to enjoy the state's four national parks, five national monuments, and over forty state parks.	Closing	Park entrance fees vary throughout the state and are subject to change.

The following steps show how to add text to the Document window and insert blank lines between sections of text.

To Add Text

1

• **Type the heading** Colorado National Parks and Monuments **as shown in Table 1-1, and then press the ENTER key.**

The heading is entered in the Document window (Figure 1-44). Pressing the ENTER key creates a new paragraph.

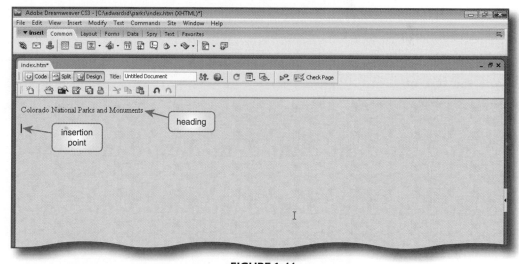

FIGURE 1-44

2

• **Type the text of Part 1 as shown in Table 1-1 on page DW 67, and then press the ENTER key.**

The introductory paragraph is entered (Figure 1-45). Pressing the ENTER key creates a new paragraph.

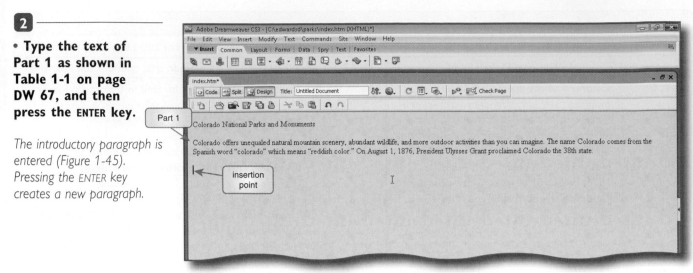

FIGURE 1-45

3

• **Type the text of Part 2 as shown in Table 1-1, and then press the ENTER key.**

The second paragraph is entered (Figure 1-46).

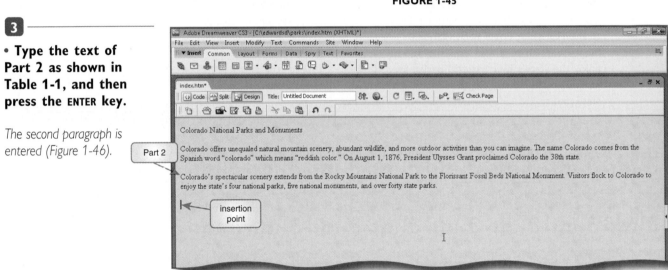

FIGURE 1-46

4

• **Type the text of Part 3 as shown in Table 1-1, and then press the ENTER key.**

The third paragraph is entered (Figure 1-47).

FIGURE 1-47

5

• **Type the three items for the bulleted list as shown in Table 1-1. Press the ENTER key after each entry.**

The items for the bulleted list are entered (Figure 1-48). Later in this chapter, you will format the list so it becomes a bulleted list.

Items list

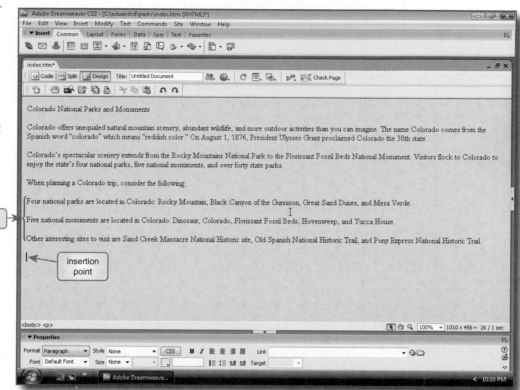

FIGURE 1-48

6

• **Type the closing paragraph shown in Table 1-1, and then press the ENTER key.**

• **Click the Save button on the Standard toolbar.**

The paragraph is entered (Figure 1-49).

Closing

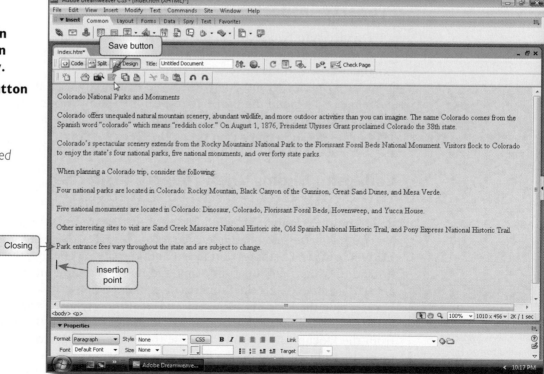

FIGURE 1-49

If you feel you need to start over for any reason, Dreamweaver makes it easy to delete a Web page or other file. Save and close the page, display the panel groups by clicking the vertical bar expander arrow, click the name of the page you want to delete, right-click to display the context menu, point to Edit, and then point to and click Delete on the Edit submenu. Click the Yes button in the Dreamweaver caution dialog box to delete the page or the No button to cancel the action. You also can select a file and press the DELETE key.

Dreamweaver will display a warning dialog box. If files are linked to other files, information will be displayed indicating how to update the links. To delete the file, click Yes in the dialog warning box or click No to cancel.

Formatting Text

The next step is to format the text on your Web page. **Formatting** means to apply different fonts, change heading styles, insert special characters, and insert other such elements that enhance the appearance of the Web page. Dreamweaver provides three options for formatting text: the Text menu, the Insert bar Text category, and the Property inspector. To format the text for the Colorado Parks index page, you use the text-related features of the Property inspector.

The Property inspector is one of the panels you will use most often when creating and formatting Web pages. The Property inspector initially displays the more commonly used attributes, or properties, of the selected object. The object can be a table, text, an image, or some other item. The Property inspector is context sensitive, so options within the Property inspector change relative to the selected object.

Property Inspector Features

Divided into two sections, the Property inspector lets you see the current properties of the selected object and allows you to alter or edit them. You can click the expander arrow in the lower-right corner of the Property inspector to collapse the Property inspector to show only the more commonly used properties for the selected element or to expand the Property inspector to show more options. Some objects, such as text, do not contain additional properties within the expanded panel (Figure 1-50). The question mark icon opens the Help window.

Collapsing/Hiding the Property Inspector

Having panels such as the Property inspector displayed in the Dreamweaver window requires considerable window space. If you are finished working with a panel, it generally is better to collapse it, hide it, or close it. **Collapsing** it leaves the title bar in the window, which allows you to expand it easily by clicking the expander arrow instead of using the Properties command on the Window menu. Pressing CTRL+F3 also collapses/expands the Property inspector. **Hiding** it hides the panel and the title bar. To hide the Property inspector and the Property inspector title bar, click the expander arrow on the horizontal bar. **Closing** it removes the Property inspector from the Document window. To close the Property inspector, display the context menu by right-clicking on the Properties title bar, and then selecting the Close panel group command — or click the Options menu button and select the Close panel group command from the pop-up menu.

By default, the Property inspector displays the properties for text on a blank document. Most changes you make to properties are applied immediately in the Document window. For some properties, however, changes are not applied until you

Q: When a change is made in the Property inspector, when is the change applied?

A: Most changes are applied immediately. You can confirm that changes are applied, however, by clicking the TAB or ENTER key.

click outside the property-editing text fields, press the ENTER key, or press the TAB key to switch to another property. The following section describes the text-related features of the Property inspector (Figures 1-50 and 1-51).

FIGURE 1-50

FIGURE 1-51

FORMAT The **Format box** allows you to apply a Paragraph, Heading, or Preformatted style to the text. Clicking the Format box arrow displays a pop-up menu from which you can select a style.

The **Paragraph style** is the normal default style for text on a Web page. **Paragraph formatting** is the process of changing the appearance of text. **Heading styles** are used to create divisions and separate one segment of text from another. These formats are displayed based on how different browsers interpret the tags, offering little consistency and control over layout and appearance. When you apply a heading tag to a paragraph, Dreamweaver automatically adds the next line of text as a standard paragraph. You can use the **Preformatted style** when you do not want a Web browser to change the line of text in any way.

FONT The **Font** box applies the selected font combination to the text and determines how a browser displays text on your Web page. The browser uses the first font in the combination that is installed on the user's system. If none of the fonts in the combination are installed, the browser displays the text as specified by the user's browser preferences.

Most font faces in common usage on the Web are serif, sans-serif, or monospace fonts. The default font used on most Web pages is Times (also called Times New Roman or New Times), which is a serif font. The most commonly used sans-serif fonts are Arial, Helvetica, Geneva, and Verdana, while the most commonly used monospace font is Courier (also called Courier New). Use the Font combination pop-up menu to apply a font combination.

STYLE By default, Dreamweaver uses Cascading Style Sheets (CSS) styles to format text. Cascading Style Sheets (CSS) are a collection of formatting rules that control the appearance of content in a Web page. The styles that you apply to text using the Property inspector or menu commands create CSS rules that are embedded in the head of the current document. To change the default from CSS tags to HTML tags, click the Edit menu and select the Preferences command. Under the General category, Editing options, deselect the Use CSS instead of HTML tags check box. Styles are discussed in detail in Chapter 5.

SIZE The **Text Size box** provides options that allow you to apply a font size to a single character or to an entire page of text. Font sizes in HTML and XHTML range from 1 through 7, with size 7 being the largest. The default font size, or **BASEFONT**, is 3, which equates to 12 points in a word-processing document. The **UNITS** box is activated when a specific size is selected.

TEXT COLOR When you create a new document in Dreamweaver, the default text color is black. The **Text Color** box contains palettes of colors available on the color picker that you can apply to emphasize, differentiate, and highlight topics. To display the text in a selected Web-safe color, click the Text Color box to access the different methods of selecting preset colors or creating custom ones. Colors also are represented by a hexadecimal value (for example, #FF0000) in the adjacent text field.

BOLD AND ITALIC The **Bold button** and the **Italic button** allow you to format text using these two font styles in the Property inspector. These are the two more commonly used styles. Dreamweaver also supports a variety of other font styles, which are available through the Text menu. To view these other styles, click Text on the menu bar and then point to Style. The Style submenu contains a list of additional styles, such as Underline, Strikethrough, and Teletype.

ALIGN LEFT, ALIGN CENTER, ALIGN RIGHT, AND JUSTIFY In Dreamweaver, the default alignment for text is left alignment. To change the default alignment, select the text you want to align or simply position the mouse pointer at the beginning of the text. Click an alignment button: Align Center, Align Right, or Justify. You can align and center complete blocks of text, but you cannot align or center part of a heading or part of a paragraph.

LINK The **Link (Hyperlink) box** allows you to make selected text or other objects a hyperlink to a specified URL or Web page. To select the URL or Web page, you can (a) click the Point to File or Browse for File icon to the right of the Link box to browse to a page in your Web site and select the file name, (b) type the URL, or (c) drag a file from the Files panel into the Link box. Links are covered in detail in Chapter 2.

TARGET In the **Target pop-up menu box**, you specify the frame or window in which the linked page should load. If you are using frames, the names of all the frames in the current document are displayed in the list. If the specified frame does not exist when the current document is opened in a browser, the linked page loads in a new window with the name you specified. Once this window exists, other files can be targeted to it.

UNORDERED LIST Web developers often use a list to structure a page. An unordered list turns the selected paragraph or heading into an item in a bulleted list. If no text is selected before the **Unordered List button** is clicked, a new bulleted list is started.

ORDERED LIST An ordered list is similar to an unordered list. This type of list, however, turns the selected paragraph or heading into an item in a numbered list. If no text is selected before the **Ordered List button** is clicked, a new numbered list is started.

INDENT AND OUTDENT To set off a block quote, you can use the Indent feature. The **Text Indent button** will indent a line or a paragraph from both margins. In XHTML and HTML, this is the blockquote tag. The **Text Outdent button** removes the indentation from the selected text by removing the blockquote tag. In a list, indenting creates a nested list, and removing the indentation unnests the list. A **nested list** is one list inside another list and is not the same as the block quote created by the Indent feature.

PAGE PROPERTIES Clicking the Page Properties button opens the Page Properties dialog box.

LIST ITEM Clicking the List Items button opens the List Properties dialog box. This button appears dimmed until an existing list is created and the insertion point is contained within the list.

Applying Property Inspector Text-Related Features

The text for your Web page is displayed in the Document window. The next step in creating your Web page is to format this text. You use commands from the Property inspector to format the text.

Within Dreamweaver, you can format text before you type, or you can apply new formats after you type. If you have used word-processing software, you will find many of the Dreamweaver formatting commands similar to the commands within a word-processing program. At this point, your Web page contains only text, so the Property inspector displays attributes related to text.

To set block formatting, such as formatting a heading or an unordered list, position the insertion point in the line or paragraph and then format the text. To set character formatting, such as choosing a font or font size, however, you must first select the character, word, or words.

Text Headings

Just as in a word-processing document, designers use the heading structure in a Web page to set apart document or section titles. The six levels of HTML headings are Heading 1 through Heading 6. **Heading 1 <h1>** produces the largest text and **Heading 6 <h6>** the smallest. By default, browsers will display the six heading levels in the same font, with the point size decreasing as the importance of the heading decreases. The following steps show how to format the heading.

More About

The Property Inspector

The Property inspector initially displays the most commonly used properties of the selected object. Click the expander arrow in the lower-right corner of the Property inspector to see more of the object's properties.

More About

Text Size

You can set the size of the text in your Web page, but viewers of your Web page also can change the size through their browser. When creating a page, use the font size that looks right for the page you are creating.

To Format Text with Heading 1

1

• **If necessary, scroll up and then position the insertion point anywhere in the heading text, Colorado National Parks and Monuments (Figure 1-52). Click the expander arrow to expand the Property inspector.**

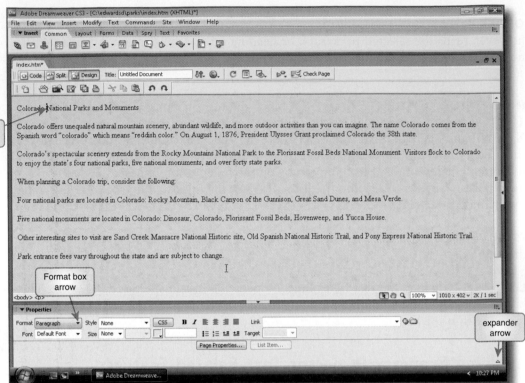

FIGURE 1-52

2

• **Click the Format box arrow in the Property inspector and then point to Heading 1.**

The Format pop-up menu is displayed with a list of formatting styles. Heading 1 is highlighted in the list (Figure 1-53).

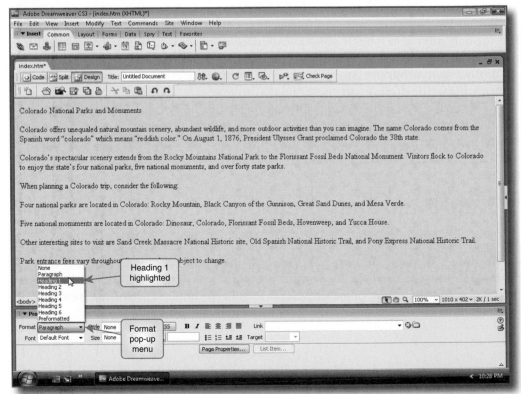

FIGURE 1-53

3

• **Click Heading 1.**

The Heading 1 style is applied to the Colorado National Parks and Monuments heading (Figure 1-54). The <h1> HTML tag is displayed in the Tag selector and Format box.

FIGURE 1-54

Other Ways

1. On Text menu point to Paragraph Format, click Heading 1 on Paragraph Format submenu
2. Right-click selected text, point to Paragraph Format on context menu, click Heading 1 on Paragraph Format submenu

Centering Text

Using the **Align Center button** in the Property inspector allows you to center text. This button is very similar to the Center button in a word-processing program. To center a single line or a paragraph, position the mouse pointer anywhere in the line or paragraph, and then click the button to center the text. You do not need to select a single line or single paragraph to center it. To center more than one paragraph at a time, however, you must select all paragraphs. The step on the next page illustrates how to center the heading.

To Center the Web Page Heading

1

• **If necessary, click anywhere in the heading, Colorado National Parks and Monuments. Click the Align Center button in the Property inspector.**

The heading, Colorado National Parks and Monuments, is centered (Figure 1-55).

FIGURE 1-55

Other Ways

1. On Text menu point to Align, click Center on Align submenu
2. Right-click selected text, point to Align on context menu, click Center on Align submenu
3. Press CTRL+ALT+SHIFT+C

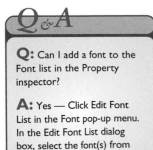

Q: Can I add a font to the Font list in the Property inspector?

A: Yes — Click Edit Font List in the Font pop-up menu. In the Edit Font List dialog box, select the font(s) from the Available fonts list, and add them to the Chosen fonts box.

Text is one of the more important elements of most Web pages. How the text displays on a Web page can impact the overall appearance of the page. Using the appropriate font type can enhance and entice viewers to browse your Web site.

Specifying Font Types

Type is important because it attracts attention, sets the style and tone of a Web page, influences how readers interpret the words, and defines the feeling of the page. The **font type** refers to the basic design of the lettering. Several methods are used to classify fonts. The most common way is to place them in different families based on shared characteristics. The five basic font type families are:

1. Serif, such as Times or Times New Roman
2. Sans-serif, such as Helvetica and Arial
3. Monospace, such as Courier
4. Cursive, such as Brush Script
5. Decorative and fantasy

Two general categories of typefaces are serif and sans-serif. **Sans-serif** typefaces are composed of simple lines, whereas **serif** typefaces use small decorative marks to embellish characters and make them easier to read. Helvetica and Arial are sans-serif types, and Times New Roman is a serif type. A **monospace** font, such as Courier, is one in which every character takes up the same amount of horizontal space. **Cursive** font styles emulate handwritten letterforms. **Decorative and fantasy** is a family for fonts that do not fit any of the other families.

Most Web pages use only the first three families. Dreamweaver provides a font combination feature available through the Property inspector. **Font combinations** determine how a browser displays your Web page's text. In the Property inspector, you can select one of six font combinations. A browser looks for the first font in the combination on the user's computer, then the second, and then the third. If none of the fonts in the combination is installed on the user's computer, the browser displays the text as specified by the user's browser preferences.

As discussed earlier in this chapter, Dreamweaver uses Cascading Style Sheets (CSS) styles to apply formatting to the text. The commands that you apply to text using the Property inspector or menu options create CSS rules that are embedded in the head of the current document. CSS styles provide you with greater flexibility and control over the appearance of your page, from the precise positioning of layout to specific fonts and text styles. When you change the font type in the following steps, Dreamweaver automatically creates a style and names it style1. The next style is named style2 and so on. If you want to apply the same attributes to other text, select the text and then select the style from the Style pop-up menu.

The following steps show how to change the font type.

To Change the Font Type

1

• **Click to the left of the heading, Colorado National Parks and Monuments, and then drag through the entire heading.**

The heading is selected (Figure 1-56).

FIGURE 1-56

2

• **Click the Font box arrow and then point to Verdana, Arial, Helvetica, sans-serif.**

The Font pop-up menu is displayed, and the Verdana, Arial, Helvetica, sans-serif combination is highlighted (Figure 1-57). The menu includes six different font combinations and the default font.

FIGURE 1-57

3

• **Click Verdana, Arial, Helvetica, sans-serif.**

The new font type is applied to the selected heading, and style1 is displayed in the Style text box (Figure 1-58).

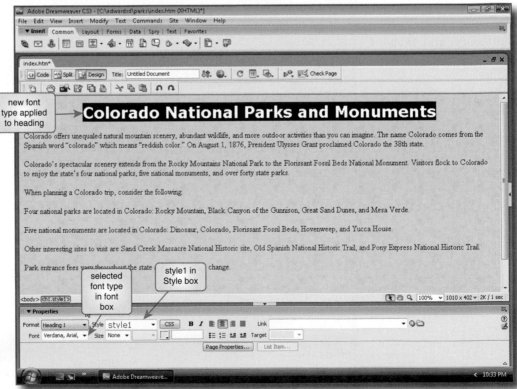

FIGURE 1-58

Other Ways

1. On the Text menu point to Font, click Verdana, Arial, Helvetica, sans-serif
2. Right-click selected text, point to Font on context menu, click Verdana, Arial, Helvetica, sans-serif

In addition to headings and font type attributes, other text design options are available. Presenting information in small chunks, such as bulleted or numbered lists, is a design element used by many Web page authors. Dreamweaver makes it easy to add lists such as these to your Web page.

Types of Lists

One way to group and organize information is by using lists. Web pages can have three types of lists: ordered (numbered), unordered (bulleted), and definition. **Ordered lists** contain text preceded by numbered steps. **Unordered lists** contain text preceded by bullets (dots or other symbols) or image bullets. You use an unordered list if the items need not be listed in any particular order. **Definition lists** do not use leading characters such as bullet points or numbers. Glossaries and descriptions often use this type of list.

The Unordered List and Ordered List buttons are available in the Property inspector. You can access the Definition List command through the Text menu List command submenu. Through the List Properties dialog box, you can set the number style, reset the count, or set the bullet style options for individual list items or for the entire list. To access the List Properties dialog box, click anywhere in the list, and then click the List Item button in the Property inspector.

You can create a new list or you can create a list using existing text. When you select existing text and add bullets, the blank lines between the list items are deleted. Later in this chapter, you add line breaks to reinsert a blank line between each list item. The following steps show how to create an unordered list using existing text.

> ### More About
>
> ### Lists
>
> You can remove the bullets or numbers from a formatted list just as easily as you added them. Select the formatted list. Click the button in the Properties inspector that you originally used to apply the formatting.

To Create an Unordered List

1

• **Click to the left of the line, Four national parks are located in Colorado: Rocky Mountain, Black Canyon of the Gunnison, Great Sand Dunes, and Mesa Verde. (Figure 1-59).**

insertion point

FIGURE 1-59

2

• **Drag to select the text, Four national parks are located in Colorado: Rocky Mountain, Black Canyon of the Gunnison, Great Sand Dunes, and Mesa Verde, and the next two lines.**

• **Point to the Unordered List button in the Property inspector.**

The text is selected (Figure 1-60).

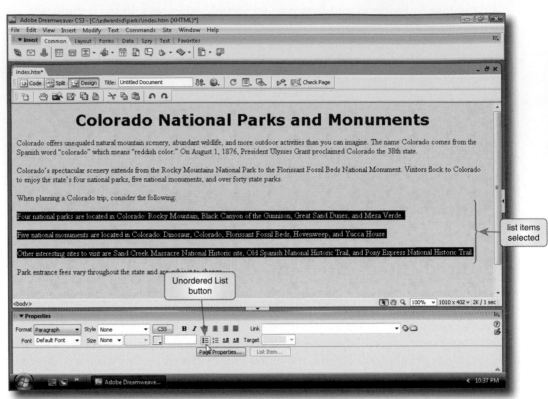

FIGURE 1-60

3

• **Click the Unordered List button.**

A bullet is added to each line, the three lines are indented, and the space between each item is deleted (Figure 1-61).

FIGURE 1-61

Other text formatting options are applying bold or italic styles to text. **Bold** characters are displayed somewhat thicker and darker than those that are not bold. **Italic** characters slant to the right. The Property inspector contains buttons for both bold and italic font styles.

Bold Formatting

To bold text within Dreamweaver is a simple procedure. If you have used word-processing software, you are familiar with this process. The next steps illustrate how to emphasize the bulleted items by applying bold formatting.

To Bold Text

1

• **If necessary, drag through the bulleted points to select all three lines.**

2

• **Click the Bold button and then click anywhere in the Document window to deselect the text (Figure 1-62).**

Bold formatting is applied to the unordered list items.

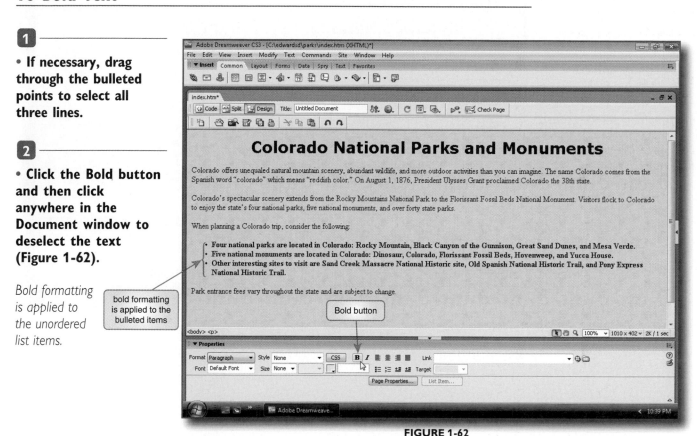

FIGURE 1-62

Understanding Line Breaks

When you added bullets to the items list earlier in this chapter, the blank line between each item was removed. Removing the blank line between items is a result of how Dreamweaver interprets the HTML code. A blank line between the bulleted items, however, will provide better spacing and readability when viewing the Web page in a browser. You can add blank lines in several ways. You might assume that pressing the ENTER key at the end of each line would be the quickest way to accomplish this. Pressing the ENTER key, however, adds another bullet. The easiest way to accomplish the task of adding blank lines is to insert line breaks. Recall that the line break starts a new single line without inserting a blank line between lines of text. Inserting two line breaks, however, adds a single blank line.

More About

HTML

For more information about HTML, visit the Dreamweaver CS3 More About Web page (scsite.com/dwcs3/more.htm) and then click HTML.

Dreamweaver provides a Line Break command through the Insert HTML Special Characters submenu. It is easier, however, to use the SHIFT+ENTER keyboard shortcut. The following steps show how to add a blank line between each of the bulleted items.

To Add a Line Break

1

• **Click at the end of the first bulleted item.**

• **Press SHIFT+ENTER two times.**

Two line breaks are inserted (Figure 1-63). When the Web page is viewed in Dreamweaver, it appears that two blank lines are inserted. When viewed in a browser, however, only one blank line is displayed between each item. You will view your Web page in a browser later in this chapter.

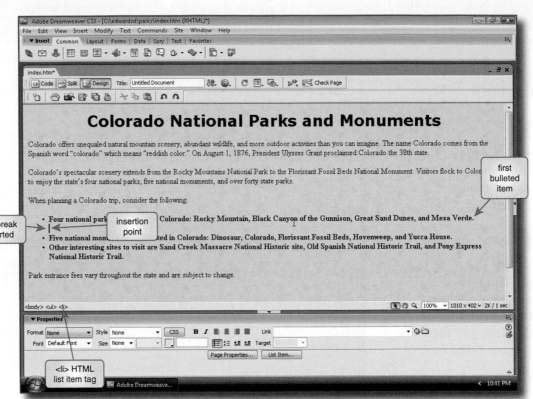

FIGURE 1-63

2

• **Press SHIFT+ENTER
two times at the end
of the second bulleted
item to insert blank
lines between the
second and third
bulleted list items.**

• **Press SHIFT+ENTER
two times at the end
of the third bulleted
list item.**

*Dreamweaver
displays the bulleted
items with blank lines
between them and a blank
line between the third
bulleted item and the last
sentence in the Document
window (Figure 1-64).*

FIGURE 1-64

When creating a Web document, it is a good idea to add your name and date to
the document. Insert a single line break between your name and the date. The steps
on the next page show how to add this information.

To Add Your Name and Date

1

• **If necessary, scroll down to display the closing paragraph. Click at the end of the closing paragraph.**

• **Press the ENTER key.**

The insertion point moves to the next paragraph (Figure 1-65).

FIGURE 1-65

2

• **Type your name and then press SHIFT+ENTER.**

The insertion point moves to the next line (Figure 1-66). No line space is displayed between the name and the insertion point. The insertion point is displayed smaller than normal.

FIGURE 1-66

3

• Type the current date and then press the ENTER key (Figure 1-67).

Your name and date are added to the Web page.

FIGURE 1-67

Web-Safe Colors

Adding color to text can attract attention to important information and emphasize different aspects of a Web page. You easily can change the color of an individual character, a word, a line, a paragraph, or the text of an entire document. In HTML, colors are expressed either as hexadecimal values (for example, #FF0000) or as color names (such as red).

Use the **color picker** to select the colors for page elements or text. Through the Property inspector, Dreamweaver provides access to five different color palettes: Color Cubes, Continuous Tone, Windows OS, Mac OS, and Grayscale. Color Cubes is the default color palette. Figure 1-68 on the next page shows the Color Cubes color palette available on the color palette pop-up menu.

More About

The Color Picker

To open the system color picker, click the Color Wheel button on the Text Color palette or click Color on the Text menu.

FIGURE 1-68

Two of the color palettes, Color Cubes and Continuous Tone, display Web-safe colors. Web-safe colors are colors that are displayed correctly on the screen when someone is viewing your Web page in a browser. A Web-safe color appears the same in Microsoft Internet Explorer, Firefox, and other browsers, on both Windows and Macintosh systems. Most experts agree that approximately 212 to 216 Web-safe colors exist. Testing by experts, however, suggests that Internet Explorer renders only 212 Web-safe colors. Table 1-2 contains a list of the color picker options.

Table 1-2 Color Picker Options	
OPTION	**FUNCTION**
Color preview box	Provides a preview of the currently selected color or the color picked up by the eyedropper
Hex value area	Displays the hexadecimal value of the current color or the color picked up by the eyedropper
Default Color button	Clears the current color and retains the default color
Color Wheel button	Opens the system color pickers via the operating system Color dialog box
Color picker pop-up menu	Displays a pop-up menu from which you can select one of five color pickers

Dreamweaver has an **eyedropper** feature that lets you select colors and make perfect color matches. When you are working with color palettes, you can use the eyedropper to choose a color from anywhere on the screen, including outside of Dreamweaver, and apply the color to a selected object in the Document window. You place the eyedropper over the color you want to select and then click the mouse button. As soon as you click the mouse button, the color automatically is applied to the selected object. If you move the eyedropper to an object outside of Dreamweaver, the eyedropper changes to the block arrow mouse pointer shape until you move it back into the Dreamweaver window.

Changing Text Color

The default color for Dreamweaver text is black. The following steps show how to change the text color of the heading to a shade of brown.

To Change the Text Color

1

• **If necessary, scroll up, select the heading, and then click the Text Color box in the Property inspector.**

The Color Cubes palette is displayed (Figure 1-69). The color palette includes Web-safe colors, the color preview box, and the six-digit hexadecimal number that represents the selected color.

FIGURE 1-69

2

• **Position the eyedropper on the shade of green represented by hexadecimal number #336633 (row 2 and column 10 from the right).**

The selected color is displayed in the color preview box, and the hexadecimal value area displays the number for the color (Figure 1-70).

FIGURE 1-70

3

• **Click the eyedropper to apply the color to the selected text, and then deselect the heading by clicking anywhere within it.**

The color is applied to the text. The heading is displayed in the selected color (Figure 1-71). Occasionally you may have to press the ESC key to close the picker. Note in the Property inspector that style1 changed to display the text color.

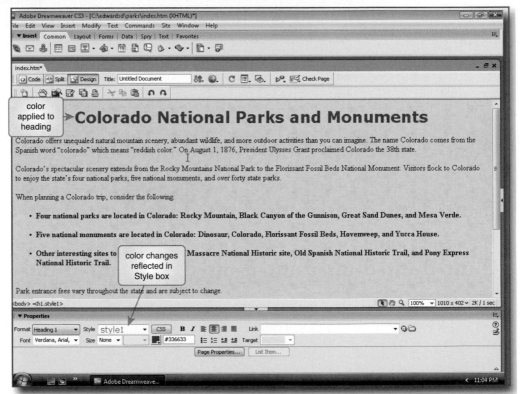

FIGURE 1-71

Web Page Titles

A **Web page title** helps Web site visitors keep track of what they are viewing as they browse. It is important to give your Web page an appropriate title. When visitors to your Web page create bookmarks or add the Web page to their Favorites lists, the title is used for the reference. If you do not title a page, the page will be displayed in the browser window, Favorites lists, and history lists as Untitled Document. Because many search engines use the Web page title, it is important to use a creative and meaningful name. Giving the document a file name when saving it is not the same as giving the page a title.

Changing a Web Page Title

The current title of your Web page is Untitled Document. Unless you change the title of the Web page, this name will be displayed on the browser title bar when the page is opened in a browser window. The following steps show how to change the name of the Web page to Colorado National Parks and Monuments.

To Change the Web Page Title

1

• **Drag through the text, Untitled Document, in the Title text box on the Document toolbar.**

The text is highlighted to indicate that it is selected (Figure 1-72).

FIGURE 1-72

• **Type** Colorado
National Parks and
Monuments **in the Title
text box and then
press the ENTER key.**

*The new name, Colorado
National Parks and
Monuments, is displayed
in the Title text box
(Figure 1-73).*

• **Click the Save button
on the Standard
toolbar.**

*The document changes are
saved. When displayed in a
browser, the title will appear
on the title bar.*

FIGURE 1-73

Other Web Page Enhancements

Dreamweaver includes many other features that you can use to enhance your Web page. One of the more commonly used enhancements that you may want to apply to a Web page is special characters.

Special Characters

Sometimes it is necessary to enter non-alphanumeric characters such as quotation marks and ampersands as well as non-keyboard symbols like trademarks and registrations into a Web page. To have the browser display these special characters requires a character code. **Character entities**, another name for character codes, allow a browser to show special characters. HTML represents these codes by a name (named entity) or a number (numbered entity). Both types of entities begin with an ampersand (&) and end with a semicolon (;). HTML includes entity names for characters such as the copyright symbol (©), the ampersand (&), and the registered trademark symbol (®). Some entities, such as the left and right quotation marks, include a number sign (#) and a numeric equivalent (such as —). Table 1-3 contains a list of HTML entities supported by Dreamweaver. To add an entity to your Web page, you click Insert on the menu bar, point to HTML, point to Special Characters on the HTML submenu, and then click the entity name on the Special Characters submenu.

Table 1-3 Character Entities

NAME	DESCRIPTION	HTML TAGS AND CHARACTER ENTITIES
Non-breaking Space	Places a non-breaking space at the insertion point	
Left Quote	Places opening, curved double quotation mark at the insertion point	“
Right Quote	Places closing, curved double quotation mark at the insertion point	”
Em Dash	Places an em dash at the insertion point	—
Pound	Places a pound (currency) symbol at the insertion point	£
Euro	Places a euro (currency) symbol at the insertion point	€
Yen	Places a yen (currency) symbol at the insertion point	¥
Copyright	Places a copyright symbol at the insertion point	©
Registered Trademark	Places a registered trademark symbol at the insertion point	®
Trademark	Places a trademark symbol at the insertion point	™
Other Characters	Provides a set of special characters from which to select	Other ASCII characters select

Check Spelling

After you create a Web page, you should check it visually for spelling errors. In addition, you can use Dreamweaver's Check Spelling command to identify possible misspellings. The Check Spelling command ignores HTML tags and attributes. Recall from the Introduction that attributes are additional information contained within an HTML tag.

The steps on the next page show how to start the Check Spelling command and check your entire document. Your Web page may contain different misspelled words depending on the accuracy of your typing.

Q: Does Dreamweaver contain a dictionary with American/British spelling options?

A: Yes — Dreamweaver contains 15 different spelling option dictionaries, including English (British) and English (Canadian). Access the dictionaries by clicking the Preferences command on the Edit menu, selecting the General category, and then clicking the Spelling dictionary pop-up menu arrow.

To Check Spelling

1

• **Click at the beginning of the document.**

• **Click Text on the menu bar and then point to Check Spelling.**

Dreamweaver displays the Text menu (Figure 1-74).

FIGURE 1-74

2

• **Click Check Spelling.**

The Check Spelling dialog box is displayed. The Dreamweaver spelling checker displays the word, Gunnison, in the Word not found in dictionary text box. Suggestions for the correct spelling are displayed in the Suggestions list (Figure 1-75).

3

• **Click the Ignore button.**

The spelling checker ignores the word, Gunnison, and continues searching for additional misspelled words. If the spelling checker identifies a word that is spelled correctly, clicking the Ignore button skips the word.

FIGURE 1-75

• **Continue to check the spelling and, as necessary, correct any misspelled word by accepting the suggested replacement, by clicking the Change or Change All buttons, or by typing the correct word in the Change to text box.**

When Dreamweaver has checked all text for misspellings, it displays an Adobe Dreamweaver dialog box informing you that the spelling check is complete (Figure 1-76).

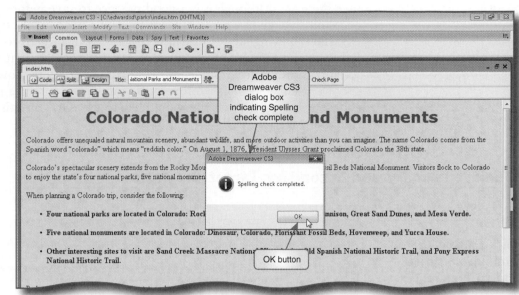

FIGURE 1-76

5

• **Click the OK button and then press CTRL+S to save any changes.**

Dreamweaver closes the Check Spelling dialog box and displays the Document window. The document is saved.

Before you can share your Web page with the world, you must select browsers to ensure your visitors can view the page properly. The two more popular browsers are Internet Explorer and Firefox.

Previewing a Web Page in a Browser

After you have created a Web page, it is a good practice to test your Web page by previewing it in Web browsers to ensure that it displays correctly. Using this strategy helps you catch errors so you will not copy or repeat them.

As you create your Web page, you should be aware of the variety of available Web browsers. More than 25 different Web browsers are in use, most of which have been released in more than one version. Most Web developers target recent versions of Microsoft Internet Explorer and Firefox, which the majority of Web visitors use. You also should know that visitors viewing your Web page might have earlier versions of these browsers. You can define up to 20 browsers for previewing. In this book, browsers are defined for Internet Explorer and Firefox.

Selecting a Browser

The browser preferences are selected in the Preferences dialog box. This dialog box provides options to select and define the settings for a primary and a secondary browser. Additionally, a Preview using temporary file option is available. When the check box for this option is checked, you can preview a page without first having to

More About

Web Page Design

Web pages reach a global audience. Therefore, to limit access to certain kinds of information, avoid including any confidential data. In particular, do not include your home address, telephone number, or other personal information.

save the page. Although it is a good practice to save before previewing in a browser, occasions will arise when you want to view a page before saving it.

The following steps show how to select your target browsers—Microsoft Internet Explorer and Firefox. To complete these steps requires that you have both Internet Explorer and Firefox installed on your computer. Note, however, that it is not necessary to install a secondary browser. If your choice is to use just one browser, you can choose to install the one you would like to use. Or, you can choose to install additional browsers as well.

To Select Primary and Secondary Target Browsers

1

• **Click Edit on the menu bar and then point to Preferences.**

Dreamweaver displays the Edit menu and Preferences is highlighted (Figure 1-77).

FIGURE 1-77

More About

Browsers

Just as you can specify a primary and secondary browser, you also can remove a browser from your list. Click Edit on the menu bar, click Preferences, and then click the Preview in Browser category. Select the name of the browser you want to remove and then click the minus (–) button.

2

• **Click Preferences and then, if necessary, click the Preview in Browser category.**

The Preferences dialog box is displayed, and the Preview in Browser category is selected (Figure 1-78). The primary browser was selected when Dreamweaver was installed on your computer. In this book, the primary browser is Internet Explorer. The browser name, IExplore, was selected automatically during the Dreamweaver installation. The browser name on your computer may be different. If you are using a different browser or the name is spelled differently, select the option appropriate for your computer and your preference.

FIGURE 1-78

3

• **Click the plus (+) button in the Preview in Browser area.**

Dreamweaver displays the Add Browser dialog box (Figure 1-79).

FIGURE 1-79

4

• **Click the Browse button and then locate the Mozilla Firefox file. Most likely this file is located on Local Drive (C:). Use the following path to locate the file: C:Program Files\Mozilla Firefox\ firefox. The path and file name on your computer may be different.**

• **Click the Open button.**

The browser name and application path are added to the Add Browser dialog box (Figure 1-80).

FIGURE 1-80

5

• **If necessary, click the Secondary browser check box to select it.**

The Name text box displays firefox.exe. The Application text box displays the path and file name (Figure 1-81). The path and spelling of Firefox on your computer may be different from those shown.

FIGURE 1-81

6

• **Click the OK button.**

Firefox is added as the secondary browser (Figure 1-82).

7

• **If necessary, click the Preview using temporary file check box to select it.**

• **Click the OK button. If a Dreamweaver CS3 dialog box appears, click the OK button.**

The target browsers are selected, and Dreamweaver displays the Document window. If the Preview using temporary file check box is unselected, Dreamweaver requires you to save the file before previewing it in a browser.

FIGURE 1-82

Previewing a Web Page

With the target browsers set up, you can preview your Web pages in the browsers at any time. You do not have to save the document first. The steps on the next page illustrate how to preview a Web page.

To Preview the Web Page

1

• **Click File on the menu bar, point to Preview in Browser, and then point to IExplore or your selected browser name.**

The File menu and Preview in Browser submenu are displayed (Figure 1-83). The Preview in Browser submenu includes the names of both your primary and secondary browsers, the Device Central command, and the Edit Browser List command. Clicking the Edit Browser List command displays the Preferences dialog box. The browser names on your computer may be different.

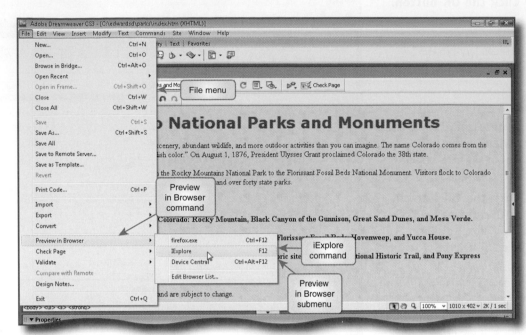

FIGURE 1-83

2

• **Click IExplore or your selected browser name.**

• **If necessary, maximize your browser window.**

Internet Explorer starts and displays the Web page in a browser window (Figure 1-84). Your browser name may be different. The file name displayed in the Address bar is a temporary name.

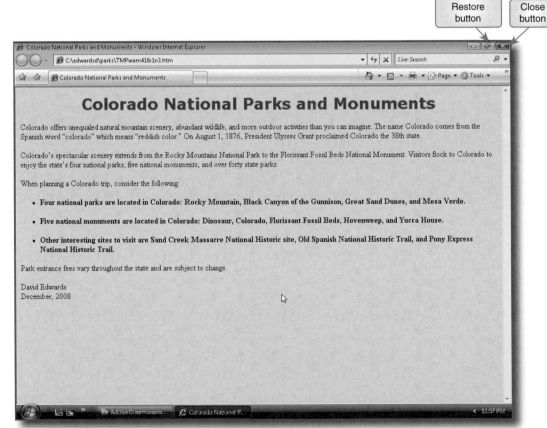

FIGURE 1-84

3

- **Click Internet Explorer's Close button.**
- **Click File on the menu bar and then point to Preview in Browser.**
- **Click firefox.exe on the Preview in Browser submenu.**

Firefox opens and displays the Web page in a browser window. Your browser name may be different. Compare how the files are displayed in the two browsers.

4

- **Click Firefox's Close button.**

Your instructor may require that you print a copy of your Web page. The next steps illustrate how to print a page.

> ### Other Ways
>
> 1. Press F12 to display primary browser
> 2. Press CTRL+F12 to display secondary browser

Printing a Web Page

You may want to print a Web page for a variety of reasons. Interestingly, Dreamweaver provides an option to print code, but does not provide an option to print the Design view. To print a Web page, you first must preview it in a browser. Printing a page from your browser is similar to printing a word-processing document. The following steps illustrate how to print the Web page in a browser.

To Print a Web Page

1

- **Press F12.**

The Web page is displayed in Internet Explorer or your selected browser.

2

- **Click the Print arrow on the Internet Explorer toolbar and then point to Print (Figure 1-85).**

FIGURE 1-85

3

• **Click Print. If necessary, select an appropriate printer.**

Internet Explorer displays the Print dialog box (Figure 1-86). Your selected printer is likely to be different from the one shown.

4

• **Click the Print button.**

The Print dialog box closes, and your Web page is sent to the printer.

FIGURE 1-86

5

• **Retrieve the printout and then click Internet Explorer's Close button.**

The browser closes, and Dreamweaver displays the Document window.

Dreamweaver Help System

Reference materials and other forms of assistance are available using the Dreamweaver Help system. You can display these documents, print them, or copy them to a word-processing document. Table 1-4 summarizes the categories of online Help available. Several methods are available to activate the first four types listed in the table. Appendix A provides detailed instructions on using Dreamweaver Help.

Table 1-4 Dreamweaver Help System

TYPE	DESCRIPTION	HOW TO ACTIVATE
Contents sheet	Use the Contents sheet option to view information organized by topic and then by subtopic, as you would in the table of contents of a book.	• Press the F1 key. If necessary, click the Contents link. • Click Help on the menu bar and then click Dreamweaver Help. • Click the Options menu button on the title bar of a panel group and then click Help on the Options pop-up menu. If necessary, click the Contents link.
Index sheet	Use the Index sheet option to look up specific terms or concepts, as you would in the index of a book.	• Press the F1 key. Click the Index link. • Click Help on the menu bar, click Dreamweaver Help, then click the Index link. • Click the Options menu button on the title bar of a panel group and then click Help on the Options pop-up menu. Click the Index link.

Table 1-4 Dreamweaver Help System (*continued*)		
TYPE	DESCRIPTION	HOW TO ACTIVATE
Search text box	Use the Search text box to find any character string, anywhere in the text of the Help system.	• Press the F1 key. Click the Search text box and type your topic. • Click the Options menu button on the title bar of a panel group and then click Help on the Options pop-up menu. Click the Search text box and type your topic.
Question Mark button or Help icon	Click the Question Mark button to find context-sensitive help in dialog boxes and panels.	• Click a Help button or Question Mark button in a dialog box. • Click the Help icon in an inspector or other kind of window.
Dreamweaver online tutorials	View online video tutorials.	• Access Dreamweaver tutorials at www.adobe.com/devnet/dreamweaver/ ?navID=gettingstarted

Disabling the Welcome Screen and Quitting Dreamweaver

After you create, save, preview, and print the Colorado Parks Web page and review how to use Help, your work in Chapter 1 is complete. The following steps show how to disable the Welcome screen, close the Web page, quit Dreamweaver CS3, and return control to Windows.

To Disable the Welcome Screen, Close the Web Site, and Quit Dreamweaver

1. Click Edit on the menu bar and then click Preferences.
2. If necessary, click General in the Category column.
3. Click the Show Welcome Screen check box under Document options to deselect it, and then click the OK button.
4. Click the Close button in the right corner of the Dreamweaver title bar.

The Document window, the Dreamweaver window, and the Colorado Parks Web site all close. If you have unsaved changes, Dreamweaver will prompt you to save the changes. Clicking the Yes button in the Dreamweaver CS3 dialog box saves the changes. The next time you start Dreamweaver, the Welcome screen will not be displayed.

Other Ways
1. On File menu, click Exit
2. Press CTRL+Q

Starting Dreamweaver and Opening a Web Page

Opening an existing Web page in Dreamweaver is much the same as opening an existing document in most other software applications: that is, you use the File menu and Open command. In addition to this common method to open a Web page, Dreamweaver provides other options. The Dreamweaver File menu also contains the Open Recent command. Pointing to this command displays the Open Recent submenu, which contains a list of the 10 most recently opened files. Additionally, if you want the page on which you currently are working to display when you next open Dreamweaver, you can select the Reopen Documents on startup command from the Open Recent submenu.

If the page you want to open is part of a Dreamweaver Web site, you can open the file from the Files panel. To open a Web page from the Files panel, you first must select the appropriate Web site. The Files pop-up menu in the Files panel lists sites you have defined. When you open the site, a list of the pages and subfolders within the site are displayed. To open the page you want, double-click the file name. After opening the page, you can modify text, images, tables, and any other elements.

Earlier in this chapter, you disabled the Welcome screen. The next time you open Dreamweaver, therefore, the Welcome screen will not be displayed. Instead, a blank window is displayed, requiring that you open an existing document or open a new document. Dreamweaver provides four options to open a new Document window:

- Click File on the menu bar, click New, and then select Blank Page
- Press CTRL+N and then select Blank Page
- Select the site's root folder, right-click, and then click New File on the context menu
- Click the Files panel Options menu, click File on the pop-up menu, and then click the New File command

The first two options display the New Document dialog box. From this dialog box, you select the Blank Page category and the HTML page type and then click the Create button. When you select option three or four, a template page or sample page is displayed. These are discussed in Chapter 5.

Chapter Summary

Chapter 1 introduced you to starting Dreamweaver, defining a Web site, and creating a Web page. You added an image background and used Dreamweaver's Property inspector to format text, change font color, and center text. You also learned how to apply color to text and use an unordered list to organize information. You added line breaks and learned about special characters. Once your Web page was completed, you learned how to save the Web page and preview it in a browser. You also learned how to print using the browser. To enhance your knowledge of Dreamweaver further, you learned basics about the Dreamweaver Help system.

What You Should Know

Having completed this chapter, you should now be able to perform the tasks below. The tasks are listed in the same order they were presented in the chapter. For a list of keyboard commands for topics introduced in this chapter, see the Quick Reference for Windows at the back of this book and refer to the Shortcut column.

1. Start Dreamweaver (DW 36)
2. Display the Standard Toolbar and Close and Open Panels (DW 43)
3. Use Site Definition to Create a Local Web Site (DW 46)
4. Copy Data Files to the Local Web Site (DW 53)
5. Hide the Rulers, Change the .htm Default, and Save a Document as a Web Page (DW 58)
6. Add a Background Image to the Index Page (DW 62)
7. Hide the Panel Groups (DW 66)
8. Add Text (DW 67)
9. Format Text with Heading 1 (DW 74)
10. Center the Web Page Heading (DW 76)
11. Change the Font Type (DW 77)
12. Create an Unordered List (DW 79)

13. Bold Text (DW 81)
14. Add a Line Break (DW 82)
15. Add Your Name and Date (DW 84)
16. Change the Text Color (DW 87)
17. Change the Web Page Title (DW 89)
18. Check Spelling (DW 92)

19. Select Primary and Secondary Target Browsers (DW 94)
20. Preview the Web Page (DW 98)
21. Print a Web Page (DW 99)
22. Disable the Welcome Screen, Close the Web Site, and Quit Dreamweaver (DW 101)

Learn It Online

Instructions: To complete the Learn It Online exercises, start your browser, click the Address bar, and then enter the Web address scsite.com/dwcs3/learn. When the Dreamweaver CS3 Learn It Online page is displayed, follow the instructions in the exercises below. Each exercise has instructions for printing your results, either for your own records or for submission to your instructor.

1 Chapter Reinforcement TF, MC, and SA

Below Dreamweaver Chapter 1, click the Chapter Reinforcement link. Print the quiz by clicking Print on the File menu for each page. Answer each question.

2 Flash Cards

Below Dreamweaver Chapter 1, click the Flash Cards link and read the instructions. Type 20 (or a number specified by your instructor) in the Number of playing cards text box, type your name in the Enter your Name text box, and then click the Flip Card button. When the flash card is displayed, read the question and then click the ANSWER box arrow to select an answer. Flip through the Flash Cards. If your score is 15 (75%) correct or greater, click Print on the File menu to print your results. If your score is less than 15 (75%) correct, then redo this exercise by clicking the Replay button.

3 Practice Test

Below Dreamweaver Chapter 1, click the Practice Test link. Answer each question, enter your first and last name at the bottom of the page, and then click the Grade Test button. When the graded practice test is displayed on your screen, click Print on the File menu to print a hard copy. Continue to take practice tests until you score 80% or better.

4 Who Wants To Be a Computer Genius?

Below Dreamweaver Chapter 1, click the Computer Genius link. Read the instructions, enter your first and last name at the bottom of the page, and then click the PLAY button. When your score is displayed, click the PRINT RESULTS link to print a hard copy.

5 Wheel of Terms

Below Dreamweaver Chapter 1, click the Wheel of Terms link. Read the instructions, and then enter your first and last name and your school name. Click the PLAY button. When your score is displayed, right-click the score and then click Print on the shortcut menu to print a hard copy.

6 Crossword Puzzle Challenge

Below Dreamweaver Chapter 1, click the Crossword Puzzle Challenge link. Read the instructions, and then enter your first and last name. Click the SUBMIT button. Solve the crossword puzzle. When you are finished, click the Submit button. When the crossword puzzle is redisplayed, click the Print Puzzle button to print a hard copy.

7 Tips and Tricks

Below Dreamweaver Chapter 1, click the Tips and Tricks link. Click a topic that pertains to Chapter 1. Right-click the information and then click Print on the shortcut menu. Construct a brief example of what the information relates to in Dreamweaver to confirm you understand how to use the tip or trick.

8 Newsgroups

Below Dreamweaver Chapter 1, click the Newsgroups link. Click a topic that pertains to Chapter 1. Print three comments.

9 Expanding Your Horizons

Below Dreamweaver Chapter 1, click the Expanding Your Horizons link. Click a topic that pertains to Chapter 1. Print the information. Construct a brief example of what the information relates to in Dreamweaver to confirm you understand the contents of the article.

10 Search Sleuth

Below Dreamweaver Chapter 1, click the Search Sleuth link. To search for a term that pertains to this chapter, select a term below the Chapter 1 title and then use the Google search engine at google.com (or any major search engine) to display and print two Web pages that present information on the term.

Apply Your Knowledge

1 Bryan's Lawn Service Web Site

Instructions: Start Dreamweaver. Perform the following tasks to define a Web site and create and format a Web page for Bryan's Lawn Service. The Web page as it is displayed in a browser is shown in Figure 1-87. The text for the Web site is shown in Table 1-5.

Software and hardware settings determine how a Web page is displayed in a browser. Your Web pages may display differently in your browser than the pages shown in the figure.

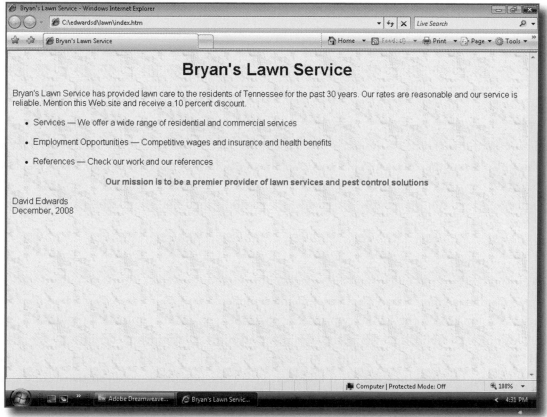

FIGURE 1-87

Table 1-5 Bryan's Lawn Service Web Page	
SECTION	**WEB PAGE TEXT**
Heading	Bryan's Lawn Service
Introductory Paragraph	Bryan's Lawn Service has provided lawn care to the residents of Tennessee for the past 30 years. Our rates are reasonable and our service is reliable. Mention this Web site and receive a 10 percent discount.
List Item 1	Services — We offer a wide range of residential and commercial services
List Item 2	Employment Opportunities — Competitive wages and insurance and health benefits
List Item 3	References — Check our work and our references
Closing	Our mission is to be a premier provider of lawn services and pest control solutions

(continued)

Bryan's Lawn Service Web Site *(continued)*

1. Click Site on the menu bar, click New Site, and use the Site Definition Advanced tab window to create a local Web site under the your name folder. In the Site Definition Site name text box, name the site Lawn Service. In the Local root folder text box, create a new subfolder under the your name folder, and name the new subfolder lawn. The path will be C:\yourname\lawn (substitute your name). In the Default images folder text box, create a new subfolder and name the folder images. The path will be C:\yourname\lawn\images.

2. Click File on the menu bar and then click New. Click Blank Page and then click Create. If necessary, display the Standard toolbar. Use the Save As command on the File menu to save the page with the name index.htm.

3. Use the Windows Computer tool to copy the data file image (lawnbg.jpg) to your lawn images folder.

4. Click the Modify menu and then click Page Properties. Apply the background image (located in the images folder) to the index page.

5. Type the Web page text shown in Table 1-5 on the previous page. Press the ENTER key after typing the text in each section and after each one of the list items in the table. The em dash, used in the three list items, is an HTML object. To insert the em dash, click the Insert menu, point to HTML, point to Special Characters, and then click Em-Dash.

6. Select the heading text and then apply the Heading 1 format. Click the Align Center button in the Property inspector to center the heading.

7. Select the three list items. Click the Unordered List button in the Property inspector to create a bulleted list with these three items.

8. Select the closing paragraph. Click the Align Center button and then click the Bold button in the Property inspector. When this is complete, do not deselect the sentence.

9. Click the Text Color box in the Property inspector and type hexadecimal color #006600 in the hexadecimal text box. This color swatch is located in the first row and sixth column from the left.

10. Click at the end of the first bulleted item. If necessary, deselect the Bold button. Insert one line break between the first and second bulleted items and then insert one line break between the second and third bulleted items.

11. Title the Web page Bryan's Lawn Service, using the Title text box on the Document toolbar.

12. Click at the end of the closing paragraph and then press the ENTER key. Click the Align Left button. Type your name, insert a line break, and then type the current date.

13. Select your name and the current date, and use the Text Color box in the Property inspector to change the text color to #000000.

14. Select the heading, introductory paragraph, list items, closing paragraph, your name, and the current date. Use the Font combination box to change the font type to Arial, Helvetica, sans-serif.

15. Click Text on the menu bar and then click Check Spelling. Spell check your document and correct any errors.

16. Click File on the menu bar and then click Save.

17. Press the F12 key to view the Web page in the primary browser. Submit the document in the format specified by your instructor.

18. Click the Dreamweaver Close button to quit Dreamweaver.

1 CandleLight Web Site

Problem: A friend of yours, Eve Perry, is starting her own business selling candles. She has asked you to assist her in preparing a Web page to help her advertise her candles (Figure 1-88).

Software and hardware settings determine how a Web page is displayed in a browser. Your Web pages may be displayed differently in your browser than those shown in the figure.

Instructions: Start Dreamweaver. Perform the tasks on the following pages to define a Web site and create and format a Web page for CandleLight. The text for the Web page is shown in Table 1-6.

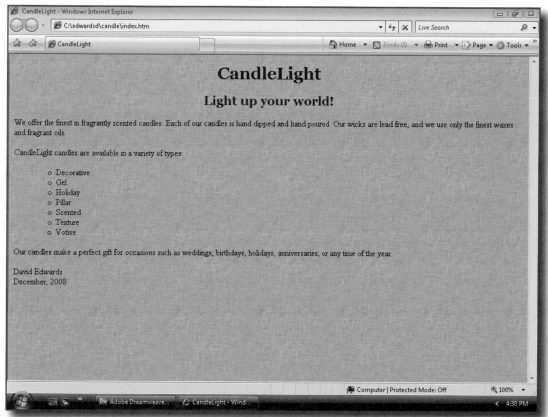

FIGURE 1-88

Table 1-6 CandleLight Web Page	
SECTION	**WEB PAGE TEXT**
Heading	CandleLight
Subheading	Light up your world!
Introductory Paragraph	We offer the finest in fragrantly scented candles. Each of our candles is hand dipped and hand poured. Our wicks are lead free, and we use only the finest waxes and fragrant oils.
Second Paragraph	CandleLight candles are available in a variety of types:
List Item 1	Decorative

(continued)

In the Lab

CandleLight Web Site *(continued)*

Table 1-6 CandleLight Web Page *(continued)*	
SECTION	**WEB PAGE TEXT**
List Item 2	Gel
List Item 3	Holiday
List Item 4	Pillar
List Item 5	Scented
List Item 6	Texture
List Item 7	Votive
Closing	Our candles make a perfect gift for occasions such as weddings, birthdays, holidays, anniversaries, or any time of the year.

1. Click Site on the menu bar and then click New Site. Use the Site Definition Advanced window option to create a local Web site under the your name folder. In the Site Definition Site name text box, name the site CandleLight. In the Local root folder text box, create a new subfolder under the your name folder, and name the new subfolder candle. The path will be C:\yourname\candle. In the Default images folder text box, create a new subfolder and name the folder images.
2. Click File on the menu bar and then click New. Click Blank Page and then click Create. Use the Save As command on the File menu to save the page with the name index.htm. If necessary, display the Standard toolbar.
3. Use the Windows Computer tool to copy the data file image (candlebg.jpg) to your candle\images folder.
4. Click the Modify menu and then click Page Properties. Apply the background image to the index page.
5. Click in the Document window and then type the Web page text shown in Table 1-6 on page DW 107 and DW 108. Press the ENTER key after typing each section and after each list item in the table.
6. Apply the Heading 1 format to the heading and apply the Heading 2 format to the subheading text. Center both headings. Select the heading and subheading text. Change the font type to Georgia, Times New Roman, Times, serif.
7. Change the text color of the heading and subheading to #990000 (fourth column from the left, sixth row from the bottom).
8. Create an unordered list for the list items. With these items still selected, click the Text Indent button in the Property inspector.
9. Title the Web page CandleLight.
10. Click at the end of the closing line and then press the ENTER key. Type your name. Insert a line break and then type the current date.
11. Check the spelling of your document and correct any errors.
12. Save the file.
13. View the Web page in the primary browser. Submit the document in the format specified by your instructor. Close the browser.
14. Quit Dreamweaver.

2 Credit Protection Web Site

Problem: Tracy Coady is an intern in a local bank. She recently lost her wallet, which contained all of her credit cards. Tracy called the credit card companies and canceled her cards. One of the employees at the bank suggested she also call the three credit bureaus to make them aware of this problem. Because searching for the names, telephone numbers, and addresses of the credit bureaus was time-consuming, Tracy decided she wants to have this information readily available for herself if she ever needs it again, and for others who might find themselves in a similar situation. Tracy also feels this Web site will serve as a valuable resource for the bank's customers. She has asked you to prepare the Web page shown in Figure 1-89.

Software and hardware settings determine how a Web page is displayed in a browser. Your Web pages may display differently in your browser than those shown in the figure.

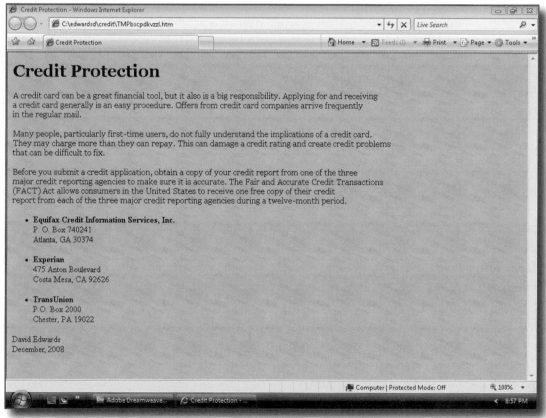

FIGURE 1-89

Instructions: Start Dreamweaver. Perform the following tasks to define a Web site and create and format an informational Web page on credit protection. The text for the Web page is shown in Table 1-7 on the next page.

(continued)

Credit Protection Web Site *(continued)*

Table 1-7 Credit Protection Web Page	
SECTION	**WEB PAGE TEXT**
Heading	Credit Protection
Introductory Paragraph	A credit card can be a great financial tool, but it also is a big responsibility. Applying for and receiving a credit card generally is an easy procedure. Offers from credit card companies arrive frequently in the regular mail.
Second Paragraph	Many people, particularly first-time users, do not fully understand the implications of a credit card. They may charge more than they can repay. This can damage a credit rating and create credit problems that can be difficult to fix.
Third Paragraph	Before you submit a credit application, obtain a copy of your credit report from one of the three major credit reporting agencies to make sure it is accurate. The Fair and Accurate Credit Transactions (FACT) Act allows consumers in the United States to receive one free copy of their credit report from each of the three major credit reporting agencies during a twelve-month period.
List Item 1	Equifax Credit Information Services, Inc. P. O. Box 740241 Atlanta, GA 30374
List Item 2	Experian 475 Anton Boulevard Costa Mesa, CA 92626
List Item 3	TransUnion P.O. Box 2000 Chester, PA 19022

1. Define a local Web site under the your name folder. Name the site Credit Protection. Create a new subfolder under the your name folder and name the new subfolder credit. Create an images folder and copy the image data file (creditbg.jpg) into the images folder.

2. Open a new Document window and use the Save As command to save the page with the name index.htm. Apply the background image to the index page.

3. Type the heading and first three paragraphs of the Web page text shown in Table 1-7. Press the ENTER key after typing each section of the text in the table.

4. Type list item 1. Insert a line break after the company name and after the address. Press the ENTER key after the line containing the city, state, and postal code. Type list items 2 and 3 in the same fashion.

5. Apply the Heading 1 format to the heading text. Align to the left (to ensure the heading is displayed properly in the browser).

6. Change the font type to Georgia, Times New Roman, Times, serif for all the text on the Web page.

7. Select the three list items (companies and addresses) and create an unordered list. Insert two line breaks between items 1 and 2, and between items 2 and 3.

8. Bold the company name of the first item in the bulleted list (Equifax Credit Information Services, Inc.). Apply the bold attribute to the names of the other two companies.

9. Title the Web page Credit Protection.

10. Click at the end of the last line of text and then press the ENTER key. If a bullet is displayed, click the Unordered List button in the Property inspector to remove the bullet. Type your name, add a line break, and then type the current date.
11. Check the spelling of your document, correct any errors, and then save the page.
12. View the Web page in your browser. Submit the document in the format specified by your instructor. Close the browser and then quit Dreamweaver.

3 Lexington, NC Web Site

Problem: Jerry Smith recently moved to Lexington, North Carolina. He discovered that Lexington has a colorful history and that many consider the city to be the Barbeque Capital of the World. He has asked you to help prepare a Web page (Figure 1-90) so he can share information with friends, relatives, and visitors to North Carolina about the city's facts.

Software and hardware settings determine how a Web page is displayed in a browser. Your Web pages may display differently in your browser than those shown in the figure.

FIGURE 1-90

(continued)

In the Lab

Lexington, NC Web Site *(continued)*

Instructions: Start Dreamweaver. Perform the following tasks to define a Web site and create and format an informational Web page on Lexington, North Carolina. The text of the Web page is shown in Table 1-8.

Table 1-8 Lexington, North Carolina Web Site

SECTION	WEB PAGE TEXT
Heading	Lexington, North Carolina
Subheading	Barbeque Capital of the World
Introductory Paragraph	Located in the heart of North Carolina's Piedmont section, about 95 miles west of Raleigh, the city is surrounded by a countryside of lush rolling hills and features a small-town atmosphere.
Second Paragraph	Each year, Uptown Lexington hosts a Barbeque Festival where an eight-block stretch of Main Street is closed to traffic. Over four hundred exhibitors sell everything from handmade crafts to home-made fudge. The festival is for people of all ages and includes a special section of rides and games for children.
Third Paragraph	Interesting Facts about Lexington:
List Item 1	Lexington's history dates back to the late 1700s.
List Item 2	Lexington was named in honor of the Revolutionary War battle site in Massachusetts.
List Item 3	Lexington is located in Davidson County, North Carolina, with a population of some 17,000 residents.
List Item 4	The barbeque festival is a Lexington annual tradition and is celebrated each year in October.
List Item 5	A section of Davidson County is known for its red dirt, called "Davidson Loam." It is considered the best agricultural soil around.
List Item 6	The first barbeque restaurant in Lexington no longer exists. The space was incorporated into the City Hall.
List Item 7	Elvis Presley was paid $200 for performing at the YMCA in Lexington on March 21, 1956.

1. Define a local Web site under the your name folder. Name the site Lexington, NC. Create a subfolder and name it city. Create an images subfolder and copy the image data file (citybg.gif) into the folder.
2. Open a new Document window and use the Save As command to save the page with the name index.htm. Apply the background image to the index page.
3. Click in the Document window and then type the Web page text shown in Table 1-8. Press the ENTER key after typing the text in each section in the table.
4. Apply Heading 1 to the heading. Apply Heading 2 to the subheading. Center both headings. Change the heading font type to Arial, Helvetica, sans-serif.
5. Select the third paragraph, Interesting Facts about Lexington:, and then apply Heading 2 to the text.
6. Select list items 1 through 7 and apply an ordered list format.
7. Title the Web page Lexington, NC.
8. Insert your name and the current date at the bottom of the Web page. Select all of the text on the page, change the text color to hexadecimal #993333, and then apply bold formatting.
9. Check the spelling of your document and correct any errors. Save the Web page.
10. View the Web page in the browser. Submit the document in the format specified by your instructor. Quit Dreamweaver.

Cases and Places

The difficulty of these case studies varies:
■ are the least difficult and ■■ are the most difficult. The last exercise is a group exercise.

1 ■ Define a Web site named Favorite Sports with a subfolder named sports. Prepare a Web page listing your favorite sports and favorite teams. Include a title for your Web page. Bold and center the title, and then apply the Heading 1 style. Include a sentence or two explaining why you like the sport and why you like the teams. Bold and italicize the names of the teams and the sports. Give the Web page a meaningful title. Apply a background image to your Web page. Check the spelling in the document. Use the concepts and techniques presented in the chapter to format the text. Save the file in the sports folder. For a selection of images and backgrounds, visit the Dreamweaver CS3 Media Web page (scsite.com/dwcs3/media).

2 ■ Your instructor has asked you to create a Web page about one of your hobbies. Define the Web site using Hobbies for the site name and hobby for the subfolder name. Italicize and center the title, and then apply the Heading 2 style. Type a paragraph of three or four sentences explaining why you selected the subject. Select and center the paragraph. Add a list of three items and create an ordered list from the three items. Include line breaks between each numbered item. Title the Web page the name of the hobby you selected. Check the spelling in your document. Use the concepts and techniques presented in the chapter to format the text. For a selection of images and backgrounds, visit the Dreamweaver CS3 Media Web page (scsite.com/dwcs3/media).

3 ■■ Define a Web site and create a Web page that gives a description and information about your favorite type of music. Name the Web site Favorite Music and the subfolder music. Apply a background image to the Web page. Include a left-aligned heading formatted with the Heading 1 style. Include a subheading formatted with Heading 2. List four facts about why you selected this type of music. Include the names of three of your favorite songs and the names of the artists. Bold and italicize the name of the songs and artists and apply a font color of your choice. Create an ordered list from the four facts. Title the Web page Favorite Music. Save the file as index in the music folder. Use the concepts and techniques presented in the chapter to format the text. For a selection of images and backgrounds, visit the Dreamweaver CS3 Media Web page (scsite.com/dwcs3/media).

Cases and Places

4 ■■ Assume you are running for office in your city's local government. Define a Web site using the name of the city in which you live and a subfolder named government. Include the following information in your Web page: your name, centered, with Heading 1 and a font color of your choice; the name of the office for which you are running, bold and italicized; and a paragraph about the duties of the office in Courier font. Create a bulleted list within your Web page. Change the title of the Web page from Untitled Document to your name. Use the concepts and techniques presented in the chapter to format the text. For a selection of images and backgrounds, visit the Dreamweaver CS3 Media Web page (scsite.com/dwcs3/media).

5 ■■ **Working Together** Your school has a budget for student trips. Your assignment and that of your teammates is to put together a Web site and Web page that list locations and trips that students can select. Apply an appropriate background image. Include a title, formatted with Heading 1, and a subtitle, formatted with Heading 2. List three locations. Bold and apply a font color to each location name. Add a bullet to each location name. Include information about each location. Title the page Student Government. Use the concepts and techniques presented in the chapter to format the text. For a selection of images and backgrounds, visit the Dreamweaver CS3 Media Web page (scsite.com/dwcs3/media).

Adding Web Pages, Links, and Images

CHAPTER

2

CASE PERSPECTIVE

Tracy Coady, a coworker at the state environmental agency, is interested in Colorado's parks and viewed the Web page that you and David created. She has offered some suggestions and asked to help with the design. Both you and David agreed, and the three of you have become a team.

Tracy suggests adding images to the home page. David proposes that the Web site include a page for Colorado's four national parks and another page with information about Colorado's five national monuments. You explain to David and Tracy that the addition of each new page will require hyperlinks from the home page and links from each page back to the home page. You assure them that Dreamweaver includes all the tools they need to add these and other types of links, including e-mail links, to related Web sites. You create a navigation map to illustrate how the links will work among the three pages. All team members agree that these two new pages should be added and that the pages will include images and links. With the addition of these two pages, the Web page you created in Chapter 1 will become a Web site.

As you read through this chapter, you will learn how to add pages to a Web site, how to add images to a Web page, and how to insert absolute, relative, and e-mail links.

ADOBE
Dreamweaver CS3

Adding Web Pages, Links, and Images

Objectives

You will have mastered the material in this chapter when you can:

- Define and set a home page
- Add pages to a Web site
- Describe Dreamweaver's image accessibility features
- Describe image file formats
- Insert, resize, and align images within a Web page
- Describe the different types of links

- Create relative, absolute, and e-mail links
- Describe how to change the color of links
- Edit and delete links
- Describe and display the Site Map
- Describe Code view, Split view, and Design view
- View Code view

Introduction

Chapter 2 introduces the addition of Web pages to the local site created in Chapter 1 and the integration of links and graphics into the Web pages that make up the site. Recall from Chapter 1 that a site or a Web site is a set of linked documents with shared attributes, such as related topics, a similar design, or a shared purpose.

The Dreamweaver site structure feature provides a way to maintain and organize your files. A Web page essentially is a text document and a collection of HTML and XHTML code. The code defines the structure and layout of a Web document and is generated automatically by Dreamweaver. Images and other media content are separate files. For example, a page that displays text and three images consists of four separate files — one for the text document and one for each of the three images.

Most Web site builders include images on their Web pages. It is important that you take the time to learn about images, image properties, and the types of images best suited for a particular situation. Image properties, such as alignment, size adjustment, and alternative text for accessibility issues, help you to understand the effects of using images on Web pages.

When a file or image is referenced within the source code, a link (or hyperlink) exists within the source code to the external file or image. A link (hyperlink) also is a Web page element that, when clicked, accesses another Web page, or a different place within the existing Web page. A Web page can contain different types of links: internal, or relative; absolute; e-mail; and named anchors. A named anchor is a link to a specific place within a document and is discussed in Chapter 3. This chapter discusses how to create relative, absolute, and e-mail links.

Chapter Two — Two New Pages, Links, and Images

In this chapter, you continue with the creation of the Colorado Parks Web site. You create two additional Web pages, add image backgrounds to the two new pages, add images to the two new pages and to the index page, add links to and from the index page, and add absolute links to the five national monuments (Figures 2-1a, 2-1b, and 2-1c).

(a) Colorado Parks Index (Home) Page

(c) Colorado National Parks Page

(b) Colorado National Monuments Page

FIGURE 2-1

In the Introduction chapter, four types of Web structures were illustrated: linear, hierarchical, web (or random), and grid. This chapter uses a hierarchical structure (Figure 2-2 on the next page). The index page is the home page, or entrance to the Web site. From this page, the visitor to this site can link to a page about Colorado National Parks or to a page about Colorado National Monuments.

FIGURE 2-2

Managing a Web Site

Organization is a key element of Web design. Dreamweaver works best with entire sites rather than individual Web pages and has many built-in tools, such as checking links and organizing files, to make site creation easy. You defined the parks Web site in Chapter 1 and created the index page. You can add pages to your site by creating a new page and saving it as part of the site, or by opening an existing page from another source and saving it as part of the site. In this chapter, you will create two new pages.

Almost all Web sites have a home page. Compare the home page to your front door. Generally, the front door is the first thing guests see when they visit you. The same applies to a Web site's home page. When someone visits a Web site, he or she usually enters through the home page.

The home page normally is named **index.htm** or **index.html**. This file name has special significance. Most Web servers recognize index.htm (or index.html) as the default home page and automatically display this page without requiring that the user type the full Uniform Resource Locator (URL), or Web address. For example, if you type http://www.symantec.com into a Web browser address box to access the Web site, what you see is http://www.symantec.com/index.htm — the actual file name of the site's home page — even though you did not type it that way.

Organizing your Web site and using Dreamweaver's site management features can assure you that the media within your Web page will be displayed correctly. Bringing all of these elements together will start you on your way to becoming a successful Web site developer.

Before you start enhancing your Web site, you need to copy the data files into the site's folder hierarchy.

Copying Data Files to the Local Web Site

Your data files contain images for Chapter 2. These images are in an images folder. You use the Windows Computer option to copy the Chapter 2 images to your parks images folder. See the inside back cover of this book for instructions for downloading the data files, or see your instructor for information about accessing the files required for this book.

The DataFiles folder for this chapter is stored on Local Disk (C:). The location on your computer may be different. If necessary, verify the location of the DataFiles folder with your instructor. The following steps show how to copy the files to the parks local root folder. This book uses the Microsoft Windows Vista operating system. If you are using a different version of Windows, the copying process will be somewhat different.

To Copy Data Files to the Parks Web Site

1 Click the Start button on the Windows taskbar and then click Computer.

2 Double-click Local Disk (C:) and then navigate to the location of the data files for Chapter 2.

3 Double-click the folder containing the data files and then double-click the Chap02 folder.

4 Double-click the parks folder and then double-click the images folder.

5 Click the dinosaur image file or the first file in the list.

6 Hold down the SHIFT key and then click the waterfall01 image file, or the last file in the list.

7 Right-click the selected files to display the context menu.

8 Click the Copy command and then click the Back button the number of times necessary to navigate to the your name folder.

9 Double-click the your name folder, double-click the parks folder, and then double-click the images folder.

10 Right-click anywhere in the open window to display the context menu.

11 Click the Paste command.

12 Click the images window Close button.

The six images are pasted into the Colorado Parks Web site images folder, and the folder now contains seven images, including the parksbg image file (Figure 2-3).

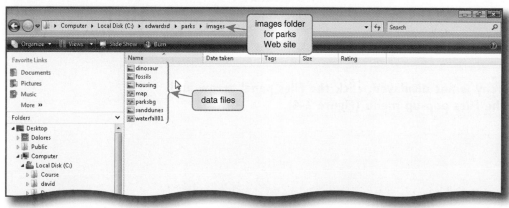

FIGURE 2-3

The data files are copied to the parks Web site file hierarchy. The next step is to start Dreamweaver.

Starting Dreamweaver and Opening a Web Site

Each time you start Dreamweaver, it opens to the last site displayed when you closed the program. It therefore may be necessary for you to open the parks Web site. Clicking the **Files pop-up menu** in the Files panel lists the sites you have defined. When you open the site, a list of pages and subfolders within the site is displayed. The following steps illustrate how to start Dreamweaver and open the Colorado Parks Web site.

To Start Dreamweaver and Open the Colorado Parks Web Site

1

• **Click the Start button on the Windows taskbar. Point to All Programs on the Start menu, point to Adobe Dreamweaver CS3 on the All Programs menu, and then click Adobe Dreamweaver CS3 submenu. If necessary, display the panel groups.**

Dreamweaver might be installed differently on your computer and appear on a submenu.

Dreamweaver opens and displays panel groups and an empty Document window. If the Start page is displayed, click Open in the Open a Recent Item column and then select the parks index.htm file.

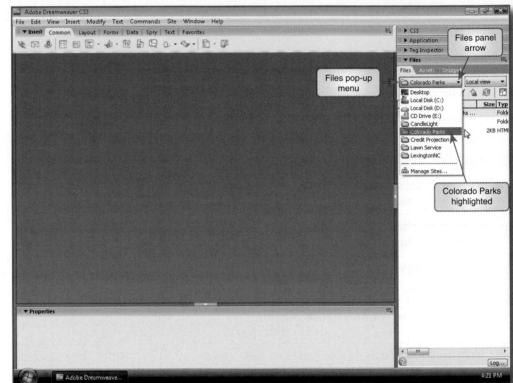

FIGURE 2-4

2

• **If the Colorado Parks hierarchy is not displayed, click the Files panel arrow and point to Colorado Parks on the Files pop-up menu (Figure 2-4).**

3

• **Click Colorado Parks.**

The Colorado Parks Web site hierarchy is displayed in the Files panel (Figure 2-5).

FIGURE 2-5

Opening a Web Page

Once you have created and saved a Web page or copied a Web page to a Web site, you often will have reason to retrieve it from disk. Opening an existing Web page in Dreamweaver is much the same as opening an existing document in most other software applications; that is, you use the File menu and Open command or you can use Dreamweaver's unique File and Open Recent command. If, however, the page is part of a Web site created with Dreamweaver, you also can open the file from the Files panel.

After opening the page, you can modify text, images, tables, and any other elements. The following step on the next page illustrates how to open a Web page from a local site in the Files panel.

To Open a Web Page from a Local Web Site

1

• **Double-click index.htm in the Files panel.**

• **If the Standard toolbar is not displayed, click View on the menu bar, point to Toolbars, and then click Standard.**

The Colorado Parks index page opens in the Document window, and the name of the page is displayed on the tab at the top of the window. The Standard toolbar is displayed (Figure 2-6).

FIGURE 2-6

Other Ways

1. On File menu, click Open, select file

The Files Panel

Organization is one of the keys to a successful Web site. Creating documents without considering where in the folder hierarchy they should go generally creates a difficult-to-manage Web site. The Dreamweaver **Files panel** provides a view of the devices and folders on your computer and shows how these devices and folders are organized. You can create new folders and files for your site through the Files panel, which is similar to the Windows file organization method. You also can use the Files panel to drag or copy and paste files from one folder to another or from one Web site to another. You cannot, however, copy a file from a Windows folder and paste it into a site in the Dreamweaver Files panel.

In Windows, the main directory of a disk is called the **root directory** or the **top-level directory**. A small device icon or folder icon is displayed next to each object in the list. The **device icon** represents a device such as the Desktop or a disk drive, and the **folder icon** represents a folder. Many of these icons have a plus or minus sign next to them, which indicates whether the device or folder contains additional folders or files. Windows arranges all of these objects — root directory, folders, subfolders, and files — in a hierarchy. The plus and minus signs are controls that you can click to expand or collapse the view of the file hierarchy. In the Files panel, Dreamweaver uses the same hierarchy arrangement, but site folders and other file icons appear in a different color than non-site folders and files so that you easily can distinguish between the two.

The Home Page and the Site Map

Most Web sites have a starting point, called a home page. In a personal home page within a Web site, for example, you probably would list your name, your e-mail address, some personal information, and links to other information on your Web site. The index page you created in Chapter 1 is the home page for the parks Web site.

Although you cannot tell which page in a Web site is the home page by viewing the site files, Dreamweaver provides a graphical option to view the site organization — the Site Map. You access the Site Map through the Files panel. To create a Site Map requires that you designate one page in the Web site as a home page. You will use the Site Map to view the Web site structure later in this chapter. The next section sets the home page.

Setting a Home Page

Each Web site you create within Dreamweaver should have a home page. A **home page** is similar to a table of contents or an index in a book. The home page generally contains links to all the other level two pages within the Web site. Most home pages are named index.htm or index.html. The following step shows how to define the home page through Dreamweaver's Files panel.

To Set a Home Page

1

• **Right-click the index.htm file name in the Files panel.**

• **Point to Set as Home Page.**

The context menu is displayed (Figure 2-7).

• **Click Set as Home Page on the context menu.**

The index.htm file is set as the home page for the parks Web site. In the files list, however, no changes are evident.

FIGURE 2-7

Q: Is it necessary to create a folder for images within the Web site?

A: Critical to Web development is the hierarchy of folders and files in a Web site. Even for the very simplest of sites, you should create a separate folder for the images. The folder name can be any name you choose, but it is best to use a descriptive, meaningful name.

Adding Pages to a Web Site

You copied the files necessary to begin creating your Web site to the parks local root folder in the Files panel, and you set the home page. It is time to start building and enhancing your site. You will create two additional pages for the Web site: Colorado National Parks and Colorado National Monuments. You will add links and Web page images to the index or home page and add links, a background image, and Web page images to the two new pages.

Opening a New Document Window

The next step is to open a new Document window. This will become the Colorado National Parks page. The following steps illustrate how to open a new document window and save the page as natl_parks.htm.

To Open a New Document Window

1

• **Click File on the menu bar and then point to New.**

The File menu is displayed (Figure 2-8).

FIGURE 2-8

2

• **Click New. If necessary, click Blank Page.**

• **Click HTML in the Page Type column. Verify that XHTML 1.0 Transitional is selected in the DocType pop-up menu.**

The New Document dialog box is displayed. Blank Page is selected and HTML is the selected Page Type (Figure 2-9).

FIGURE 2-9

3

• **Click the Create button.**

A new Untitled-2 Document window opens (Figure 2-10). The number following Untitled increases each time you open a new Document window. Your computer may display a different number.

FIGURE 2-10

4

• **Click the Save button on the Standard toolbar.**

The Save As dialog box is displayed and Untitled-2 is highlighted in the File name text box (Figure 2-11).

FIGURE 2-11

5

• **Type** natl_parks **for the file name.**

The natl_parks file name is displayed in the File name text box (Figure 2-12).

FIGURE 2-12

6

• **Click the Save button.**

The natl_parks.htm page is saved in the parks local folder and is displayed in Dreamweaver's Files panel. The .htm extension is added automatically by Dreamweaver. The path and file name [C:\edwardsd\parks\natl_parks.htm] appear on the Dreamweaver title bar (Figure 2-13).

FIGURE 2-13

To organize your workspace, you collapse the lower portion of the Property inspector. This gives you additional window space in the Dreamweaver Document window. The following step on the next page shows how to organize your workspace by collapsing the lower portion of the Property inspector.

To Prepare the Workspace

1 **If necessary, click the Property inspector expander arrow.**

The natl_parks.htm Document window is open, and the Property inspector is collapsed (Figure 2-14).

FIGURE 2-14

With the workspace prepared and the Document window displayed, you can begin creating the Web page for Colorado National Parks.

Creating the National Parks Web Page

To create the page for Colorado National Parks, you type the text in the Document window. Table 2-1 includes the text for the Colorado National Parks Web page. Press the ENTER key after typing each section as indicated in Table 2-1.

Table 2-1 Colorado National Parks Web Page Text

SECTION	WEB PAGE TEXT
Heading	Colorado National Parks<ENTER>
Part 1	Rocky Mountain National Park, located in the northern part of Colorado, is world renowned for the beauty of its ancient mountains and the diversity of its plant and animal life. The park was established on January 26, 1915 and contains 60 peaks rising above 12,000 feet.<ENTER>
Part 2	Black Canyon of the Gunnison National Park, located in the western part of the state, is unique. The spectacular landscape was formed slowly by the action of water and rock scouring down through hard Proterozoic crystalline rock.<ENTER>
Part 3	Mesa Verde National Park is located near the New Mexico border. Spanish for "green table," Mesa Verde is rich in cultural heritage. The well-preserved site presents an archeological glimpse of the lives of the Ancestral Pueblo people.<ENTER>
Part 4	Great Sand Dunes National Park and Preserve, located along the edge of the Sangre de Cristo Mountains in southern Colorado, is a pile of sand over 700 feet tall and covering over 54 square miles. This geologic wonderland became a national monument in 1932.<ENTER>
Closing	Home<ENTER>

The following steps show how to create the Web page.

To Create the National Parks Web Page

1

• **Type the heading** Colorado National Parks **as shown in Table 2-1. Press the** ENTER **key.**

The heading is entered in the Document window (Figure 2-15). Pressing the ENTER *key creates a new paragraph.*

FIGURE 2-15

2

• **Type the rest of the text as shown in Table 2-1 on the previous page. Press the ENTER key as indicated in the table.**

The text for the Colorado National Parks Web page is entered (Figure 2-16).

text for Web page entered

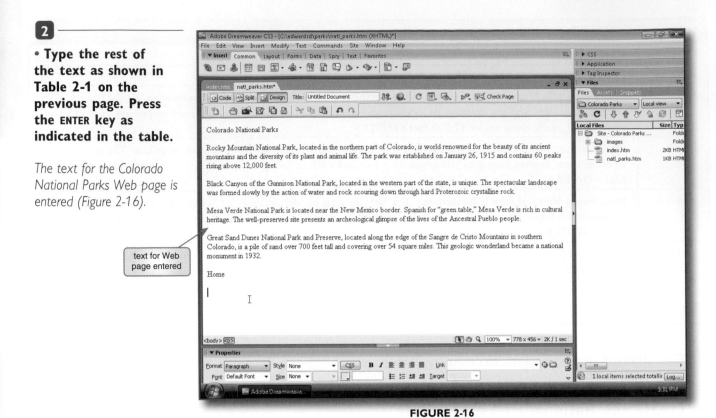

FIGURE 2-16

In Chapter 1, you formatted the index page by adding headings and bullets and by centering and bolding text. The following steps show how to apply similar formatting to the Colorado National Parks page.

To Format the Colorado National Parks Page

1 If necessary, scroll up to the top of the Web page, and then apply Heading 1 to the heading text.

2 Center the heading.

3 Add bullets to the following four lines that begin: Rocky Mountain National Park, Black Canyon of the Gunnison National Park, Mesa Verde National Park, and Great Sand Dunes National Park and Preserve.

4 Bold the park names at the beginning of each of the four lines: Rocky Mountain National Park, Black Canyon of the Gunnison National Park, Mesa Verde National Park, and Great Sand Dunes National Park and Preserve.

5 Add two line breaks after the bullet paragraphs describing the Rocky Mountain National Park, Black Canyon of the Gunnison National Park, and the Mesa Verde National Park.

6 At the top of the page, type Colorado National Parks as the Web page title.

7 Save the natl_parks.htm Web page.

8 Press F12 to view the page in the browser and to verify that the line spacing is correct, as shown in Figure 2-17.

9 Close the browser.

The Colorado National Parks Web page text is entered, formatted, and saved.

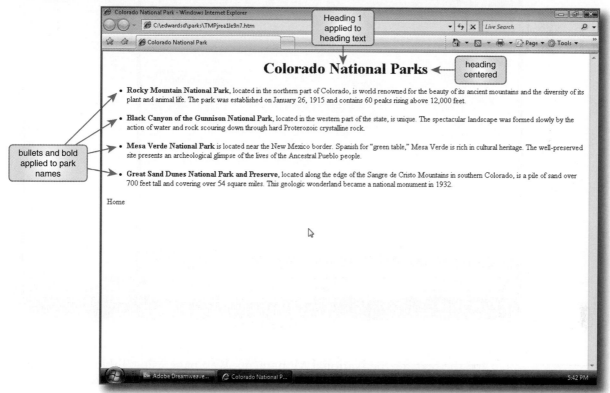

FIGURE 2-17

Creating the National Monuments Web Page

You will enter the text for the Colorado National Monuments page the same way you entered the text for the Colorado National Parks page. Table 2-2 on the next pages DW 132 and DW 133 includes all the text for the Colorado National Monuments Web page.

To Open a New Document Window

1 Click File on the menu bar, click New, and then, if necessary, click Blank Page.

2 Click HTML in the Page Type column.

3 Click the Create button.

4 Save the Web page as monuments.htm in the parks folder.

A new Document window opens, and the name of the saved page is displayed on the title bar (Figure 2-18 on the next page).

monuments.htm saved in Files panel

FIGURE 2-18

Type the text for the National Monuments Web page using Table 2-2 and the following steps. Press the ENTER key or insert a line break, or <br>, as indicated in the table.

Table 2-2 Colorado National Monuments Web Page Text	
SECTION	**WEB PAGE TEXT**
Heading	Colorado National Monuments<ENTER>
Part 1	Dinosaur National Monument This monument, located in Colorado and Utah, was designated as a national monument in 1915. It was discovered by paleontologist Earl Douglass on August 17, 1909. The 200,000 acre area was layered with prehistoric plant and animal fossils and contained 350 tons of fossils, including full skeletons and remains of some dinosaur species that previously were unknown.<ENTER>
Part 2	Colorado National Monument The Colorado National Monument, located in Fruita, Colorado, covers about 20,000 acres. The sheer walls and deep canyons are considered one of the grand landscapes of the American West. <ENTER>
Part 3	Florissant Fossil Bed National Monument Volcanic eruptions formed fossil beds when they sent lava and mud into the Florissant Basin millions of years ago. The monument is known for more than 80,000 identified animal and plant specimens and is located just west of Pikes Peak. <ENTER>
Part 4	Hovenweep National Monument Hovenweep National Monument was established in 1923 and is found in Colorado and Utah. Located on 784 acres, the monument includes six unique prehistoric villages that date back to the mid-thirteenth century. <ENTER>

Table 2-2 Colorado National Monuments Web Page Text *(continued)*	
SECTION	WEB PAGE TEXT
Part 5	Yucca House National Monument This historic site is located in southwest Colorado and contains the unexcavated ruins of Ancestral Puebloan villages. <ENTER>
Closing	Home<ENTER>

To Create the National Monuments Web Page

1 Type the text of the Web page as shown in Table 2-2, and then click the Save button.

The text for the Colorado National Monuments Web page is entered (Figure 2-19).

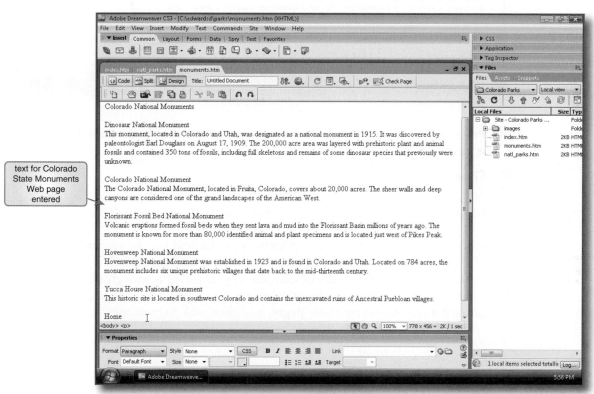

text for Colorado
State Monuments
Web page
entered

FIGURE 2-19

To Format the Colorado National Monuments Page

1 If necessary, scroll to the top of the Web page and then apply Heading 1 to the heading.

2 Center the heading.

3 Bold the names of each of the five monuments where they are used as subtitles.

4 Type Colorado National Monuments as the Web page title (Figure 2-20 on the next page).

5 Click the Save button on the Standard toolbar.

FIGURE 2-20

6 Press F12 to view the page in the browser and to verify that the line spacing is correct.

7 Close the browser.

The text for the Colorado National Monuments page is entered, formatted, and saved.

You have completed entering and formatting the text for the two new pages and copied the images to the parks local root folder in the Files panel. It is time to add other enhancements to your site. In Chapter 1, you added a background image to the index page. In this chapter, you learn more about images. You will add the same background image to the two new pages, and then add page images and links to all three pages.

Images

If used correctly and with an understanding of the Web site audience, images add excitement and interest to a Web page. When you are selecting images for a Web site, it is important to understand that the size and type of image or images used within a Web page affect how fast the Web page downloads and is displayed in the viewer's Web browser. A Web page that downloads too slowly will turn away visitors.

Image File Formats

Graphical images used on the Web are in one of two broad categories: vector and bitmap. **Vector** images are composed of key points and paths, which define shapes and coloring instructions, such as line and fill colors. The vector file contains a description of the image expressed mathematically. The file describes the image to the computer, and the computer draws it. This type of image generally is associated with Adobe Flash or LiveMotion animation programs. One of the benefits of vector images is the small file size, particularly relative to the larger file size of bitmap images.

Bitmap images are the more common type of image file. A bitmap file maps out or plots an image on a pixel-by-pixel basis. A **pixel**, or **picture element**, is the smallest point in a graphical image. Graphic monitors display images by dividing the display screen into thousands (or millions) of pixels, arranged in a **grid** of rows and columns. The pixels appear connected because they are so close together. This grid of pixels is a **bitmap**. The **bit-resolution** of an image is described by the number of bits used to represent each pixel. There are 8-bit images as well as 24- or 32-bit images, where each bit represents a pixel. An 8-bit image supports up to 256 colors, and a 24- or 32-bit image supports up to 16.7 million colors.

Web browsers currently support three bitmap image file types: GIF, JPEG, and PNG.

GIF (.gif) is an acronym for **Graphics Interchange Format**. The GIF format uses 8-bit resolution, supports up to a maximum of 256 colors, and uses combinations of these 256 colors to simulate colors beyond that range. The GIF format is best for displaying images such as logos, icons, buttons, and other images with even colors and tones. GIF images come in two different versions: GIF87 format and GIF89a format. The GIF89a format contains three features not available in the GIF87 or JPEG formats: transparency, interlacing, and animation. The **transparency** feature allows you to specify a transparency color, which allows the background color or image to display. The **interlacing** feature lets the browser begin to build a low-resolution version of the full-sized GIF picture on the screen while the file is still downloading, so there is something visible to the visitor as the Web page downloads. The **animation** feature allows you to include moving images. Animated GIF images are simply a number of GIF images saved into a single file and looped, or repeated, over and over. A number of shareware GIF editors are available to create animated GIFs. If you do not want to create your own animations, you can find thousands of free animated GIFs on the Internet available for downloading.

JPEG (.jpg) is an acronym for **Joint Photographic Experts Group**. JPEG files are the best format for photographic images because JPEG files can contain up to 16.7 million colors. **Progressive JPEG** is a new variation of the JPEG image format. This image format supports a gradually-built display similar to the interlaced GIFs. Older browsers do not support progressive JPEG files.

PNG (.png) stands for **Portable Network Graphics**. PNG, which is the native file format of Adobe Fireworks, is a GIF competitor normally used for images. Many browsers do not support this format without a special plug-in. Generally, it is better to use GIF or JPEG images in your Web pages.

When developing a Web site that consists of many pages, you should maintain a consistent, professional layout and design throughout all of the pages. The pages in a single site, for example, should use similar features such as background colors or images, margins, and headings.

Background Colors and Background Images

Most Web pages are displayed with a default white or gray background. Generally, the browser used to display the Web page determines the default background. You can enhance your Web page by adding a background image and/or background color.

If you use a background color, the same cautions apply to background color as they do to text color. You want to use Web-safe colors. This means the colors will be displayed correctly on the computer screen when someone is viewing your Web page. To insert an image or color for the page background, you use the Page Properties dialog box.

Q: Is it necessary to add a background image to a Web page?

A: No, you do not need to add a background image. If you do add a background image to your Web page, however, select an image that does not clash with the text and other content. The background image should not overwhelm the Web page.

Background images add texture and interesting color to a Web page and set the overall appearance of the document. Most browsers support background images. A background image can be a large image, but more frequently it is a smaller image. The image tiles to fill the screen in the Dreamweaver Document window and in the browser window. In Chapter 1, you added a background image to the index page. Now you add the same image to the National Parks Web page and the National Monuments page. The following steps illustrate how to add a background image to these two pages.

To Add a Background Image to the Colorado National Parks Web Page

1 Click the natl_parks.htm tab.

2 Click Modify on the menu bar and then click Page Properties.

3 Click the Browse button to the right of the Background image box.

4 If necessary, navigate to the images folder.

5 Click parksbg.gif and then click the OK button in the Select Image Source dialog box.

6 Click the OK button in the Page Properties dialog box.

7 Click the Save button on the Standard toolbar.

The background image is applied to the Colorado National Parks page (Figure 2-21).

FIGURE 2-21

To Add a Background Image to the Colorado National Monuments Web Page

Other Ways

1. Right-click Document window, click Page Properties on context menu
2. Expand the Property inspector, click Page Properties button

1 Click the monuments.htm tab.

2 Click Modify on the menu bar and then click Page Properties.

3 Click the Browse button to the right of the Background image box.

4 Click parksbg.gif and then click the OK button in the Select Image Source dialog box.

5 Click the OK button in the Page Properties dialog box.

6 Click the Save button on the Standard toolbar.

The background image is applied to the Colorado National Monuments page (Figure 2-22).

FIGURE 2-22

Besides adding background images, you also can add images to your Web pages. To enhance your index.htm Web page further, you will add two images. One of the images will be displayed at the top left of the document, and the second image will be displayed to the right of the bulleted list. Dreamweaver has features to assist with placement and enhancement of images. The Assets panel provides visual cues for your images, the invisible element feature provides placement control for the images, and the accessibility feature provides information for individuals with disabilities.

Assets Panel

Assets are elements, such as images or Flash files, that you use in building a page or a site. The **Assets panel**, which is grouped with the Files panel, helps you manage and organize your Web site's assets (Figure 2-23 on the next page). This panel contains a list of all the asset types (images, colors, URLs, Flash and Shockwave files, movies, scripts, templates, and library items) within the selected local root folder. The Site option shows the assets in your site. The Favorites list shows only the assets you have selected and added to the list. To add an asset to the Favorites list, select the item in the Site list and then click the Add to Favorites button. Remove an item from the list by selecting the Favorites option button, selecting the item, and then clicking the Remove from Favorites button. The Assets panel in Figure 2-23 is resized to show all options. You resize the panels by moving the mouse pointer over the vertical bar until it displays as a two-headed arrow. Then you hold down the mouse button and drag.

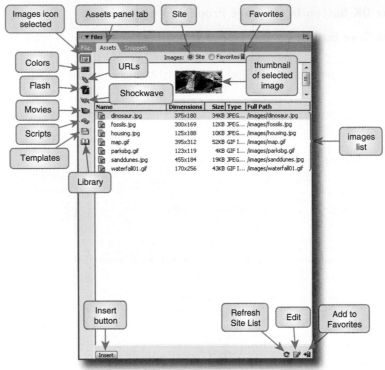

FIGURE 2-23

You can insert most asset types into a document by dragging them into the Document window or by using the Insert button at the bottom of the Assets panel. Also, you either can insert colors and URLs or apply them to selected text in Design view. Additionally, you can apply URLs to other elements in Design view, such as images. When an image file name is selected, a thumbnail of the image displays at the top of the Assets panel. You will use the Assets panel to insert the images into the Colorado Parks Web pages.

Accessibility

When developing a Web page, the Web page developer needs to consider the full spectrum of visitors who may access the site. Dreamweaver provides accessibility tools that allow the Web site developer to create pages to meet the needs of all visitors, including those with disabilities. The four accessibility object tools included in Dreamwaver are form objects, frames, media, and images. This chapter includes accessibility information relative to images. The three other objects are covered in later chapters.

When you insert an image, the Image Tag Accessibility Attributes dialog box may be displayed (Figure 2-24). This dialog box contains two text boxes — one for Alternate text and one for Long description. Screen readers translate and read the information you enter in both text boxes. The information you enter for Alternate text displays when a Web site visitor moves the mouse pointer over the image. You should limit your alternate text entry to 50 characters or less. For a more detailed description of the image, create and save a text file and then add it as a link to the file. When the link is activated, the screen reader recites the text for visually impaired visitors. It is not required that you enter text in either text box. For images in this chapter and other chapters, however, instructions are included to add alternate text. Clicking Cancel removes the dialog box and inserts the image. Appendix B contains a full overview of Dreamweaver's accessibility features.

FIGURE 2-24

Invisible Elements

Dreamweaver's Document window displays basically what you see in a Web browser window. It sometimes is helpful, however, when designing a Web page to see the placement of certain code elements. For example, viewing the Line Break code <br /> provides a visual cue regarding the layout. Dreamweaver enables you to control the visibility of 13 different codes, including those for image placement, through the Preferences dialog box.

When you insert into and then align an image in a Document window, Dreamweaver can display an **invisible element marker** that shows the location of the inserted image within the HTML code. This visual aid is displayed as a small yellow icon. When you select the icon, it turns blue, and you can use it to cut and paste or drag and drop the image. When using invisible elements with images, however, the invisible element marker is not displayed if the image is aligned to the left. Dreamweaver provides the invisible element marker for 13 other elements, including tables, ActiveX objects, plug-ins, and applets. To hide all invisible elements temporarily, select Hide All on the View menu Visual Aids submenu.

The following steps on the next page illustrate how to display the invisible element marker for aligned elements such as images and how to turn on invisible elements through the Visual Aids submenu command.

To Set Invisible Element Preferences and Turn on Visual Aids

1

• **Click Edit on the menu bar and then click Preferences.**

• **Click Invisible Elements in the Category list.**

The Preferences dialog box is displayed, and Invisible Elements is selected in the Category list (Figure 2-25).

FIGURE 2-25

2

• **Click the Anchor points for aligned elements check box (Figure 2-26).**

FIGURE 2-26

3

- **Click the OK button.**

The Document window is displayed with no visible change.

4

- **Click View on the menu bar, point to Visual Aids, and then point to Invisible Elements.**

The View menu and the Visual Aids submenu are displayed. Invisible Elements is highlighted (Figure 2-27). Note: If a check mark already appears to the left of the Invisible Elements command, do not complete the next step.

FIGURE 2-27

5

- **Click Invisible Elements.**

A check mark is added to the Invisible Elements command, and the Document window is displayed with no visible changes.

Inserting an Image into a Web Page

Inserting images into your Web page is easy and quick with Dreamweaver — just drag and drop the image from the Files panel or the Assets panel. Image placement, however, can be more complex. When you view the Web page in a browser, the image may be displayed somewhat differently than in the Document window. If the images are not displayed correctly, you can select and modify the placement of the images in the Document window by dragging the invisible element marker to move the image.

To Insert an Image into the Index Page

1

• **Click the index.htm page tab. If necessary, scroll to the top of the page.**

• **If necessary, click the Assets panel tab. Verify that the Images icon is selected.**

• **Click sanddunes.jpg in the Assets panel.**

The index page is displayed and the Assets panel is available. The file, sanddunes.jpg, is selected (Figure 2-28).

FIGURE 2-28

2

• **Drag sanddunes.jpg from the Assets panel to the left of the first line of the first paragraph.**

The Image Tag Accessibility Attributes dialog box is displayed (Figure 2-29).

FIGURE 2-29

3

• **Type Sand Dunes National Park in the Alternate text text box.**

The alternate text is entered for the image (Figure 2-30).

FIGURE 2-30

4

• **Click the OK button.**

The image appears in the Document window. The border and handles around the image indicate that it is selected. The attributes change in the Property inspector to reflect the selected object (Figure 2-31). The alternate text you entered in the Alternate text text box is displayed in the Alt box in the Property inspector.

FIGURE 2-31

In addition to the visual aid feature, you use the Property inspector to help with image placement and to add other attributes. When you select an image within the Document window, the Property inspector displays properties specific to that image.

Property Inspector Image Features

The Property inspector lets you see the current properties of the selected element. The Property inspector is divided into two sections. Clicking the expander arrow in the lower-right corner of the Property inspector expands/collapses the Property inspector. When it is in collapsed mode, it shows only the more commonly used properties for the selected element. Expanded mode shows more advanced options. The Property inspector for images contains several image-related features in the top and lower sections.

The following section describes the image-related features of the Property inspector (Figure 2-32).

FIGURE 2-32

W AND H The **W** and **H** boxes indicate the width and height of the image, in pixels. Dreamweaver automatically displays the dimensions when an image is inserted into a page. You can specify the image size in the following units: pc (picas), pt (points), in (inches), mm (millimeters), cm (centimeters), and combinations, such as 2in+5mm. Dreamweaver converts the values to pixels in the source code.

LINK The **Link** box allows you to make the selected image a hyperlink to a specified URL or Web page. To create a relative link, you can click the Point to File or Browse for File icons to the right of the Link box to browse to a page in your Web site, or you can drag a file from the Files panel into the Link box. For an external link, you can type the URL directly into the Link box or use copy and paste.

ALIGN Set the alignment of an image in relation to other elements in the same paragraph, table, or line with **Align**. This property option is discussed in more detail later in this chapter.

ALT Use Alt to specify alternate text that appears in place of the image for text-only browsers or for browsers that have been set to download images manually. For visually impaired users who utilize speech synthesizers with text-only browsers, the text is spoken aloud. In some browsers, this text also appears when the mouse pointer is over the image.

MAP AND HOTSPOT TOOLS Use the **Map** box and the **Hotspot tools** to label and create an image map.

V SPACE AND H SPACE Use V Space and H Space to add space, in pixels, along the sides of the image. **V Space** adds space along the top and bottom of an image. **H Space** adds space along the left and right of an image.

TARGET Use **Target** to specify the frame or window in which the linked page should load. This option is not available when the image is linked to another file.

LOW SRC Use **Low Src** to specify the image that should load before the main image. Many designers use a small black-and-white version of the main image because it loads quickly and gives visitors an idea of what they will see when the page has fully loaded.

BORDER The **Border** is the width, in pixels, of the image's border. The default is no border.

EDIT Use **Edit** to select from six different editing option tools: (a) Edit, which opens the computer's default image editor; (b) **Optimize**, which opens the Image Preview dialog box; (c) **Crop**, which lets you edit images by reducing the area of the image; (d) **Resample**, which adds or subtracts pixels from a resized JPEG or GIF image file to match the appearance of the original image as closely as possible; (e) **Brightness and Contrast**, which modifies the contrast or brightness of pixels in an image; and (f) **Sharpening**, which adjusts the focus of an image by increasing the contrast of edges found within the image. Editing tools (c) through (f) do not require an external image-editing application. These editing functions are discussed in more detail later in this chapter.

RESET SIZE If you change an image size, the **Reset Size** tool is displayed after an image size has been changed. Use this tool to reset the W and H values to the original size of the image.

LEFT, CENTER, AND RIGHT In Dreamweaver, the default alignment for an image is left alignment. To change the default alignment, select the image you want to align. Click an alignment button: Align Left, Align Center, or Align Right.

SRC Use **Src** to specify the source file for the image.

After you insert the image into the Web page and then select it, the Property inspector displays features specific to the image. As discussed earlier, alignment is one of these features. **Alignment** determines where on the page the image displays and if and how text wraps around the image.

Aligning an Image

When you insert an image into a Web page, by default, the text around the image aligns to the bottom of the image. The image alignment options on the Align pop-up menu in the Property inspector let you set the alignment for the image in relation to other page content. Dreamweaver provides 10 alignment options for images. Table 2-3 on the next page describes these image alignment options.

Table 2-3 Image Alignment Options

ALIGNMENT OPTION	DESCRIPTION
Default	Aligns the image with the baseline of the text in most browser default settings
Baseline	Aligns the image with the baseline of the text regardless of the browser setting
Top	Aligns the image with the top of the item; an item can be text or another object
Middle	Aligns the image with the baseline of the text or object at the vertical middle of the image
Bottom	Aligns the image with the baseline of the text or the bottom of another image regardless of the browser setting
TextTop	Aligns the image with the top of the tallest character in a line of text
Absolute Middle	Aligns the image with the middle of the current line of text
Absolute Bottom	Aligns the image with the bottom of the current line of text or another object
Left	Aligns the image at the left margin
Right	Aligns the image at the right margin

The more widely used options are left and right. The following steps show how to align the sanddunes image to the right and create text wrapping to the left of the image. To have a better overview of how the page will display in a browser, you will collapse the panel groups.

To Align an Image

1

• **Click the panel groups expander arrow to collapse the panel groups.**

• **If necessary, click the sanddunes image to select it and then click the Align box arrow in the Property inspector. Point to Right on the pop-up menu.**

The Align pop-up menu is displayed, and Right is highlighted (Figure 2-33).

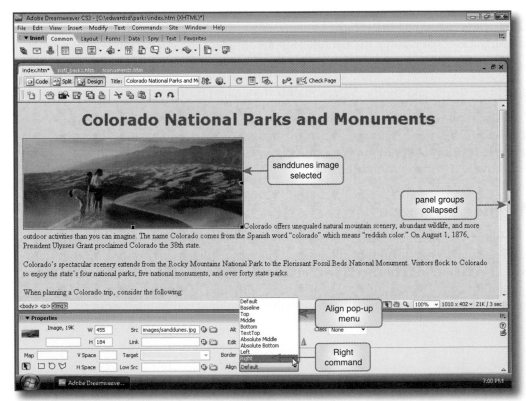

FIGURE 2-33

2

• Click Right.

The image moves to the right side of the window and is selected (Figure 2-34). An element marker is displayed to indicate the location of the insertion point.

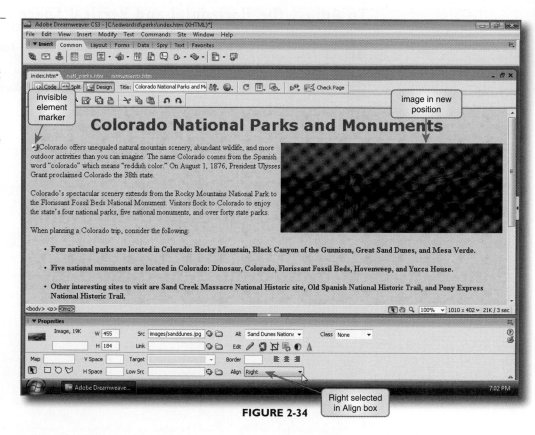

FIGURE 2-34

Adjusting Space around Images

When aligning an image, by default, only about three pixels of space are inserted between the image and adjacent text. You can adjust the amount of vertical and horizontal space between the image and text by using the V Space and H Space settings in the Property inspector. The V Space setting controls the vertical space above or below an image. The H Space setting controls the horizontal space to the left or right side of the image. The following steps on the next page show how to add vertical and horizontal spacing.

To Adjust the Horizontal and Vertical Space

1 **Verify that the image is selected. Click the V Space text box and type** 6 **as the vertical space.**

2 **Press the TAB key and type** 12 **as the H Space text box. Press the TAB key.**

3 **Click the image to remove the highlighting.**

Dreamweaver adds horizontal and vertical space between the image and the text (Figure 2-35).

FIGURE 2-35

More About

Accessibility Issues

For more information about authoring for accessibility, visit the Dreamweaver CS3 More About Web page (scsite.com/dwcs3/more) and then click Dreamweaver CS3 Accessibility Issues.

To enhance your Web page further, you will add a waterfall image. This image will appear on the left side of the page, to the left of the bulleted items. The following steps show how to insert an image of a waterfall in the Web page.

To Insert the Waterfall Image

1

• If necessary, scroll down and position the insertion point so it is to the left of the sentence introducing the bulleted list (Figure 2-36).

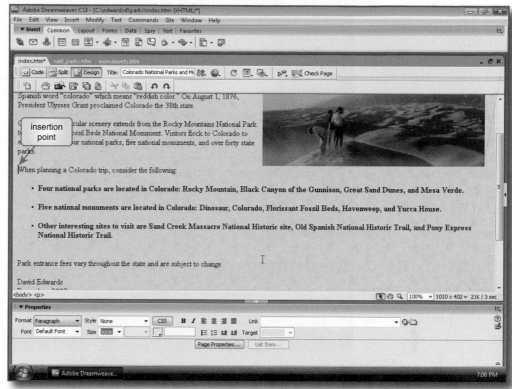

FIGURE 2-36

2

• Display the Assets panel and click waterfall01.gif.

• Drag the image to the insertion point. Type Rocky Mountain waterfall in the Alternate text text box, and then click the OK button.

• Collapse the panel groups.

The waterfall image is displayed (Figure 2-37). The border and handles around the image indicate that it is selected. The panel groups are collapsed.

FIGURE 2-37

3

• **Click the Align box
arrow and then click
Left in the Align pop-
up menu.**

*The image moves to the left
side of the window, and the
text adjusts to the right
(Figure 2-38). The bullets and
some of the text is hidden by
the image. Adjusting the
spacing will make the bullets
and text visible.*

FIGURE 2-38

4

• **Click the V Space box
and type 6 as the
vertical space.**

• **Click the H Space box
and type 20 as the
horizontal space.**

• **Press the TAB key.**

• **Click anywhere in the
Document window to
deselect the image.**

*Additional horizontal and
vertical space is added
between the image and the
text, and the bullets are now
visible (Figure 2-39).*

FIGURE 2-39

5

• **Click the Save button on the Standard toolbar.**

• **Press the F12 key.**

• **Move the mouse pointer over the sanddunes and waterfall images to display the Alt text.**

The index page is displayed in your browser and all changes to the index page are saved (Figure 2-40). Web pages may appear differently in your browser. The browser and selected text size affect how a Web page is displayed. In Figure 2-40, the text size is set to Medium.

FIGURE 2-40

6

• **Close the browser to return to Dreamweaver.**

The second page in your Web site is the National Parks page. To develop the National Parks page further and add information showing the locations of the four Colorado national parks, you will add a Colorado map. References to each park are contained on the map. The following steps on the next page show how to add the Colorado map image to the National Parks Web page.

Adobe
Dreamweaver CS3

To Insert and Align an Image in the National Parks Web Page

1

- **Click the natl_parks.htm Web page tab. Display the panel groups. If necessary, click the Assets tab.**

- **Position the insertion point to the left of the first bulleted text item (Rocky Mountain National Park).**

The insertion point is positioned to the left of Rocky Mountain National Park (Figure 2-41).

FIGURE 2-41

2

- **Drag the map.gif file from the Assets panel to the insertion point.**

- **Type** Colorado National Parks **in the Alternate text text box and then click the OK button.**

- **Collapse the panel groups.**

The image is selected (Figure 2-42). The attributes change in the Property inspector to reflect the selected object.

FIGURE 2-42

3

• **Click the Align box arrow and then click Right.**

The selected image is aligned to the right in the Document window (Figure 2-43).

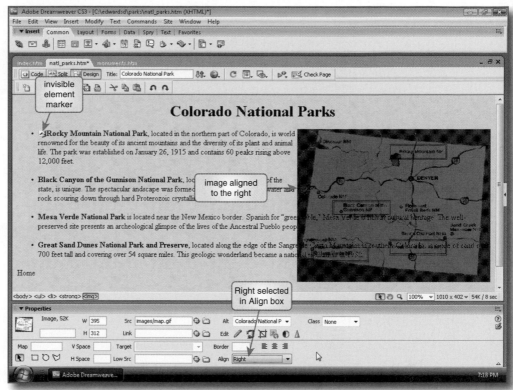

FIGURE 2-43

4

• **Click the V Space box and type 8 as the vertical space.**

• **Click the H Space box and type 10 as the horizontal space.**

• **Press the ENTER key.**

• **Click anywhere in the Document window to deselect the image (Figure 2-44).**

FIGURE 2-44

5

• **Click the Save button on the Standard toolbar.**

The Colorado National Parks Web page is saved.

• **Press the F12 key.**

The Colorado National Parks Web page is displayed in the browser (Figure 2-45).

• **Close the browser to return to Dreamweaver.**

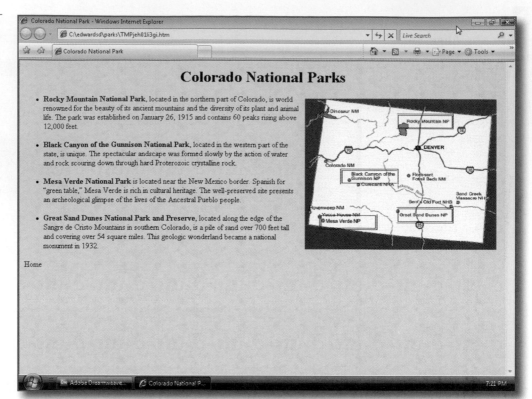

FIGURE 2-45

The third page in your Web site is the Colorado National Monuments page. To add interest to this page, you will add three images. You will align two of the images to the left and one to the right. When you added images to the index.htm and natl_parks.htm pages, you expanded and collapsed the panel groups. In the following steps, you leave the panel groups expanded. This enables you to experience both methods and determine the one which works best for you. The following steps illustrate how to add the images to the Colorado National Monuments Web page.

To Insert and Align Images in the National Monuments Web Page

1

• **Click the monuments.htm Web page tab. Display the panel groups and click the Assets tab, if necessary.**

• **Position the insertion point to the left of the paragraph following the Dinosaur National Monument subhead.**

The insertion point is to the left of the first sentence in the first paragraph (Figure 2-46).

FIGURE 2-46

2

• **Drag the dinosaur.jpg file from the Assets panel to the insertion point.**

• **Type** Dinosaur National Park **in the Alternate text text box and then click the OK button.**

• **Click the Align box arrow in the Property inspector and then click Left on the Align pop-up menu.**

The image aligns to the left (Figure 2-47).

FIGURE 2-47

3

• **Click the V Space box and then type** 8 **as the vertical space.**

• **Click the H Space box, type** 10 **as the horizontal space, and then press the ENTER key.**

The image is highlighted. The V Space and H Space attributes are added for the Dinosaur image (Figure 2-48).

FIGURE 2-48

4

• **If necessary, scroll down and then position the insertion point to the left of the word, Volcanic, in the first line in the Florissant Fossil Bed National Monument paragraph.**

The insertion point is to the left of the first sentence in the fourth paragraph (Figure 2-49).

FIGURE 2-49

5

- **Drag the fossils.jpg image to the insertion point.**

- **Type** Florissant Basin **in the Alternate text text box and then click the OK button. If necessary, scroll down to view the image.**

The image is inserted into the Document window and is selected (Figure 2-50).

FIGURE 2-50

6

- **Click the Align box arrow and then click Right on the Align pop-up menu.**

- **Click the V Space box and then type** 35 **as the vertical space.**

- **Click the H Space box and then type** 20 **as the horizontal space. Press the ENTER key.**

The image is positioned on the page (Figure 2-51).

FIGURE 2-51

7

• **Position the insertion point to the left of the Hovenweep National Monument subhead.**

• **Drag the housing.jpg image from the Assets panel to the insertion point.**

• **Type** Yucca House prehistoric village **in the Alternate text text box and then press the ENTER key. If necessary, scroll down to view the image.**

The housing image is inserted on the page (Figure 2-52).

FIGURE 2-52

8

• **Click the Align box arrow and then click Left on the Align pop-up menu.**

• **Click the V Space box and then type** 5 **as the vertical space.**

• **Click the H Space box and then type** 10 **as the horizontal space. Press the ENTER key.**

• **Click anywhere on the page to deselect the image.**

• **Click the Save button on the Standard toolbar.**

The image is positioned on the page and the Web page is saved (Figure 2-53).

FIGURE 2-53

9

• **Press the F12 key.**

The National Monuments page is displayed in the browser (Figure 2-54).

• **Close the browser.**

FIGURE 2-54

Image Editing Tools

Dreamweaver makes available several basic image editing tools to modify and enhance an image. You access these functions through the Property inspector.

- Use an external image editor: Adobe Fireworks is the default image editor, but you can specify which external editor should start for a specified file type. To select an external editor, click Edit on the menu bar and display the Preferences dialog box. Select File Types/Editors from the Category list to display the Preferences File Types/Editors dialog box. Select the image extension and then browse for the External Code Editor executable file.

- Optimize: The process of compressing and setting display options for Web graphics is called **optimization**. Options include quality, smoothing, matte, image size, and progressively increasing an image's resolution during download. Fireworks is the default program used for optimization in Dreamweaver.

- Crop an image: **Cropping** lets you edit an image by reducing the area of the image and allows you to eliminate unwanted or distracting portions of the image. Cropping can be very effective for improving the appearance of a photo by highlighting the main point of interest in an image. To return the image to its original size, click the Undo button on the Standard toolbar. When you crop an image and then save the page, the source image file is changed on the disk. Prior to saving, you may want to keep a backup copy of the image file in the event you need to revert to the original image.

- Resampling: The process of **resampling** adds or subtracts pixels from a resized JPEG or GIF image file to match the appearance of the original image as closely as possible. Resampling an image also reduces an image's file size, resulting in improved download performance. When you resize an image in Dreamweaver, you can resample it to accommodate its new dimensions. To resample a resized image, resize the image as previously described and then click the Resample button in the Property inspector.

- Brightness and Contrast: The **Brightness and Contrast** tool modifies the contrast or brightness of the pixels in an image. Recall that a pixel is the smallest point in a graphical image. Brightness makes the pixels in the image lighter or darker overall, while Contrast either emphasizes or de-emphasizes the difference between lighter and darker regions. This affects the highlights, shadows, and midtones of an image. The values for the brightness and contrast settings range from –100 to 100.

- Sharpening: **Sharpening** adjusts the focus of an image by increasing the contrast of edges found within the image.

The fossils image in the Colorado National Monuments page extends somewhat below the last line of the text. Cropping the image and emphasizing the fossil bed in the image will enhance the page. The following steps show how to crop the image, and then modify the brightness/contrast.

To Crop and Modify the Brightness/Contrast of an Image

1

- **Select the fossils.jpg image.**

- **Click the Crop Tool icon in the Property inspector. If an Adobe Dreamweaver CS3 caution dialog box is displayed, click the OK button.**

A bounding box with crop handles appears around the selected image (Figure 2-55).

FIGURE 2-55

2

• **Click the crop handle in the lower-right corner and adjust the handles until the bounding box surrounds the area of the image similar to that shown in Figure 2-56.**

The area of the image to retain is selected (Figure 2-56).

FIGURE 2-56

3

• **Double-click inside the bounding box.**

• **Click the image.**

The image is cropped and selected (Figure 2-57). If you need to make changes, click the Undo button on the Standard toolbar and repeat Steps 1 through 3.

FIGURE 2-57

4

• **Click the housing.jpg image to select it. Click the Brightness and Contrast tool. If an Adobe Dreamweaver CS3 caution dialog box appears, click the OK button.**

The Brightness/Contrast dialog box is displayed (Figure 2-58).

FIGURE 2-58

5

• **Drag the Brightness slider to the left and adjust the setting to -10.**

• **Drag the Contrast slider to the right and adjust the setting to 35.**

The brightness and contrast are changed in the image (Figure 2-59).

6

• **Click the OK button.**

• **Click the Save button on the Standard toolbar.**

The two images are adjusted and the National Monuments page is saved.

FIGURE 2-59

• **Press the F12 key to view the Monuments page in your browser.**

The Colorado National Monuments page is displayed in your browser (Figure 2-60).

8

• **Close the browser to return to the Dreamweaver window.**

FIGURE 2-60

To connect the pages within the Web site and to display the navigation structure of the pages in the Site Map, you create links. The next section discusses the different types of links.

Understanding Different Types of Links

Links are the distinguishing feature of the World Wide Web. A link, also referred to as a hyperlink, is the path to another document, to another part of the same document, or to other media such as an image or a movie. Most links are displayed as colored and/or underlined text, although you also can link from an image or other object. Clicking a link accesses the corresponding document, other media, or another place within the same document. If you place the mouse pointer over the link, the Web address of the link, or path, usually appears at the bottom of the window, on the status bar.

Three types of link paths are available: absolute, relative, and root-relative. An **absolute link** provides the complete URL of the document. This type of link also is referred to as an **external link**. Absolute links generally contain a protocol (such as http://) and primarily are used to link to documents on other servers.

You use **relative links** for local links. This type of link also is referred to as a **document-relative link**, or an **internal link**. If the linked documents are in the same folder, such as those in your parks folder, this is the best type of link to use. You also can use a relative link to link to a document in another folder, such as the images folder. All the files you see in the Files panel Local View are internal files and are referenced as relative links. You accomplish this by specifying the path through the folder hierarchy from the current document to the linked document. Consider the following examples.

- To link to another file in the same folder, specify the file name. Example: monuments.htm.
- To link to a file in a subfolder of the current Web site folder (such as the images folder), the link path would consist of the name of the subfolder, a forward slash (/), and then the file name. Example: images/sanddunes.jpg.

You use the **root-relative link** primarily when working with a large Web site that requires several servers. Web developers generally use this type of link when they must move HTML files from one folder or server to another folder or server. Root-relative links are beyond the scope of this book.

Two other types of links are named anchor and e-mail. A **named anchor** lets the user link to a specific location within a document. To create a named anchor, click the Named Anchor command on the Insert menu. An **e-mail link** creates a blank e-mail message containing the recipient's address. Another type of link is a **null**, or **script, link**. This type of link provides for attaching behaviors to an object or executes JavaScript code.

Named Anchor

To create a named anchor, place the insertion point where you want the named anchor. Then click the Named Anchor command on the Insert menu. Type a name for the anchor in the Named Anchor text box.

Relative Links

Dreamweaver offers a variety of ways in which to create a relative link. Three of the more commonly used methods are point to file, drag-and-drop, and browse for file. The point to file and drag-and-drop methods require that the Property inspector and the Files or Assets panels be open. To use the **point to file method**, you drag the Point to File icon to the file or image in the Files or Assets panel. In the **drag-and-drop method**, you drag the file from the Files or Assets panel to the Link text box in the Property inspector. The **browse for file method** is accomplished through the Select File dialog box. A fourth method is to use the context menu. To do this, you select the text for the link, right-click to display the context menu, and then select the Make Link command.

The next step is to add the text to create the relative links from the home page to the National Parks and National Monuments pages. You will use the drag-and-drop method to create a relative link from the text to a specific Web page.

Adding Text for the Relative Links

To create relative links from the index page, you add text to the index page and use the text to create the links to the other two Web pages in your Web site. You will center the text directly below the Colorado National Parks and Monuments heading. The following steps show how to add the text for the links.

To Add Text for Relative Links

1

• **Click the Files panel tab.**

• **Click the index.htm tab in the Document window. If necessary, scroll to the top of the page and then position the insertion point at the end of the title, Colorado National Parks and Monuments.**

• **Press the ENTER key.**

• **If style1 (or another style number) is displayed in the Style text box in the Property inspector, click the Style pop-up menu and select None.**

The insertion point is centered below the title, and the text color is returned to the default. The Files panel is displayed (Figure 2-61).

FIGURE 2-61

2

• **Type** National Parks **and then press the SPACEBAR.**

The text for the first link, National Parks, is displayed in the Document window (Figure 2-62).

FIGURE 2-62

3

• Hold down the SHIFT key and then press the vertical line key (|). Press the SPACEBAR and then type National Monuments.

The text for both links is displayed in the Document window (Figure 2-63).

FIGURE 2-63

You will use the text, National Parks, to create a link to the National Parks Web page and the text, National Monuments, to create a link to the National Monuments page.

Creating a Relative Link Using Drag-and-Drop

A relative link is used to create links between local files or files within one Web site. The drag-and-drop method requires that the Property inspector be displayed and that the site files are displayed in the Files or Assets panel. The following steps illustrate how to use the drag-and-drop method to create a relative link from the Colorado Parks home page to the National Parks Web page.

To Create a Relative Link Using Drag-and-Drop

1

• **Drag to select the text, National Parks.**

The National Parks text is selected (Figure 2-64).

FIGURE 2-64

2

• **Use the Point to File tool to drag the natl_parks.htm file from the Files panel to the Link box in the Property inspector. Do not release the mouse button.**

When you start to drag, a circle icon with a diagonal line through it appears as the mouse pointer (Figure 2-65).

FIGURE 2-65

3

• **When the pointer is over the Link box, release the mouse button.**

The link text is displayed underlined and in a different color in the Document window, and the linked text is displayed in the Link box (Figure 2-66). If you click anywhere else in the document, the linked document name is not displayed in the Link box.

FIGURE 2-66

Creating a Relative Link Using the Context Menu

The context menu is a second way to create a link. Using this method, you select the file name in the Select File dialog box. The following steps illustrate how to use the context menu to create a link to the National Monuments page.

To Create a Relative Link Using the Context Menu

1

• **Drag to select the text, National Monuments, and right-click to display the context menu. Point to Make Link.**

The text, National Monuments, is selected, and the context menu is displayed. The Make Link command is highlighted (Figure 2-67).

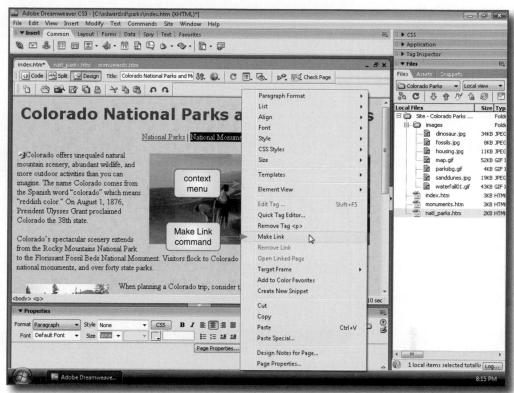

FIGURE 2-67

2

• **Click the Make Link command and then click monuments.**

The Select File dialog box is displayed and monuments is selected (Figure 2-68).

FIGURE 2-68

3

• **Click the OK button and then click the selected text, National Monuments, to display the link.**

• **Click the Save button on the Standard toolbar.**

The linked text is displayed underlined and in a different color in the Document window, and the link text is displayed in the Link box (Figure 2-69). If you click anywhere else in the document, the linked document name is not displayed in the Link box.

4

• **Press the F12 key to view the index page in your browser.**

• **Click the National Parks link to verify that the link works and then click the browser Back button to return to the index page.**

• **Click the National Monuments link to verify that the link works.**

• **Close the browser.**

FIGURE 2-69

Other Ways

1. Click Link box, type file name
2. Click Point to File icon in Property inspector, drag to file name

Creating a Relative Link to the Home Page

Visitors can enter a Web site at any point, so it is important always to include a link from each page within the site back to the home page. To accomplish this, you create a relative link to the home page from the National Parks page and from the National Monuments page. The following steps show how to create a link from the National Parks page and a link from the National Monuments page to the home page.

To Create a Relative Link to the Home Page

1

• **Click the natl_parks.htm tab and then scroll to the bottom of the page. Drag to select Home.**

The text, Home, is selected (Figure 2-70). This text will become a link.

FIGURE 2-70

2

• **Drag the index.htm file name from the Files panel to the Link box.**

• **Click the Save button on the Standard toolbar.**

The link is created (Figure 2-71). The National Parks page is saved.

FIGURE 2-71

3

• **Press the F12 key to view the National Parks page in your browser.**

• **Click the Home link.**

The index page is displayed in the browser (Figure 2-72). Note that the links change color after they have been clicked.

FIGURE 2-72

4

• **Close the browser.**

The browser is closed, and Dreamweaver is displayed.

5

• **Click the monuments.htm tab. If necessary, scroll to the end of the document and then drag to select the text, Home (Figure 2-73). If necessary, press ENTER to move Home below the image.**

FIGURE 2-73

6

- **Collapse the Property inspector.**
- **Drag the index.htm file name from the Files panel to the Link box.**
- **Click the Save button on the Standard toolbar.**

The link is created, and index.htm is displayed in the Link box (Figure 2-74). The National Monuments page is saved.

7

- **Press the F12 key to view the National Monuments page in your browser.**
- **Click the Home link to verify that it works.**
- **Close the browser.**

FIGURE 2-74

Other Ways

1. Click Link box, type file name

Creating an Absolute Link

Recall that an absolute link (also called an external link) contains the complete Web site address of a document. You create absolute links the same way you create relative links — select the text and paste or type the Web site address. You now will create five absolute links in the National Monuments page. These links are from the name of each of the five monuments to a Web page about the selected monument. The following steps show how to create the five absolute links. Keep in mind that Web site addresses change. If the absolute links do not work, check the Dreamweaver CS3 companion site at http://www.scsite.com/dwcs3/ for updates.

To Create an Absolute Link

1 If necessary, scroll to the top of the page. Drag to select the text, Dinosaur National Monument.

2 Click the Link box and then type http://www.nps.gov/dino/ as the link. Press the ENTER key.

3 Drag to select the text, Colorado National Monument. Click the Link box and then type http://www.nps.gov/colm/ as the link. Press the ENTER key.

4 Drag to select the text, Florissant Fossil Bed National Monument. Click the Link box and then type http://www.nps.gov/flfo/ as the link. Press the ENTER key.

5 If necessary, scroll down and then drag to select the text, Hovenweep National Monument. Click the Link box and then type http://www.nps.gov/hove/ as the link. Press the ENTER key.

6 Drag to select the text, Yucca House National Monument. Click the Link box and then type http://www.nps.gov/yuho/ as the link. Press the ENTER key, and then deselect the linked text, if necessary (Figure 2-75).

7 Click the Save button on the Standard toolbar.

8 Press the F12 key and then click each link to verify that they work.

9 Close the browser.

Other Ways

1. Start browser, open Web page, select URL, copy URL, close browser, paste in Link box

The five absolute links to the respective national monuments pages are added (Figure 2-75), and the Web page is saved.

FIGURE 2-75

E-Mail Links

An **e-mail link** is one of the foundation elements of any successful Web site. It is important for visitors to be able to contact you for additional information or to comment on the Web page or Web site. When visitors click an e-mail link, their default e-mail program opens a new e-mail message. The e-mail address you specify is inserted automatically in the To box of the e-mail message header.

Creating an E-Mail Link

The following steps show how to create an e-mail link for your home page using your name as the linked text. You do this through the Insert menu.

To Add an E-Mail Link

1

• **Click the index.htm tab, scroll down, and then drag to select your name. Click Insert on the menu bar and then point to Email Link.**

In this figure, David Edwards is selected, and the Insert menu is displayed (Figure 2-76). Your name should be selected on your screen. (It might be displayed to the right of the image instead of below the image.)

FIGURE 2-76

2

• **Click Email Link.**

The Email Link dialog box is displayed. In this figure, David Edwards is selected in the Text text box (Figure 2-77). On your computer, your name is displayed in the Text text box.

FIGURE 2-77

• Click the E-Mail text box and then type your e-mail address.

In this figure, the e-mail address for David Edwards is displayed in the E-Mail text box (Figure 2-78). On your computer, Dreamweaver will display your e-mail address.

• Click the OK button.

• Click the expander arrow on the vertical bar to hide the panel groups.

• Click anywhere in the selected text of your name.

• Click the Save button on the Standard toolbar.

The selected text for the e-mail link, David Edwards, is displayed as linked text and the index page is saved. The Link box displays the e-mail address (Figure 2-79). On your computer, Dreamweaver displays your name as the linked text.

5

• Press the F12 key to view the page in your browser. Click your name.

Your e-mail program opens with your e-mail address in the To text box.

• Close your e-mail program and then close the browser.

FIGURE 2-78

FIGURE 2-79

Changing the Color of Links

The Page Properties dialog box provides three options for link colors: Link (the link has not been clicked), Active Link (the link changes color when the user clicks it), and Visited Link (the link has been visited). The default color for the three options is black. You easily can make changes to these default settings and select colors that complement the background and other colors you are using on your Web pages. This is accomplished through the Page Properties dialog box. You display the Page Properties dialog box by clicking Modify on the menu bar or by clicking the Page Properties button in the Property inspector. You then can click the box that corresponds to one of the three types of links and select a color to match your color scheme.

Editing and Deleting Links

Web development is a never-ending process. At some point, it will be necessary to edit or delete a link. For instance, an e-mail address may change, a URL to an external link may change, or an existing link may contain an error.

Dreamweaver makes it easy to edit or delete a link. First, select the link or click the link you want to change. The linked document name is displayed in the Link box in the Property inspector. To delete the link without deleting the text on the Web page, delete the text from the Link box in the Property inspector. To edit the link, make the change in the Link box.

A second method to edit or delete a link is to use the context menu. Right-click the link you want to change, and then click Remove Link on the context menu to eliminate the link or click Change Link on the context menu to edit the link. Clicking the URLs icon in the Assets panel displays a list of all absolute and e-mail links within the Web site.

The Site Map

Earlier in this chapter, you set the index page as the home page. Dreamweaver provides a visual site map for viewing the relationships among files. The **Site Map** is a graphical representation of the structure of a Web site. You visually can design and modify the Web site structure through the Site Map. The home page is displayed at the top level of the map, and linked pages are displayed at the lower levels. The Site Map view allows you to create, change, display, save, and print a Web site's structure and navigation. As previously discussed, a Web site's structure is the relationship among the pages in the Web site.

Viewing the Site Map

The home page now contains links to other pages in the site, and each page in the site contains links back to the home page. The National Monuments page contains a link to five external Web sites, which are outside of the local site and located on a different server. You can use the Site Map to view a graphical image of these links. In addition to allowing you to view the Site Map, another Dreamweaver option lets you view your file list and Site Map simultaneously.

Displaying the Site Map and Local Files

The Site Map shows the pages as icons and displays links in the order in which they are encountered in the HTML source code. Starting from the home page, the Site Map default displays the site structure two levels deep. The relative links have a

More About

Targeting Links

By default, when you click a link, the linked Web page will open in the current browser window. You can specify, however, that a linked Web page open in a new browser window. To do this, first select the item and create the link. Then, in the Property inspector, click the Target box arrow and click _blank on the Target pop-up menu. When you view the page in a browser and click the link, it will display in a new window.

plus sign to their left. If you click the plus (+) sign, pages below the second level display. Some pages have a minus sign to their left. If you click the minus (-) sign, pages linked below the second level are hidden. Text displayed in blue and marked with a globe icon indicates a file on another site or a special link such as an e-mail link. Text displayed in red indicates a broken link. You access the Site Map through the Files panel. The following steps show how to display the site map with the newly created links among the pages in the Colorado Parks Web site.

To Display the Site Map and Local Files List

1

• If necessary, click the index.htm tab.

• Click the expander arrow on the panel groups vertical bar to display the Files panel.

• Click the View box arrow and then point to Map view in the View pop-up menu (Figure 2-80).

FIGURE 2-80

2

- **Click Map view.**

Dreamweaver displays a graphical view of the Web site in the Files panel, including all links from the index page (Figure 2-81).

FIGURE 2-81

3

- **Click the Expand/Collapse button.**

The Site Map expands and displays a graphical structure of the links between the index page and the other two pages and external links (Figure 2-82). The plus signs to the left of the natl_parks.htm and monuments.htm pages indicate that additional files or links are below these pages.

FIGURE 2-82

4

• **Click the plus sign to the left of the natl_parks.htm icon.**

• **Click the plus sign to the left of monuments.htm.**

The structure expands and displays the relative link to the index page from the national parks page and from the national monuments page. The five external links are displayed under the monuments icon (Figure 2-83).

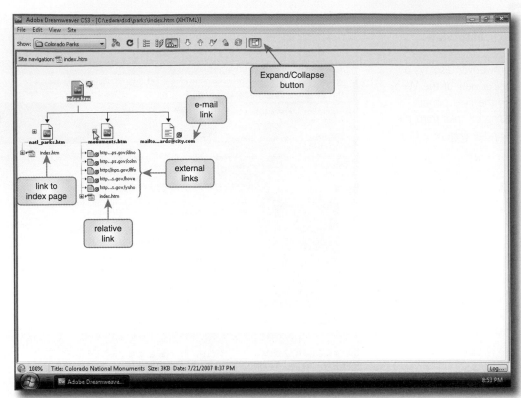

FIGURE 2-83

5

• **Click the Expand/Collapse button to collapse the Site Map.**

• **Click the View box arrow and then point to Local view in the View pop-up menu (Figure 2-84).**

 6

• **Click Local view.**

The local site is displayed.

FIGURE 2-84

Source Code View

Dreamweaver provides two views, or ways, to look at a document: **Design view** and **Code view**. Thus far, you have been working in Design view. As you create and work with documents, Dreamweaver automatically generates the underlying source code. Recall that the source code defines the structure and layout of a Web document by using a variety of tags and attributes. Even though Dreamweaver generates the code, occasions occur that necessitate the tweaking or modifying of code.

Dreamweaver provides several options for viewing and working with source code. You can split the Document window so that it displays both the Code view and the Design view. You can display only the Code view in the Document window, or you can open the Code inspector. The **Code inspector** opens in a separate window, so you can keep the whole Document window reserved for Design view.

Using Code View and Design View

In Split view, you work in a split-screen environment. You can see the design and the code at the same time. Splitting the Document window to view the code makes it easier to view the visual design while you make changes in the source code. When you make a change in Design view, the HTML code also is changed but is not visible in the Document window. You can set word wrapping, display line numbers for the code, highlight invalid HTML code, set syntax coloring for code elements, and set indenting through the View menu's Code View Options submenu. Viewing the code at this early stage may not seem important, but the more code you learn, the more productive you will become.

Within HTML source code, tags can be entered in uppercase, lowercase, or a combination of upper- and lowercase. The case of the tags has no effect on how the browser displays the output.

If the code is XHTML compliant, however, all tags are lowercase. In this book, if you use the instructions provided in Chapter 1 to create a new Web page, then your page is XHTML compliant. XHTML was discussed in the Introduction chapter. Therefore, in this book, when describing source code tags, we use lowercase letters for tags and attributes to make it easier to differentiate them from the other text and to coordinate with the XHTML standard.

The following steps on the next page show how to use the Code View and Design View option to look at the code for the
 (line break) and <p> (paragraph) tags. The paragraph tag has an opening tag, <p>, and a closing tag, </p>. The
 (line break) tag does not have a closing tag.

More About

Dreamweaver CS3 Quick Tag Editor

For more information about using the Quick Tag Editor to review and edit HTML tags, visit the Dreamweaver CS3 More About Web page (scsite.com/dwcs3/more) and then click Dreamweaver CS3 Quick Tag Editor.

To View Design View and Code View Simultaneously

1

• Click the natl_parks.htm tab.

• Hide the Files panel and collapse the Property inspector, if necessary.

• Position the insertion point to the left of the heading, Colorado National Parks. (Figure 2-85).

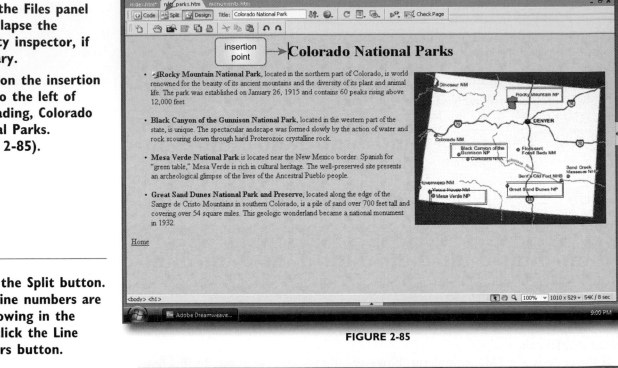

FIGURE 2-85

2

• Click the Split button. If the line numbers are not showing in the code, click the Line Numbers button.

The window splits. The upper window displays Code view and the lower window displays Design view (Figure 2-86). The insertion point is displayed in Code view in the same location as in Design view (to the left of the heading). The lines are numbered in Code view. The source code is displayed in color and in lowercase surrounded by < (less than) and > (greater than) symbols. Your window may display Design view in the upper window and Code view in the lower window.

3

• Click the Design button.

The Design view is displayed.

FIGURE 2-86

Modifying Source Code

One of the more common problems within Dreamweaver and the source code relates to line breaks and paragraphs. Occasionally, you inadvertently press the ENTER key or insert a line break and need to remove the tag. Or, you may copy and paste or open a text file that contains unneeded paragraphs or line breaks.

Pressing the BACKSPACE key or DELETE key may return you to the previous line, but does not always delete the line break or paragraph tag within the source code. The deletion of these tags is determined by the position of the insertion point when you press the BACKSPACE or DELETE keys. If the insertion point is still inside the source code, pressing the BACKSPACE key will not delete these tags and your page will not display correctly. When this occurs, the best solution is to delete the tag through Code view.

Formatting Titles for Consistency

To further create consistency among the Web pages, the titles of the two new pages (monuments and natl_parks) need to be formatted with the same style as that of the index page.

To Format the National Parks and National Monuments Titles

1 **If necessary, display the Property inspector. Select the text, Colorado National Parks. Click the color hexadecimal text box and type** #336633. **Press the ENTER key.**

2 **Click the monuments.htm tab. Select the text, Colorado National Monuments. Click the color hexadecimal text box and type** #336633. **Press the ENTER key.**

Quitting Dreamweaver

After you add pages to your Web site, including images and links, and then verify links using the Site Map, Chapter 2 is complete. The next step shows how to close the Web site, quit Dreamweaver CS3, and return control to Windows.

To Close the Web Site and Quit Dreamweaver

1 **Click the Close button on the right corner of the Dreamweaver title bar.**

The Dreamweaver window, the Document window, and the Colorado Parks Web site all close. If you have unsaved changes, Dreamweaver will prompt you to save the changes. Clicking the Yes button in the Dreamweaver CS3 dialog box saves the changes.

Chapter Summary

Chapter 2 introduced you to images, links, the Site Map, and how to view source code. You began the chapter by using the Windows Computer option to copy data files to the local site. You added two new pages, one for Colorado National Parks and one for Colorado National Monuments, to the Web site you started in Chapter 1. Next, you added page images to the index page. Following that, you added a background image and page images to the National Parks and National Monuments pages. Then, you added relative links to all three pages. You added an e-mail link to the index page and absolute links to the National Monuments page. You also learned to use the Site Map. Finally, you learned how to view source code.

What You Should Know

Having completed this chapter, you should be able to perform the tasks below. The tasks are listed in the same order they were presented in this chapter. For a list of keyboard commands for topics introduced in this chapter, see the Quick Reference for Windows at the back of this book and refer to the Shortcut column.

1. Copy Data Files to the Parks Web Site (DW 119)
2. Start Dreamweaver and Open the Colorado Parks Web Site (DW 120)
3. Open a Web Page from a Local Web Site (DW 122)
4. Set a Home Page (DW 123)
5. Open a New Document Window (DW 124)
6. Prepare the Workspace (DW 128)
7. Create the National Parks Web Page (DW 129)
8. Format the Colorado National Parks Page (DW 130)
9. Open a New Document Window (DW 131)
10. Create the National Monuments Web Page (DW 133)
11. Format the Colorado National Monuments Page (DW 133)
12. Add a Background Image to the Colorado National Parks Web Page (DW 136)
13. Add a Background Image to the Colorado National Monuments Web Page (DW 137)
14. Set Invisible Element Preferences and Turn on Visual Aids (DW 140)
15. Insert an Image into the Index Page (DW 142)
16. Align an Image (DW 146)
17. Adjust the Horizontal and Vertical Space (DW 148)
18. Insert the Waterfall Image (DW 149)
19. Insert and Align an Image in the National Parks Web Page (DW 152)
20. Insert and Align Images in the National Monuments Web Page (DW 155)
21. Crop and Modify the Brightness/Contrast of an Image (DW 160)
22. Add Text for Relative Links (DW 165)
23. Create a Relative Link Using Drag-and-Drop (DW 167)
24. Create a Relative Link Using the Context Menu (DW 169)
25. Create a Relative Link to the Home Page (DW 171)
26. Create an Absolute Link (DW 173)
27. Add an E-Mail Link (DW 175)
28. Display the Site Map and Local Files List (DW 178)
29. View Design View and Code View Simultaneously (DW 182)
30. Format the National Parks and National Monuments Titles (DW 183)
31. Close the Web Site and Quit Dreamweaver (DW 183)

Learn It Online

Instructions: To complete the Learn It Online exercises, start your browser, click the Address bar, and then enter the Web address scsite.com/dwcs3/learn. When the Dreamweaver CS3 Learn It Online page is displayed, follow the instructions in the exercises below. Each exercise has instructions for printing your results, either for your own records or for submission to your instructor.

1 Chapter Reinforcement TF, MC, and SA

Below Dreamweaver Chapter 2, click the Chapter Reinforcement link. Print the quiz by clicking Print on the File menu for each page. Answer each question.

2 Flash Cards

Below Dreamweaver Chapter 2, click the Flash Cards link and read the instructions. Type 20 (or a number specified by your instructor) in the Number of playing cards text box, type your name in the Enter your Name text box, and then click the Flip Card button. When the flash card is displayed, read the question and then click the ANSWER box arrow to select an answer. Flip through the Flash Cards. If your score is 15 (75%) correct or greater, click Print on the File menu to print your results. If your score is less than 15 (75%) correct, then redo this exercise by clicking the Replay button.

3 Practice Test

Below Dreamweaver Chapter 2, click the Practice Test link. Answer each question, enter your first and last name at the bottom of the page, and then click the Grade Test button. When the graded practice test is displayed on your screen, click Print on the File menu to print a hard copy. Continue to take practice tests until you score 80% or better.

4 Who Wants To Be a Computer Genius?

Below Dreamweaver Chapter 2, click the Computer Genius link. Read the instructions, enter your first and last name at the bottom of the page, and then click the PLAY button. When your score is displayed, click the PRINT RESULTS link to print a hard copy.

5 Wheel of Terms

Below Dreamweaver Chapter 2, click the Wheel of Terms link. Read the instructions, and then enter your first and last name and your school name. Click the PLAY button. When your score is displayed, right-click the score and then click Print on the shortcut menu to print a hard copy.

6 Crossword Puzzle Challenge

Below Dreamweaver Chapter 2, click the Crossword Puzzle Challenge link. Read the instructions, and then enter your first and last name. Click the SUBMIT button. Work the crossword puzzle. When you are finished, click the Submit button. When the crossword puzzle is redisplayed, click the Print Puzzle button to print a hard copy.

7 Tips and Tricks

Below Dreamweaver Chapter 2, click the Tips and Tricks link. Click a topic that pertains to Chapter 2. Right-click the information and then click Print on the shortcut menu. Construct a brief example of what the information relates to in Dreamweaver to confirm that you understand how to use the tip or trick.

8 Newsgroups

Below Dreamweaver Chapter 2, click the Newsgroups link. Click a topic that pertains to Chapter 2. Print three comments.

9 Expanding Your Horizons

Below Dreamweaver Chapter 2, click the Expanding Your Horizons link. Click a topic that pertains to Chapter 2. Print the information. Construct a brief example of what the information relates to in Dreamweaver to confirm that you understand the contents of the article.

10 Search Sleuth

Below Dreamweaver Chapter 2, click the Search Sleuth link. To search for a term that pertains to this chapter, select a term below the Chapter 2 title and then use the Google search engine at google.com (or any major search engine) to display and print two Web pages that present information on the term.

Apply Your Knowledge

1 Modifying the Bryan's Lawn Service Web Site

Instructions: Start Dreamweaver. Data and image files for the Bryan's Lawn Service Web site are included with the data files. See the inside back cover of this book for instructions for downloading the data files or see your instructor for information on accessing the files in this book.

You need to add three new pages to the Bryan's Lawn Service Web site: a services page, an employment page, and a references page. In this exercise, you will add relative and absolute links to each page. You also will add a background image to the new pages. Next, you will insert images on all pages and use the settings in Table 2-4 on page DW 188 to align the images and enter the alternate text. You then will add an e-mail link to the home page and relative links from the three new pages to the home page. The pages for the Web site are shown in Figures 2-87a through 2-87d on pages DW 186 through DW 188.

Software and hardware settings determine how a Web page is displayed in a browser. Your Web pages may display differently in your browser than those in the figures do.

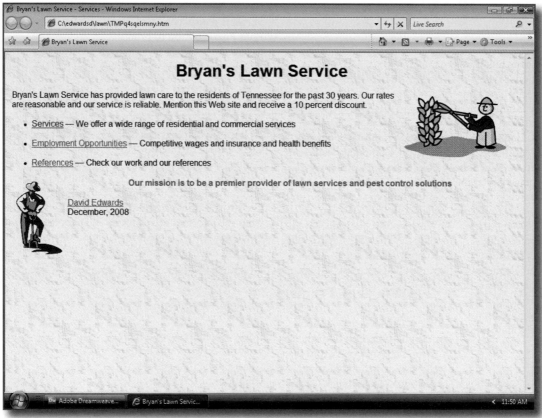

FIGURE 2-87 (a) Lawn Services Index (Home) Page

Apply Your Knowledge

(b) Lawn Services - Services Page

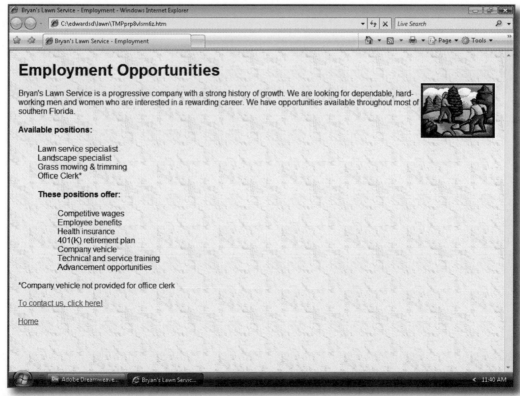

(c) Lawn Services - Employment Opportunities Page

FIGURE 2-87

(continued)

Apply Your Knowledge

Modifying the Bryan's Lawn Service Web Site *(continued)*

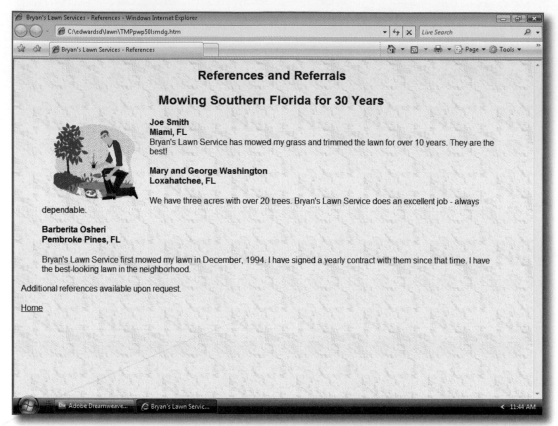

FIGURE 2-87 (d) References and Referrals Page

Table 2-4 Image Property Settings for the Bryan's Lawn Service Web Site

IMAGE NAME	W	H	V SPACE	H SPACE	ALIGN	ALT
trimming.gif	206	130	6	6	Right	Tree trimming
shovel.gif	93	141	6	8	Left	Shovel
mowing.gif	150	112	None	20	Left	Grass mowing
shakehands.gif	264	114	None	75	Right	Shaking hands
planting.gif	150	112	6	None	Right	Tree planting
planting2.gif	197	177	8	8	Left	Tree planting

Perform the following tasks:

1. Use the Windows Computer tool to copy the data files and images to your lawn folder.
2. If necessary, display the panel groups. Select Lawn Service on the Files pop-up menu in the Files panel. Double-click the index.htm file in the Files panel. If necessary, click the expander arrow to expand the Property inspector. If necessary, display the Standard toolbar.
3. Click index.htm in the Files panel to select it. Right-click index.htm and then click Set as Home Page on the context menu.

Apply Your Knowledge

4. If necessary, click the Expand/Collapse button to the left of the images folder in the Files panel to display the contents of the images folder. Position the insertion point to the left of the first line of the first paragraph. Drag the trimming.gif image to the insertion point, add the alternate text as indicated in Table 2-4, and then select the image. Apply the settings shown in Table 2-4 to align the image. If necessary, scroll down. Position the insertion point to the left of the last sentence on the Web page. Drag the shovel.gif image to the insertion point and then apply the settings shown in Table 2-4.

5. If necessary, scroll up. Select Services (the first bulleted item heading). Use the drag-and-drop file method to create a link to the Services page. Repeat this process to add links from Employment Opportunities and References (the second and third bulleted item headings) to their respective Web pages. Select your name. Use the Insert menu to create an e-mail link using your name. Save the index page (Figure 2-87a on page DW 186).

6. Open services.htm. Click Modify on the menu bar and click Page Properties. Click the Background image Browse button to add the background image (lawnbg.jpg) to the services.htm page.

7. Position the insertion point to the left of the page heading, drag the mowing.gif image to the insertion point, and then apply the settings shown in Table 2-4. Position the insertion point to the right of the first bulleted item and then drag the shakehands.gif image to the insertion point. Apply the settings shown in Table 2-4.

8. If necessary, scroll down. Select Home and then create a relative link to the index page. Title the page Bryan's Lawn Service - Services. Save the Services page (Figure 2-87b on page DW 187).

9. Open employment.htm. Add the background image to the employment.htm page, as you did in Step 6 to the services.htm page.

10. Position the insertion point to the right of the heading and then drag the planting.gif image to the insertion point. Apply the settings shown in Table 2-4.

11. Scroll to the bottom of the page. Select the words, To contact us, click here!. Use the Insert menu to create an e-mail link using your e-mail address. Select Home at the bottom of the page and then drag index.htm to the Link box in the Property inspector to create a relative link to the index.htm file. Title the page Bryan's Lawn Service - Employment. Save the Employment page (Figure 2-87c on page DW 187).

12. Open references.htm and apply the lawnbg.jpg background image.

13. Create a link from Home to the index page.

14. Position the insertion point to the left of the text, Joe Smith. Drag the planting2.gif image to the insertion point. If necessary, select the image. Apply the settings in Table 2-4. Title the page Bryan's Lawn Service - References. Save the References page (Figure 2-87d).

15. View the Web site in your browser. Check each link to verify that it works. Submit the documents in the format specified by your instructor. Close the browser. Quit Dreamweaver.

1 Modifying the CandleLight Web Site

Problem: Eve Perry, for whom you created the CandleLight Web site and Web page, is very pleased with the response she has received. She has asked you to create a second page with links and images added to the index page. Eve wants the new page to include information about her company's history. The revised Web site is shown in Figures 2-88a and 2-88b. Table 2-5 includes the settings and alternate text for the images. Software and hardware settings determine how a Web page displays in a browser. Your Web pages may display differently in your browser than those in the figures do.

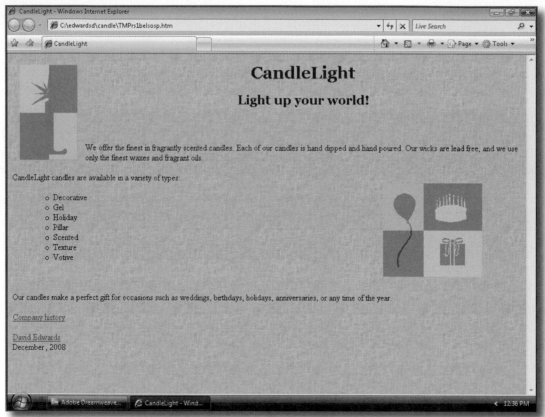

FIGURE 2-88 (a) CandleLight Index (Home) Page

In the Lab

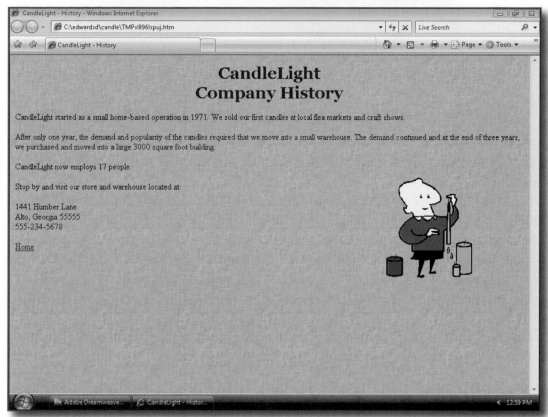

FIGURE 2-88 (b) CandleLight - History Web Page

Table 2-5   Image Property Settings for the CandleLight Web Site

IMAGE NAME	W	H	V SPACE	H SPACE	ALIGN	ALT
candle1.gif	112	180	6	15	Left	Logo
candle2.gif	192	178	None	75	Right	Candles
candle_dip.gif	164	191	10	100	Right	Candle dipping

Instructions: Perform the following tasks:

1. Use the Windows Computer tool to copy the data files and images to your candle folder.
2. Start Dreamweaver. Display the panel groups. Select CandleLight on the Files pop-up menu in the Files panel. Open the index.htm file. If necessary, click the expander arrow to expand the Property inspector and display the Standard toolbar.
3. Click index.htm in the Files panel to select it. Right-click index.htm and then click Set as Home Page on the context menu.
4. Position the insertion point to the left of the heading and then drag the candle1.gif image to the insertion point. Enter the Alt text, and then apply the settings shown in Table 2-5 to align the image.

(continued)

In the Lab

Modifying the CandleLight Web Site *(continued)*

5. Position the insertion point to the right of the text, CandleLight candles are available in a variety of types:, and then drag the candle2.gif image to the insertion point. Apply the settings shown in Table 2-5 on the previous page.

6. Position the insertion point to the right of the text, Our candles make a perfect gift for occasions such as weddings, birthdays, holidays, anniversaries, or any time of the year, and then press the ENTER key. Type Company history. Select the Company history text and use the drag-and-drop method to create a link to the history.htm page. Select your name. Use the Insert menu to create an e-mail link using your e-mail address. Save the index page (Figure 2-88a on page DW 190).

7. Open history.htm. Open the Page Properties dialog box. Click the Background image Browse button, and then add the background image (candlebg.jpg) to the history.htm page.

8. Position the insertion point at the end of the sentence, CandleLight now employs 17 people, and then drag the candle_dip.gif image to the insertion point. Apply the settings shown in Table 2-5. Title the page CandleLight - History.

9. Select Home and then create a relative link to the index page. Save the History page (Figure 2-88b on the previous page).

10. View your pages in your browser and verify that your links work. Submit the documents in the format specified by your instructor. Close your browser. Quit Dreamweaver.

2 Modifying the Credit Protection Web Site

Problem: Linda Reyes has received favorable comments about the Web page and site you created on credit information. Her bank wants to utilize the Web site to provide additional information to its customers. Linda has asked you and another intern at the bank to work with her to create two more Web pages to add to the site. They want one of the pages to discuss credit protection and the other page to contain information about identity theft. The revised pages for the Web site are shown in Figures 2-89a, 2-89b, and 2-89c on pages DW 193 and DW 194. Table 2-6 on page DW 194 includes the settings and Alt text for the images. Software and hardware settings determine how a Web page displays in a browser. Your Web pages may display differently in your browser than those in the figures do.

In the Lab

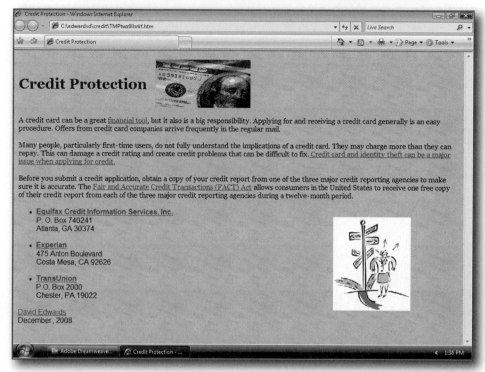

(a) Credit Protection Index (Home) Page

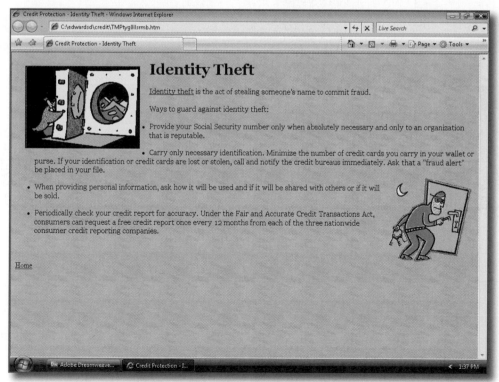

(b) Credit Protection - Identity Theft Web Page

FIGURE 2-89

(continued)

Modifying the Credit Protection Web Site *(continued)*

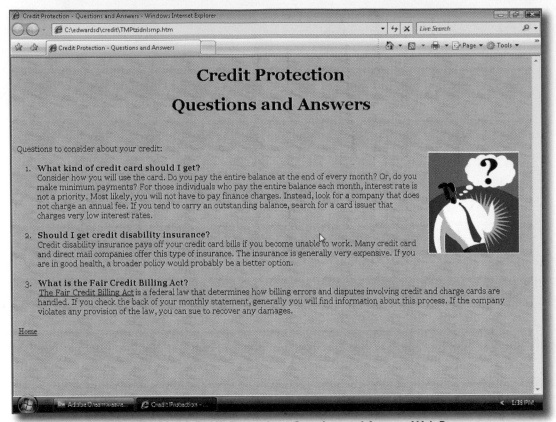

FIGURE 2-89 (c) Credit Protection - Questions and Answers Web Page

Table 2-6 Image Property Settings for the Credit Protection Web Site						
IMAGE NAME	W	H	V SPACE	H SPACE	ALIGN	ALT
money.gif	211	107	None	20	Absolute Middle	Money
answer.gif	172	204	None	100	Right	Reporting options
protection.gif	240	170	14	20	Left	Identity theft
theft.gif	179	183	20	None	Right	Protect personal information
question.gif	175	193	None	15	Right	Questions?

Instructions: Perform the following tasks:

1. Use the Windows Computer tool to copy the data files to your credit folder. The data files consist of five image files and two data files, questions.htm and theft.htm.
2. Start Dreamweaver. Display the panel groups. Select Credit Protection on the Files pop-up menu in the Files panel. Open index.htm.
3. If necessary, display the Property inspector and the Standard toolbar. Expand the Property inspector.
4. Right-click the index.htm file and set the page as the home page.

In the Lab

5. Position the insertion point to the right of the heading and then drag the money.gif image to the insertion point. Apply the settings shown in Table 2-6. Position the insertion point to the right of the text, Equifax Credit Information Services, Inc. Drag the answer.gif image to the insertion point. Apply the settings shown in Table 2-6.

6. Select the text, financial tool, located in the first sentence of the first paragraph. Create a relative link from the selected text to questions.htm. Select the text, Fair and Accurate Credit Transactions (FACT) Act, located in the second sentence of the third paragraph. Create an absolute link to http://www.annualcreditreport.com. Select the name of the company in the first bulleted list item (Equifax Credit Information Services, Inc.) and create an absolute link using http://www.equifax.com. Create absolute links from the other two company names, using http://www.experian.com and http://www.transunion.com, respectively.

7. Position the insertion point at the end of the second paragraph. Press the SPACEBAR. Type Credit card and identity theft can be a major issue when applying for credit. Select the text you just typed and then create a relative link to the theft.htm file. Add an e-mail link to your name. Save the index page (Figure 2-89a on page DW 193).

8. Open theft.htm and apply the background image (creditbg.jpg) to the theft.htm page.

9. Position the insertion point to the left of the second line and then drag the protection.gif image to the insertion point. Apply the settings shown in Table 2-6. Position the insertion point after the first sentence in the second bulleted point and then drag the theft.gif image to the insertion point. Apply the settings shown in Table 2-6.

10. Drag to select the text, Identity theft, at the beginning of the first sentence and then create an absolute link using http://www.consumer.gov/idtheft/ as the URL. Create an absolute link from the protection.gif image using the same URL. Select the image and then type the URL in the Link box. Select Home and then create a relative link to the index.htm page. Title the page Credit Protection - Identity Theft. Save the Theft page (Figure 2-89b on page DW 193).

11. Open questions.htm. Apply the background image that you added to the theft.htm page in Step 8. Use the text, Home, at the bottom of the page to create a relative link to the index page.

12. Position the insertion point to the right of the first line of text, Questions to consider about your credit:, and then drag the question.gif image to the insertion point. Apply the settings in Table 2-6.

13. Create an absolute link from the Fair Credit Billing Act text in question 3. In this link, use the following as the URL: http://www.ftc.gov/bcp/conline/pubs/credit/fcb.htm. Title the page Credit Protection - Questions and Answers. Save the Questions page (Figure 2-89c).

14. View the site in the Site Map. Then view the Web site in your browser and verify that your external and relative links work. *Hint*: Remember to check the link for the image on the theft.htm page. Submit the documents in the format specified by your instructor. Close your browser and quit Dreamweaver.

3 Modifying the Lexington, NC Web Page

Problem: Jerry Smith recently became a member of a marketing group promoting Lexington's annual Barbecue Festival. He wants to expand the Web site you created for him by adding two new Web pages that will highlight other features of Lexington, North Carolina. You inform Jerry that you can create the new pages. The revised

(continued)

Modifying the Lexington, NC Web Page *(continued)*

pages for the Web site are displayed in Figures 2-90a, 2-90b, and 2-90c. Table 2-7 on page DW 198 includes the settings and alternative text for the images. Software and hardware settings determine how a Web page displays in a browser. Your Web pages may display differently in your browser than those in the figures do.

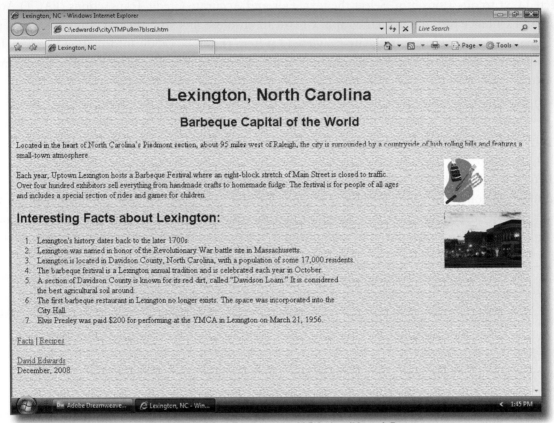

FIGURE 2-90   (a) Lexington, NC Index (Home) Page

In the Lab

(b) Lexington, NC - Barbecue Festival Facts Web Page

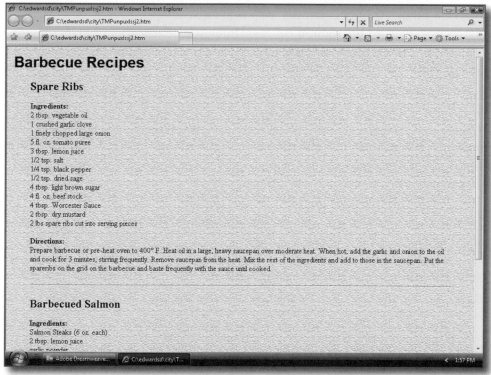

(c) Lexington, NC - Barbecue Recipes Web Page

FIGURE 2-90

(continued)

In the Lab

Modifying the Lexington, NC Web Page *(continued)*

Table 2-7 Image Property Settings for the Lexington, NC Web Site						
IMAGE NAME	W	H	V SPACE	H SPACE	ALIGN	ALT
bbq1.gif	77	87	None	80	Right	Barbecue
lexington.jpg	149	106	6	8	Right	Lexington
bbq2.gif	200	155	None	25	Left	Barbecue

Instructions: Perform the following tasks:

1. Use the Windows Computer tool to copy the data files. The data files consist of three images and two Web pages, facts.htm and recipes.htm.
2. Start Dreamweaver. Display the panel groups. Select Lexington, NC on the Files pop-up menu.
3. Open index.htm. If necessary, display the Property inspector and the Standard toolbar. Expand the Property inspector.
4. Set the index.htm page as the home page.
5. Position the insertion point after the last numbered item (7) on the page and then press the ENTER key. Click the Ordered List button to deselect the numbered list. Type Facts | Recipes as the link text.
6. Create a relative link from the text, Facts, to the facts.htm page and then create a relative link from the text, Recipes, to the recipes.htm page.
7. Position the insertion point to the right of the first line of the first paragraph and then drag the bbq1.gif image to the insertion point. Apply the settings shown in Table 2-7.
8. Insert the lexington.jpg image to the right of the text, Interesting Facts about Lexington:, and apply the settings shown in Table 2-7. Insert an e-mail link. Save the index page (Figure 2-90a on page DW 196).
9. Open facts.htm and apply the citybg.gif image to the background.
10. Position the insertion point to the left of the heading and then drag the bbq2.gif image to the insertion point. Apply the settings shown in Table 2-7.
11. Scroll to the bottom of the page and then select Home. Create a relative link to the index.htm page. Click to the right of Home. Press the ENTER key and then type Barbecue Festival. Select the text and create an absolute link to http://www.barbecuefestival.com. Title the page Lexington, North Carolina - Barbecue Festival. Save the Facts page (Figure 2-90b on the previous page).
12. Open recipes.htm. Apply the citybg.gif image to the background.
13. Create a relative link to the index page. Title the page Lexington, North Carolina - Barbecue Recipes. Save the Recipes page (Figure 2-90c on the previous page).
14. View the Web site in your browser and verify the links. Submit the documents in the format specified by your instructor. Close your browser and quit Dreamweaver.

Cases and Places

The difficulty of these case studies varies:
■ are the least difficult and ■■ are the most difficult. The last exercise is a group exercise.

1 ■ In Chapter 1, you created a Web site and a Web page listing your favorite sport. Now, you want to add another page to the site. Create and format the page. The page should include general information about your selected sport. Create a relative link from the home page to the new page and from the new page to the home page. Add a background image to the new page and insert an image on one of the pages. Include an appropriate title for the page. Save the page in the sports subfolder. For a selection of images and backgrounds, visit the Dreamweaver CS3 Media Web page (scsite.com/dwcs3/media) and then click Media below Chapter 2.

2 ■ Several of your friends were impressed with the Web page and Web site you created about your favorite hobby in Chapter 1. They have given you some topics they think you should include on the site. You decide to create an additional page that will consist of details about your hobby and the topics your friends suggested. Format the page. Add an absolute link to a related Web site and a relative link from the home page to the new page and from the new page to the home page. Add a background image to the new page. Create an e-mail link on the index page. Title the page with the name of the selected hobby. Save the page in the hobby subfolder. For a selection of images and backgrounds, visit the Dreamweaver CS3 Media Web page (scsite.com/dwcs3/media) and then click Media below Chapter 2.

3 ■■ Modify the favorite type of music Web site you created in Chapter 1 by creating a new page. Format the page. Discuss your favorite artist or band on the new page. Add a background image to the new page. On the index page, align the image to the right, and on the new page, align the image to the left. Add appropriate alternative text for each image. Position each image appropriately on the page by using the H Space and V Space property features. Add an e-mail link on the index page, and add text and a relative link from the new page to the index page. View your Web pages in your browser. Give the page a meaningful title and then save the page in your music subfolder. For a selection of images and backgrounds, visit the Dreamweaver CS3 Media Web page (scsite.com/dwcs3/media) and then click Media below Chapter 2.

Cases and Places

4 ■■ In Chapter 1, you created a Web site and a Web page to publicize your campaign for public office. Develop two additional pages to add to the site. Apply a background image to the new pages. Apply appropriate formatting to the two new pages. Scan a picture of yourself or take a picture with a digital camera and include the picture on the index page. Add a second image illustrating one of your campaign promises. Include at least two images on one of the new pages and one image on the other new page. Add alternative text for all images, and then add appropriate H Space and V Space property features to position the images. Create e-mail links on all three pages and create relative links from the home page to both pages and from each of the pages to the home page. Create an absolute link to a related site on one of the pages. Set the index page as the home page. Give each page a meaningful title and then save the pages in the office subfolder. For a selection of images and backgrounds, visit the Dreamweaver CS3 Media Web page (scsite.com/dwcs3/media) and then click Media below Chapter 2.

5 ■■ **Working Together** The student trips Web site you and your classmates created in Chapter 1 is a success. Everyone loves it. The dean is so impressed that she asks the group to continue with the project. Your team creates and formats three additional Web pages, one for each of three possible locations for the trip. Add a background image to all new pages. Add two images to each of the pages, including the index page, and set the index page as the home page. Resize one of the images. Add the Alt text for each image, and then position each image appropriately using the H Space and V Space property features. Create a link from the index page to each of the three new pages and a link from each page to the index page. Create an absolute link to a related informational Web site on each of the three new pages. Add an appropriate title to each page. Preview in a browser to verify the links. Save the pages in your trips subfolder. For a selection of images and backgrounds, visit the Dreamweaver CS3 Media Web page (scsite.com/dwcs3/media) and then click Media below Chapter 2.

ADOBE
Dreamweaver CS3

Tables and Page Layout

CASE PERSPECTIVE

The Colorado Parks Web site has been very successful thus far. David has received several e-mail messages asking for additional information about the four national parks. Tracy suggests a separate page for Rocky Mountains and Mesa Verde and a combination page for the two smaller parks — Black Canyon and Great Sand Dunes parks. Both David and you agree this is a good idea and would be a good addition to the Web site. The two of you volunteer to research various sources and to create the content for the three new pages.

Tracy further suggests that, in addition to adding the same background to these pages as that on the rest of the site, the three new pages also should have some consistency in the displayed information. The team decides that each page should include a heading with the name of the park, that the information contained in the body content should describe the location and contain some interesting facts, and that each page should list the park's address, including an e-mail link. The footer will contain links to the home page and to all four national parks. Everyone is eager to get started on this new addition to the Colorado Parks Web site.

As you read through this chapter, you will learn how to plan and design Web pages and how to create pages using tables. You also will learn how to modify and delete tables.

ADOBE
Dreamweaver CS3

Tables and Page Layout

CHAPTER

3

Objectives

You will have mastered the material in this chapter when you can:

- Understand and plan page layout
- Describe Standard mode and Layout mode
- Design a Web page using tables in Standard mode
- Design a Web page using tables in Layout mode
- Describe visual guides
- Modify a table structure

- Describe HTML table tags
- Add content to a table
- Format table content
- Format a table
- Create head content

Introduction

Chapter 3 introduces the use of tables for page layout and the addition of head content elements. Page layout is an important part of Web design because it determines the way your page will be displayed in the browser, which is one of the major challenges for any Web designer.

Dreamweaver's table feature is a great tool for designing a Web page. The table feature is very similar to the table feature in word processing programs such as Microsoft Word. A table allows you to add vertical and horizontal structure to a Web page. Using a table, you can put just about anything on your page and have it be displayed in a specific location. You can lay out tabular data. Using the many table features, you can create columns of text or navigation bars. You can delete, split, and merge rows and columns; modify table, row, or cell properties to add color and alignment; and copy and paste cells in the table structure.

Dreamweaver provides three views, or ways, to use the table feature: Standard mode, Layout mode, and Expanded mode. Standard mode uses the Insert Table dialog box, and Layout mode is a freeform process in which you draw the table and the individual cells. Expanded mode allows you to edit table elements. In Expanded mode, Dreamweaver adds cell padding and spacing to the tables, thus temporarily increasing the tables' borders. This provides easy access to items that are difficult to select and allows for precise insertion point placement. This chapter discusses the three views and the advantages and disadvantages of each.

The second part of this chapter discusses the addition and value of head content. When you create a Web page, the underlying source code is made up of two main sections: the head section and the body section. The body section contains the page content that is displayed in the browser. In Chapters 1 and 2, you created your Web pages in the body section. The head section contains a variety of information. With the exception of the page title, all head content is invisible when viewed in the Dreamweaver Document window or in a browser. Some head content is accessed by other programs, such as search engines, and some content is accessed by the browser. This chapter discusses the head content options and the importance of this content.

Chapter Three — Colorado Parks Page Layout

In this chapter, you continue with the creation of the Colorado Parks Web site. You use tables to create three new Web pages focusing on Colorado's four national parks — a separate page for Rocky Mountains and Mesa Verde and a combination page for Black Canyon and Great Sand Dunes. You then add these new pages to the parks Web site and link to them from the natl_parks.htm Web page (Figures 3-1a, 3-1b, and 3-1c on pages DW 203 through 205). When you complete your Web page additions, you will add keywords and a description as the head content.

(a) Rocky Mountain National Park Page

FIGURE 3-1 (*continued*)

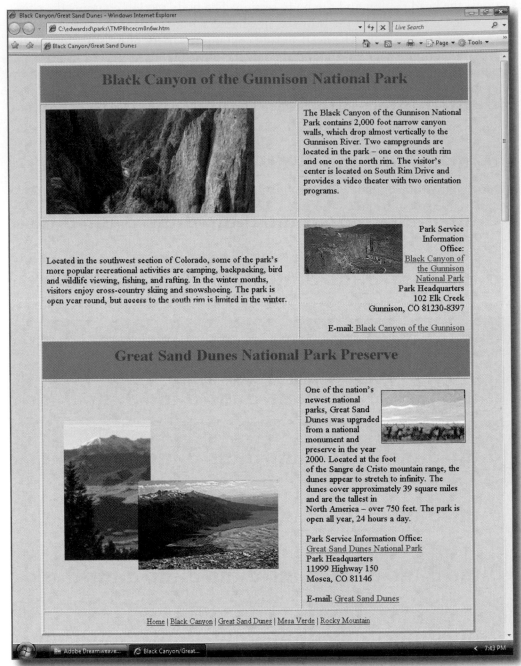

(b) Black Canyon and Great Sand Dunes National Park Page

FIGURE 3-1 (*continued*)

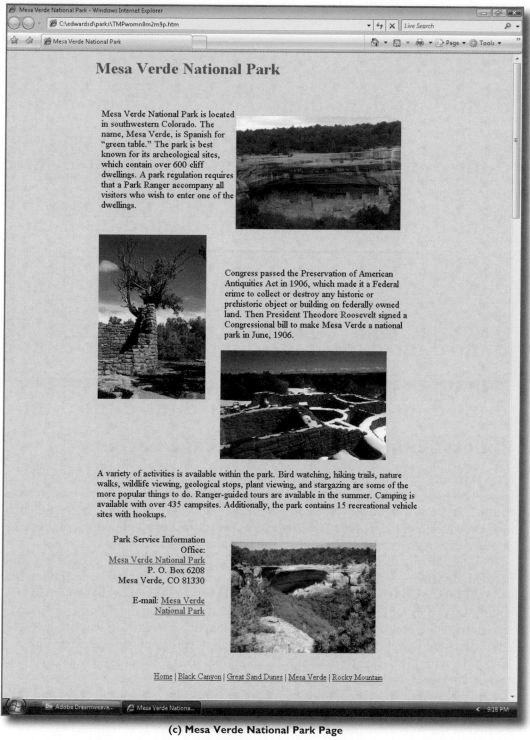

(c) Mesa Verde National Park Page

FIGURE 3-1 (continued)

This chapter uses a hierarchical structure. The structure now is expanded to include the three new pages (Figure 3-2 on the next page).

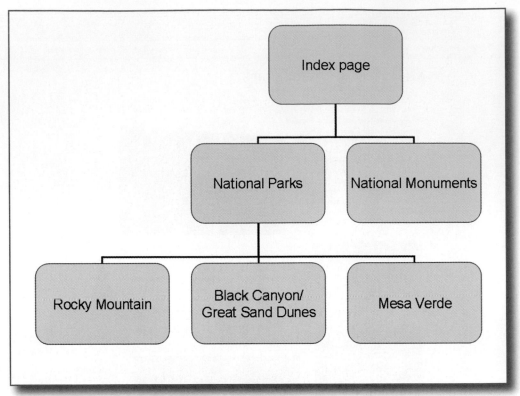

FIGURE 3-2

Understanding and Planning Page Layout

Page layout is the process of arranging the text, images, and other elements on the page. The basic rules of page layout are that your site should be easy to navigate, easy to read, and quick to download. Studies indicate that visitors will lose interest quickly in your Web site if the majority of a page does not download within 15 seconds. One popular design element that downloads quickly is tables.

Tables download very fast because they are created with HTML code. They can be used anywhere — for the home page, menus, images, navigation bars, frames, and so on. Tables originally were intended for presenting data arranged by rows and columns, such as tabular data within a spreadsheet. Web designers, however, quickly seized upon the use of tables to produce specific layout effects. You can produce good designs by using tables creatively. Tables allow you to position elements on a Web page with much greater accuracy. Using tables for layout provides the Web page author with endless design possibilities.

A typical Web page is composed of three sections: the header, the body, and the footer, such as those shown in Figure 3-3 on the next page. The **header**, generally located at the top of the page, can contain logos, images, or text that identifies the Web site. The header also may contain hyperlinks to other pages within the Web site.

The **body** of the Web page contains informational content about your site. This content may be in the form of text, graphics, animation, video, and audio, or a combination of any of these elements.

The **footer** provides hyperlinks for contact information and navigational controls. This may be in addition to the navigation controls in the header. Other common items contained within a footer are the name and e-mail address of the author or of the Webmaster. Sometimes, hyperlinks to other resources or to Help information are part of the footer.

FIGURE 3-3

With tables, it is easy to create this header/body/footer structure or to create any other layout structure applicable to your specific Web page needs. The entire structure can be contained within one table or a combination of multiple and nested tables. A nested table is a table inside another table. You will use a structure similar to that shown in Figure 3-3 to create the three new pages for the Colorado Parks Web site.

Standard Mode and Layout Mode

Dreamweaver provides two options for creating tables: Standard mode and Layout mode. In **Standard mode**, a table is presented as a grid of rows and columns. This view is similar to a Microsoft Excel spreadsheet or a table created in a word processing program such as Microsoft Word. In **Layout mode**, you can draw, resize, and move boxes on the page while Dreamweaver still uses tables for the underlying structure. If you have used a desktop publishing program such as Microsoft Publisher or Adobe InDesign, then you are familiar with the format in which tables are created in Layout mode. Using Layout mode, you can place content at any location in the Document window.

Copying Data Files to the Local Web Site

Your data files contain images for Chapter 3. These images are in an images folder. You use the Windows Computer option to copy the Chapter 3 images to your parks images folder. See the inside back cover for instructions for downloading the data files or see your instructor for information about accessing the files required for this book.

The DataFiles folder for this chapter is stored on Local Disk (C:). The location on your computer may be different. If necessary, verify with your instructor the location of the DataFiles folder. The following steps illustrate how to copy the files to the parks local root folder.

To Copy Data Files to the Parks Web Site

1 Click the Start button on the Windows taskbar and then click Computer.

2 Double-click Local Disk (C:) and then navigate to the location of the data files for Chapter 3.

3 Double-click the folder containing your data files, and then double-click the Chap03 folder.

4 Double-click the parks folder and then double-click the images folder.

5 Click the alberta_falls.gif image file or the first file name in the list.

6 Hold down the SHIFT key and then click the winter_view.jpg image file (or the last file name in the list) to select the eleven image files.

7 Right-click the selected files to display the context menu.

8 Click the Copy command and then click the Back button the number of times necessary to navigate to the your name folder.

9 Double-click the your name folder, double-click the parks folder, and then double-click the images folder.

10 Right-click anywhere in the open window to display the context menu, and then click Paste (Figure 3-4).

11 Click the images window Close button.

The 11 new image files are pasted into the Colorado Parks Web site images folder (Figure 3-4).

FIGURE 3-4

Starting Dreamweaver and Opening a Web Site

Each time you start Dreamweaver, it opens to the last site displayed when you closed the program. It, therefore, may be necessary for you to open the parks Web site. The Files pop-up menu in the Files panel lists sites you have defined. When you open the site, a list of pages and subfolders within the site are displayed. The following steps show how to start Dreamweaver and open the Colorado Parks Web site.

To Start Dreamweaver and Open the Colorado Parks Web Site

1 Click the Start button on the Windows taskbar.

2 Point to All Programs on the Start menu, point to Adobe Dreamweaver CS3 on the All Programs menu, if necessary, and then click Adobe Dreamweaver CS3.

3 Click the Files panel box arrow and point to Colorado Parks on the Files panel pop-up menu.

4 Click Colorado Parks. If necessary, double-click the images folder.

The Colorado Parks Web site hierarchy is displayed in the Files panel (Figure 3-5).

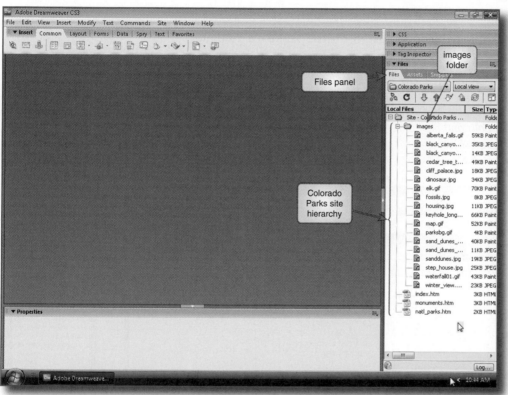

FIGURE 3-5

Adding Pages to a Web Site

You copied the images necessary to begin creating your new Web pages to the parks local root folder in the Files panel. You will add three additional pages to the Web site: separate pages for Rocky Mountain and Mesa Verde and a combination page for the two smaller parks — Black Canyon and Great Sand Dunes. You first create the Rocky Mountain National Park Web page. You then add the background image and a heading to the new page. Next, you use Dreamweaver's Standard mode to insert tables and add text, images, and links into the cells within the table.

Opening a New Document Window

The next step is to open a new Document window. This will become the Rocky Mountain National Park page. The following steps illustrate how to open a new Document window and save the page as rocky-mt.htm.

To Open a New Document Window

1 Click File on the menu bar and then point to New.

2 Click New. If necessary, click Blank Page.

3 Click HTML in the Page Type list.

4 Click the Create button.

5 Click the Save button on the Standard toolbar.

6 Type rocky-mt as the file name. If necessary, select the parks folder, and then click the Save button.

The rocky-mt page is saved in the parks local folder and is displayed in Dreamweaver's Files panel. The path and file name (edwards\parks\rocky-mt.htm) appear on the Dreamweaver title bar (Figure 3-6).

FIGURE 3-6

Creating the Rocky Mountain National Park Web Page

You start creating the Rocky Mountain National Park page by applying a background image. This is the same background image you used for the Colorado Parks Web site pages in Chapters 1 and 2. To provide additional space in the Document window and to create a better overview of the layout, you hide the panel groups. You expand the Property inspector to display the additional table options. The following steps illustrate how to apply the background image.

To Add a Background Image to the Rocky Mountain National Park Web Page

1 Click the panel groups expander arrow to hide the panel groups.

2 If necessary, click the Property inspector expander arrow to display both the upper and lower sections.

3 Click Modify on the menu bar and then click Page Properties.

4 Click the Browse button to the right of the Background image box.

5 If necessary, navigate to the parks\images folder.

6 Click parksbg.gif and then click the OK button in the Select Image Source dialog box.

7 Click the OK button in the Page Properties dialog box. If necessary, click the Document window.

The background image is applied to the Rocky Mountain National Park page. The panel groups are hidden, and the Property inspector is expanded. The insertion point is aligned at the left (Figure 3-7).

FIGURE 3-7

Next, you add, format, and change the color of the heading. You apply the same heading style and color you applied to the heading in the index page. Recall that Dreamweaver designated this as style1. The following steps on the next page show how to add the heading, apply the Heading 1 format, and change the text color.

To Insert and Format the Heading

1 **Click the Document window. Type** Rocky Mountain National Park **as the heading.**

2 **Apply Heading 1; click the Align Center button in the Property inspector.**

3 **Drag to select the title. Type** #336633 **in the color hexadecimal value box in the Property inspector. Press the ENTER key.**

4 **If necessary, click anywhere on the page to deselect the heading.**

5 **Title the page Rocky Mountain National Park.**

6 **Click the Save button on the Standard toolbar.**

The heading is centered and formatted, and the title is added (Figure 3-8). The style is turned off.

FIGURE 3-8

Understanding Tables

Tables have many uses in HTML design. The most obvious is a table of data, but, as already mentioned, tables also are used for page layout, such as placing text and graphics on a page at just the right location. **Tables** provide Web designers with a method to add vertical and horizontal structure to a page. A table consists of three basic components: rows, columns, and cells. A **row** is a horizontal collection of cells, and a **column** is a vertical collection of cells. A **cell** is the container created when the row and column intersect. Each cell within the table can contain any standard element you use on a Web page. This includes text, images, and other objects.

Inserting a Table into the Rocky Mountain National Park Page

You will add two tables to the Rocky Mountain National Park page and then add text and images to the cells within the tables. The first table will consist of three rows and two columns, with a cell padding of 2 and cell spacing of 20. **Cell padding** is the amount of space between the edge of a cell and its contents, whereas **cell spacing** is the amount of space between cells. The border will be set to 0. When the table is displayed in Dreamweaver, a border outline appears around the table. When the table's border is set to 0 and the table is viewed in a browser, however, this outline does not appear.

The table width is 90 percent. When specifying the width, you can select percent or pixels. A table with the width specified as a **percent** expands with the width of the window and the monitor size in which it is being viewed. A table with the width specified as **pixels** will remain the same size regardless of the window and monitor size. If you select percent and an image is larger than the selected percent, the cell and table will expand to accommodate the image. Likewise, if the **No Wrap** property is enabled and the text will not fit within the cell, the cell and table will expand to accommodate the text. It is not necessary to declare a table width. When no value is specified, the table is displayed as small as possible and then expands as content is added. If modifications are necessary to the original specified table values, these values can be changed in the Property inspector.

The second table is a one-cell table, consisting of one row and one column. This table will contain links to the Home page and to the four national parks pages. You use the Insert bar with the Layout category and the Property inspector to control and format the tables.

Q: Need Help?

A: Press the F1 key for comprehensive information about all Dreamweaver features.

The Insert Bar

The Insert bar appears at the top of the window below the menu bar. This toolbar contains buttons for creating and inserting objects such as tables, layers, and images. The Insert bar contains seven separate categories, and is fully customizable through the Favorites tab. When the current document contains server-side code (such as that related to a database), additional categories are displayed. Server-side code is an advanced topic and is not discussed in this book.

Some categories have buttons with pop-up menus. When you select an option from a pop-up menu, it becomes the default action for the button. Any time you select a new option from the pop-up menu, the default action for the button changes. The Insert bar is displayed when you start Dreamweaver. You can, however, hide or display the Insert bar as necessary. All selections within the categories also are available through the menu bar and many of the selections also are available through the Property inspectors.

Category Types

The default Insert bar contains the following categories, each on a different tab:

COMMON CATEGORY The **Common category** contains buttons for the most frequently used Web publishing tasks.

LAYOUT CATEGORY The **Layout category** contains buttons pertaining to the design modes for Web publishing and enables you to insert tables, Spry objects, Spry frameworks for Ajax (not covered in this book), and frames. You also can choose from among two table modes: Standard (default), and Expanded Tables. Dreamweaver also contains a Layout Mode, which provides the following: Draw Layout Cell and Layout Table. Layout Mode is accessed by clicking View on the menu bar, clicking Table Mode, and then clicking Layout Mode, or by pressing ALT+F6.

FORMS CATEGORY The **Forms category** contains buttons for creating forms and inserting form elements.

DATA CATEGORY The **Data category** contains buttons that can be used to insert Spry objects and other dynamic elements.

SPRY CATEGORY The **Spry category** contains buttons that enable you to build Spry pages.

TEXT CATEGORY The **Text category** contains buttons for text formatting.

FAVORITES CATEGORY The **Favorites category** enables you to group and organize the Insert bar buttons you use the most in one common place.

You use the Layout category to assist with the page design and to insert tables. The following steps illustrate how to display the Insert bar if necessary and select the Layout category. If the Insert bar already is displayed on your computer, skip Step 1.

To Display the Insert Bar and Select the Layout Category

1

• **If necessary, click Window on the menu bar. If the Insert command is not checked, click Insert.**

2

• **Point to the Layout tab (Figure 3-9).**

Layout is underlined on the Insert bar.

FIGURE 3-9

3

• **Click the Layout tab.**

The Insert bar for the Layout category is displayed (Figure 3-10).

FIGURE 3-10

Layout Category

The Layout category (Figure 3-11 on the next page) enables you to work with tables and other features. Dreamweaver provides two ways to create tables — Standard mode and Layout mode. In Standard mode, a table is displayed as a grid and expands as you add text and images. You define the structure of the table using the Insert Table dialog box. In Layout mode, you create tables and cells by drawing them. You will work with Layout mode later in this chapter.

The Layout category also contains a button for Expanded Tables mode. This mode temporarily expands the cells, enabling you to select items in individual cells and to place the insertion point precisely. Use this mode as a temporary visual aid for insertion point placement. After placing the insertion point, return to Standard or Layout mode to make your edits and to provide a better visualization of your changes.

FIGURE 3-11

Table 3-1 lists the button names and descriptions available in the Insert bar Layout category.

Table 3-1 Buttons on the Layout Insert Bar	
Standard Mode	Displays a table as a grid of lines
Expanded Tables Mode	Temporarily adds cell padding and spacing
Insert Div Tag	Inserts a <div> tag
Draw AP Div	A fixed absolute point within a Web document
Spry Menu Bar	An AJAX predefined control
Spry Tabbed Panels	Inserts a tabbed panel widget directly into the Web page
Spry Accordion	Creates horizontal regions on a Web page that can be expanded or collapsed
Spry Collapsible Panel	Displays collapsible panels that have a clickable tab and a content area that displays/hides when a tab is clicked
Table	Places a table at the insertion point
Insert Row Above	Used to insert a row above the selected row
Insert Row Below	Used to insert a row below the selected row
Insert Column to the Left	Used to insert a column to the left of the selected column
Insert Column to the Right	Used to insert a column to the right of the selected column
IFrame	Displays data (text and image) that is stored in a separate page
Frames	Displays Frames pop-up menu
Draw Layout Table	Lets you draw a layout table in the Design view of the Document window
Draw Layout Cell	Lets you draw individual table cells in the Design view of the Document window

More About

Dreamweaver CS3 Tables

For more information about Dreamweaver CS3 table views, visit the Dreamweaver CS3 More About Web page (scsite.com/dwcs3/more.htm) and then click Dreamweaver CS3 Tables.

Table Defaults and Accessibility

When you insert a table, the Table dialog box is displayed and contains default settings for each of the table attributes. The Table dialog box in Figure 3-12 contains the values shown in Table 3-2. After you have created a table and made changes to these defaults, the settings that are displayed for the next table you create are the settings from the last table created.

FIGURE 3-12

Table 3-2 Table Dialog Box Default Values

ATTRIBUTE	DEFAULT	DESCRIPTION
Rows	3	Determines the number of rows in the table
Columns	3	Determines the number of columns in the table
Table width	200 pixels	Specifies the width of the table in pixels or as a percentage of the browser window's width
Border thickness	1 pixel	Specifies the border width in pixels
Cell padding	0	Specifies the number of pixels between a cell's border and its contents
Cell spacing	0	Specifies the number of pixels between adjacent table cells
Header	None	Specifies if the top row and/or column is designated as a header cell
Caption	None	Provides a brief description of the table; used for accessibility
Align caption	default	Specifies where the table caption appears in relation to the table
Summary	None	Provides a table description; used by screen readers

It is advisable to use headers for tables when the table presents tabular information. Screen readers read table headings and help screen-reader users keep track of table information. Additionally, the Caption option provides a table title that displays outside of the table, the Align caption option specifies where the table caption appears in relation to the table, and the Summary option provides a table description. Screen readers read the summary text, but the text does not appear in the user's browser. Summary text is similar to the Alt text you added for images in Chapter 2. You add Summary text to the tables you create in this chapter.

Standard Mode

As indicated previously, the Header and Caption options are important when a table displays tabular data. When using a table for layout, however, other options apply. Structurally and graphically, the elements in a table used for layout should be invisible in the browser. For instance, when using a table for layout, use the None option for Headers. The None option prevents the header tags <th> and </th> from being added to the table. Because the table does not contain tabular data, a header would be of no benefit to the screen-reader user. Screen readers, however, read table content from left to right and top to bottom. Therefore, it is important to structure the table content in a linear arrangement.

The following steps illustrate how to use Standard mode to insert a table with three rows and two columns into the Rocky Mountain National Park Web page.

Q: What is the Web site address for Adobe online support?

A: You can find Adobe online support at www.adobe.com/support/dreamweaver/.

To Insert a Table Using Standard Mode

1

• **If necessary, click the Standard button on the Insert bar and then click the Table button.**

The Table dialog box is displayed (Figure 3-13). The settings displayed are the default settings from the last table created, so your dialog box most likely will contain different values.

FIGURE 3-13

2

• **If necessary, type** 3 **and then press the** TAB **key to move to the Columns box.**

• **Type** 2 **as the new value in the Columns box and then press the** TAB **key.**

• **Type** 90 **as the new value in the Table width box and then click the Table width arrow.**

• **Click percent and then press the** TAB **key.**

• **Type** 0 **in the Border thickness box and then press the** TAB **key.**

• **Type** 2 **in the Cell padding box and then press the** TAB **key.**

• **Type** 20 **in the Cell spacing box and then press the** TAB **key.**

• **If necessary, select None for the Header.**

• **Click the Summary text box and type** Table layout for Rocky Mountain National Park Web page. The table contains three rows and two columns with images and text in the table cells.

The Table dialog box is displayed with the new settings, as shown in Figure 3-14.

FIGURE 3-14

3

• **Click the OK button.**

The table is inserted into the Document window (Figure 3-15). The dark border around the table and the three handles on the lower and right borders indicate that the table is selected. The <table> tag is selected in the tag selector, also indicating that the table is selected. The cell spacing between each cell is 20 pixels. The default alignment for the table is left. The border is set to 0 and appears as an outline when the table is viewed in Dreamweaver. When the table is viewed in a browser, however, no border is displayed.

FIGURE 3-15

Other Ways

1. On Insert menu, click Table, select table properties, click OK button
2. Press CTRL+ALT+T

Property Inspector Table Features

As you have seen, the Property inspector options change depending on the selected object. You use the Property inspector to modify and add table attributes. When a table is selected, the Property inspector displays table properties in both panels. When another table element — a row, column, or cell — is selected, the displayed properties change and are determined by the selected element. The following section describes the table-related features of the Property inspector shown in Figure 3-16.

FIGURE 3-16

TABLE ID An identifier used for Cascading Style Sheets, scripting, and accessibility. A table ID is not required; however, it is a good idea to always add this identifier.

ROWS AND COLS The number of rows and columns in the table.

W Used to specify the minimum width of the table in either pixels or percent. If a size is not specified, the size can vary depending on the monitor and browser settings. A table width specified in pixels is displayed at the same size in all browsers. A table width specified in percent is altered in appearance based on the user's monitor resolution and browser window size.

CELLPAD The number of pixels between the cell border and the cell content.

CELLSPACE The number of pixels between adjacent table cells.

ALIGN Determines where the table appears, relative to other elements in the same paragraph such as text or images. The default alignment is to the left.

BORDER Specifies the border width in pixels.

CLEAR COLUMN WIDTHS AND CLEAR ROW HEIGHTS Deletes all specified row height or column width values from the table.

CONVERT TABLE WIDTHS TO PIXELS Sets the width of each column in the table to its current width expressed as pixels.

CONVERT TABLE WIDTHS TO PERCENT Sets the width of each column in the table to its current width expressed as a percentage of the Document window's width and also sets the width of the whole table to its current width as a percentage of the Document window's width.

BG COLOR The table background color.

HEXADECIMAL NUMBER The hexadecimal value for the bg color.

BRDR COLOR The table border color.

BG IMAGE The table background image.

CLASS An attribute used with Cascading Style Sheets.

Cell, Row, and Column Properties

When a cell, row, or column is selected, the properties in the upper pane of the Property inspector are the same as the standard properties for text. You can use these properties to incorporate standard HTML formatting tags within a cell, row, or column. The part of the table selected determines which properties are displayed in the lower pane of the Property inspector. The properties for all three features (cell, row, and column) are the same, except for one element — the icon displayed in the lower-left pane of the Property inspector. The following section describes the row-related features (Figure 3-17), cell-related features (Figure 3-18), and column-related features (Figure 3-19) of the Property inspector.

FIGURE 3-17

FIGURE 3-18

column image

Split cells into rows or columns button

column properties

Merge selected cells using spans

FIGURE 3-19

HORZ Specifies the horizontal alignment of the contents of a cell, row, or column. The contents can be aligned to the left, right, or center of the cells.

VERT Specifies the vertical alignment of the contents of a cell, row, or column. The contents can be aligned to the top, middle, bottom, or baseline of the cells.

W AND H Specifies the width and height of selected cells in pixels or as a percentage of the entire table's width or height.

BG (UPPER TEXT FIELD) The file name of the background image for a cell, column, or row.

BG (LOWER COLOR BOX AND TEXT FIELD) The background color of a cell, column, or row, using the color picker.

BRDR The border color for the cells.

NO WRAP Prevents line wrapping, keeping all text in a given cell on a single line. If No Wrap is enabled, cells widen to accommodate all data as it is typed or pasted into a cell.

HEADER Formats the selected cells as table header cells. The contents of table header cells are bold and centered by default.

MERGE CELLS Combines selected cells, rows, or columns into one cell (available when two or more cells, rows, or columns are selected).

SPLIT CELLS Divides a cell, creating two or more cells (available when a single cell is selected).

Table Formatting Conflicts

When formatting tables in Standard mode, you can set properties for the entire table or for selected rows, columns, or cells in the table. When you are applying these properties, however, a potential for conflict exists. To resolve this potential conflict,

HTML assigns levels of precedence. The order of precedence for table formatting is cells, rows, and table. When a property, such as background color or alignment, is set to one value for the whole table and another value for individual cells, cell formatting takes precedence over row formatting, which in turn takes precedence over table formatting.

For example, if you set the background color for a single cell to green, and then set the background color of the entire table to red, the green cell does not change to red, because cell formatting takes precedence over table formatting. Dreamweaver, however, does not always follow the precedence. The program will override the settings for a cell if you change the settings for the row that contains the cell. To eliminate this problem, you should change the cell settings last.

Understanding HTML Structure within a Table

As you work with and become more familiar with tables, it is helpful to have an understanding of the HTML structure within a table. Suppose, for example, you have a table with two rows and two columns, displaying a total of four cells, such as the following:

First cell	Second cell
Third cell	Fourth cell

The general syntax of the table is:

```
<table>
<tr>
    <td> First cell </td>
    <td> Second cell </td>
</tr>
<tr>
    <td> Third cell </td>
    <td> Fourth cell </td>
</tr>
</table>
```

More About

Table Formatting Conflicts

For more information about Dreamweaver CS3 table formatting conflicts, visit the Dreamweaver CS3 More About Web page (scsite.com/dwcs3/more.htm) and then click Dreamweaver CS3 Tables.

When you view your table in Dreamweaver, the tag selector displays the <table>, <td>, and <tr> tags. The <table> tag indicates the whole table. Clicking the <table> tag in the tag selector selects the whole table. The <td> tag indicates table data. Clicking the <td> tag in the tag selector selects the cell containing the insertion point. The <tr> tag indicates table row. Clicking the <tr> tag in the tag selector selects the row containing the insertion point.

Selecting the Table and Selecting Cells

The Property inspector displays table attributes only if the entire table is selected. To select the entire table, click the upper-left corner of the table, anywhere on the top or bottom edge of the table, or click in a cell and then click <table> in the tag selector. When you move the pointer over the border, the pointer changes to a table grid icon, indicating that when the mouse button is clicked, the table is selected (Figure 3-20).

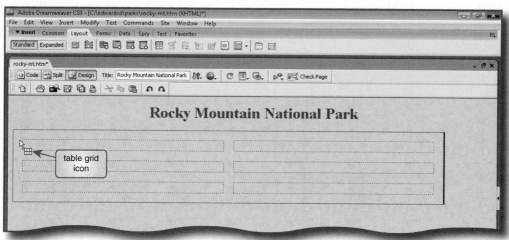

FIGURE 3-20

As discussed previously, another method for selecting a table is to click anywhere in the table and then click the <table> tag in the tag selector. When selected, the table will display with a dark border and selection handles on the table's lower and right edges (Figure 3-21).

FIGURE 3-21

Selecting a row, column, or cell is easier than selecting the entire table. When a cell, row, or column is selected, the selected item has a dark border. To select a cell, click inside the cell. When you click inside the cell, the <td> tag displays as selected on the status bar. To select a row or column, click inside one of the cells in the row or column and drag to select the other cells. When you select a row, the <tr> tag is displayed on the status bar. A second method for selecting a row or column is to point to the left edge of a row or the top edge of a column. When the pointer changes to a selection arrow, click to select the row or column. In Figure 3-22, the selection arrow is pointing to a row.

FIGURE 3-22

Adobe
Dreamweaver CS3

Centering a Table

When a table is inserted into the Document window with a specified width, it defaults to the left. Using the Property inspector, you can center the table by selecting it and then applying the Center command. The following steps illustrate how to select and center the table.

More About

Formatting a Table

Tabular data, saved in a delimited text format, can be imported into Dreamweaver from another program, such as Microsoft Excel, and then formatted as a table.

To Select and Center a Table

1

- **Click in row 1, column 1.**

The insertion point is in the first cell of the first row and the first column (Figure 3-23).

FIGURE 3-23

2

- **Click <table> in the tag selector.**

- **Click the Align box arrow in the Property inspector and then point to Center.**

The table is selected, and handles are displayed on the lower and right borders of the table. The <table> tag is selected. Center is selected in the Align pop-up menu (Figure 3-24).

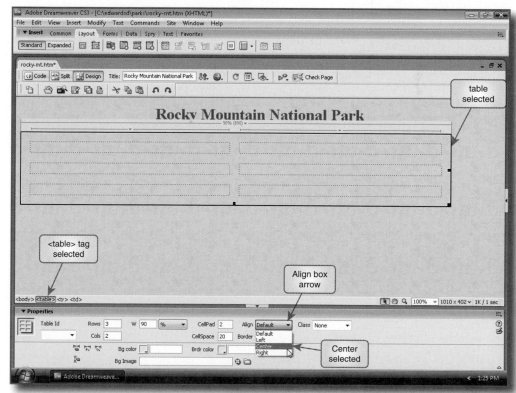

FIGURE 3-24

3

• **Click Center.**

The table is centered in the Document window (Figure 3-25).

FIGURE 3-25

Changing the Default Cell Alignment

The default horizontal cell alignment is left. When you enter text or add an image to a cell, it defaults to the left margin of the cell. You can change the left alignment through the Property inspector by clicking the cell and then changing the default to Center or Right. The default vertical cell alignment is Middle, which aligns the cell content in the middle of the cell. Other vertical alignment options include the following:

Top — aligns the cell content at the top of the cell
Bottom — aligns the cell content at the bottom of the cell
Baseline — aligns the cell content at the bottom of the cell (same as Bottom)

You can change the vertical alignment through the Property inspector by clicking the cell and then selecting another vertical alignment option.

The following steps show how to select all of the cells and change the default vertical alignment from middle to top.

To Change Vertical Alignment from Middle to Top

1

• **Click in row 1, column 1 and then drag to the right and down to select the three rows and two columns in the table.**

• **Click the Vert box arrow and then point to Top in the Vert pop-up menu.**

The three rows in the table are selected. The Property inspector changes to reflect the properties for a row. The Vert pop-up menu is displayed, and Top is selected (Figure 3-26).

FIGURE 3-26

2

• **Click Top.**

The vertical alignment is changed to Top (Figure 3-27). This change is not displayed in the Document window.

FIGURE 3-27

Specifying Column Width

When a table width is specified as a percentage, each column's width expands to accommodate the text or image. When you add content to the table, this expansion can distort the table appearance and make it difficult to visualize how the final page will be displayed. You can control this expansion by setting the column width. The objective for the Rocky Mountain National Park page is to display the page in two columns of equal widths of 50 percent. The following steps show how to specify column width.

To Specify Column Width

1

• **Click the cell in row 1, column 1 and then drag to select all cells in column 1.**

• **Click the W box in the Property inspector. Type** 50% **and then press the ENTER key.**

• **Click the cell in row 1, column 2, and then drag to select all cells in column 2.**

• **Click the W box in the Property inspector. Type** 50% **and then press the ENTER key.**

The width for column 1 and column 2 is specified as 50% at the top of the table (Figure 3-28). The percentage bar located at the top of the table sometimes appears below the table, depending on available screen space and screen location.

FIGURE 3-28

2

• **Click anywhere in the table to deselect the column.**

Table ID and Accessibility

Earlier in this chapter, the accessibility options available through the Table dialog box were discussed. The Property inspector for tables contains another accessibility option — table ID. For accessibility purposes, it is recommended that you add a table ID. This provides a name for the table within the HTML code. The table ID is similar to the alternate text for an image, identifying the object to devices that read browser screens. You must select the table to display the Table ID text box. The following step illustrates how to select the table and add a table ID to the Rocky Mountain National Park feature table.

To Add a Table ID to the Rocky Mountain National Park Feature Table

1

• **Click <table> in the status bar to select the table.**

• **Click the Table Id text box and then type** Rocky Mountain National Park feature page **as the Table ID text.**

• **Press the ENTER key.**

The Table ID is added to the Table ID text box and appears on the status bar (Figure 3-29).

FIGURE 3-29

Adding Text to the Rocky Mountain National Park Web Page

Next, you will enter and format the text for the Rocky Mountain National Park Web page. Table 3-3 on the next page includes the text for the first table. The text is entered into the table cells. If you have not set the width and height of a cell, when you begin to enter text into a table cell, the cell expands to accommodate the text. The other cells may appear to shrink, but they also will expand when you type in the cells or add an image to the cells.

The following steps on the next page show how to add text to the Rocky Mountain National Park page. Press the ENTER key or insert a line break, <br>, as indicated in Table 3-3. Press SHIFT+ENTER to insert a line break. Press the TAB key to move from cell to cell.

SECTION	TEXT FOR ROCKY MOUNTAIN NATIONAL PARK WEB PAGE
Table 3-3	**Rocky Mountain National Park Web Page Text**
Part 1	Rocky Mountain National Park is more than 415 square miles and has 114 named peaks over 10,000 feet. One of the more popular hiking trails is the Keyhole Route on Longs' Peak. At 14,255 feet, Longs' Peak is the highest peak in the Rocky Mountain National Park and the fifteenth tallest in Colorado. \<ENTER\> The park contains three distinct ecosystems which correspond to elevation: the montane, which is 7,000 to 9,000 feet above sea level; the subalpine ecosystem which is 9,000 to 11,500 feet and spans the tree line; and the alpine tundra, at the top, which is over 11,500 feet. \<ENTER\> Birds and animals add color and interest to the landscape. The park contains 65 species of mammals, 260 species of birds, and 900 species of plants. Black bears, mountain lions, and bobcats live in the park, but seldom are seen. Moose and mule deer are more visible. In autumn, herds of American elk roam the park and frequently are visible, even at the lower elevations.
Part 2	The park is open 24 hours a day year round.\<ENTER\> Park Service Information Office:\<br\> Rocky Mountain National Park\<br\> 1000 Highway 36\<br\> Estes Park, CO 80517-8397\<ENTER\> E-mail: Rocky Mountain National Park\<br\>

To Add Rocky Mountain National Park Text

1

• **Type the three paragraphs of Part 1 in Table 3-3 in row 1, column 2 of the table in the Document window. Press the ENTER key as indicated in the table.**

The three paragraphs are entered into row 1, column 2 (Figure 3-30).

text entered into row 1, column 2

FIGURE 3-30

2

• **If necessary, scroll down to display the rest of the table. Type the text of Part 2, as shown in Table 3-3, into row 3, column 1 of the Document window. Use SHIFT+ENTER to insert the line breaks.**

The text is entered (Figure 3-31). The insertion point still is within the cell below the last line and may not be displayed because a line break was added. A line break moves the insertion point to the next line, but does not create a blank space within a table cell such as when the ENTER key is pressed.

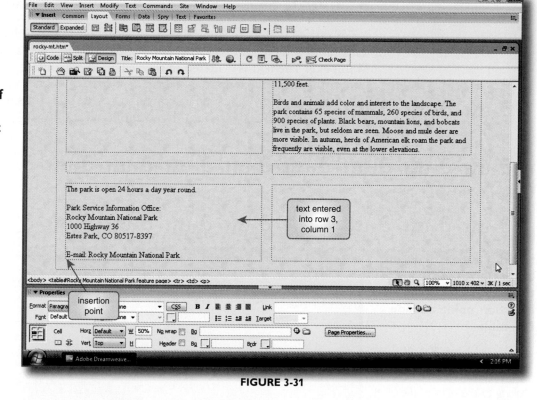

FIGURE 3-31

3

• **Select the text in row 3, column 1.**

• **Click the Align Right button in the Property inspector.**

The text is aligned to the right in the cell (Figure 3-32).

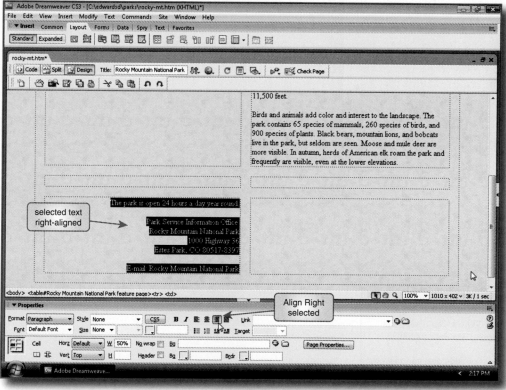

FIGURE 3-32

Other Ways

1. Right-click selected text, point to Align on context menu, click Right on Align submenu

Adding a Second Table to the Rocky Mountain National Park Web Page

Next, you add a second table to the Rocky Mountain National Park Web page. This table will contain one row and one column and will serve as the footer for your Web page. The text is centered in the cell and will contain links to the home page and to the other three national parks Web pages. When you create the pages for the other parks, you will be able to copy and paste these links into those pages. The following steps show how to add the second table and text.

To Add a Second Table to the Rocky Mountain National Park Web Page

1

• **Click outside the right border of the existing table to position the insertion point outside the table.**

The insertion point, a long dark line, is located and blinking to the right of the table border (Figure 3-33).

FIGURE 3-33

2

• **Press the ENTER key.**

• **Click the Table button on the Layout Insert bar.**

The Table dialog box is displayed (Figure 3-34). The dialog box retains the settings from the first table. The dialog box on your computer may show different settings.

FIGURE 3-34

3

• **Change the number of rows to 1, the number of columns to 1, the width to 75, the cell padding to 0, and the cell spacing to 10.**

• **Type** Links table **in the Summary text box.**

• **If necessary, change other settings to match the settings shown in Figure 3-35.**

The Table dialog box is displayed with the new table settings.

FIGURE 3-35

4

• **Click the OK button.**

• **If necessary, click the Align box arrow and then click Center.**

The table is inserted into the Document window (Figure 3-36). The dark border and handles indicate that the table is selected. The table contains one cell and is centered.

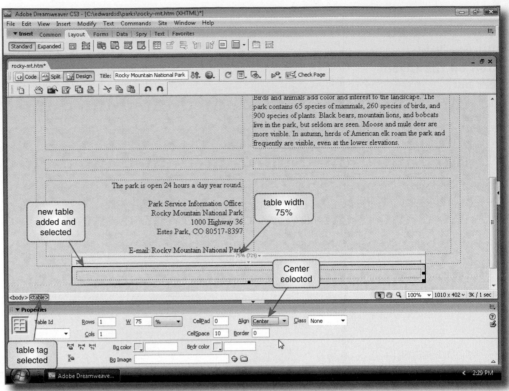

FIGURE 3-36

5

• **Click the cell in the table. Type** Home **and then press the SPACEBAR. Press SHIFT + | (vertical bar) and then press the SPACEBAR.**

• **Type** Black Canyon **and then press the SPACEBAR. Press SHIFT + | and then press the SPACEBAR.**

• **Type** Great Sand Dunes **and then press the SPACEBAR. Press SHIFT + | and then press the SPACEBAR.**

• **Type** Mesa Verde **and then press the SPACEBAR. Press SHIFT + | and then press the SPACEBAR.**

Type Rocky Mountain **as the last link text.**

FIGURE 3-37

The text is entered into the table (Figure 3-37).

Adjusting the Table Width

Determining table width is a matter of judgment. You may overestimate or underestimate the table width when first inserting it into the Document window. When this happens, it is easy to make adjustments to the table width through the Property inspector. The table with the names that will contain links is too wide for the text it contains and needs to be adjusted. You adjust the table width by selecting the table and then changing the width in the Property inspector. The following steps illustrate how to adjust the width and add the table ID.

To Adjust the Table Width, Center the Text, and Add the Table ID

1

• **If necessary, click the cell in table 2. Click <table> in the tag selector to select the table.**

• **Double-click the W box in the Property inspector.**

• **Type** 60 **and then press the ENTER key.**

The dark border around the table indicates that the table is selected. The Property inspector displays table properties. The table width is decreased (Figure 3-38).

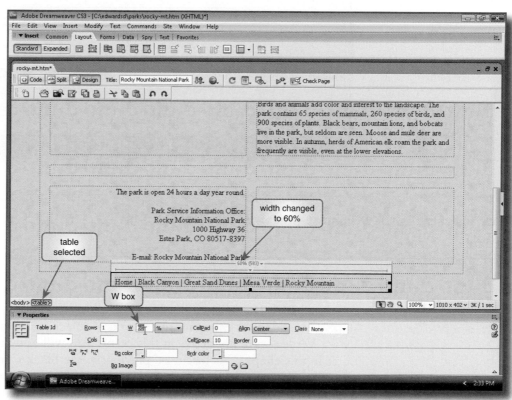

FIGURE 3-38

2

• **Click anywhere in the cell in the table.**

• **Click the Align Center button.**

• **Click <table> in the tag selector to select the table.**

• **Click the Table Id text box, type** `Colorado Parks links table`, **and then press the ENTER key.**

The text is centered in the cell, and the table is named (Figure 3-39).

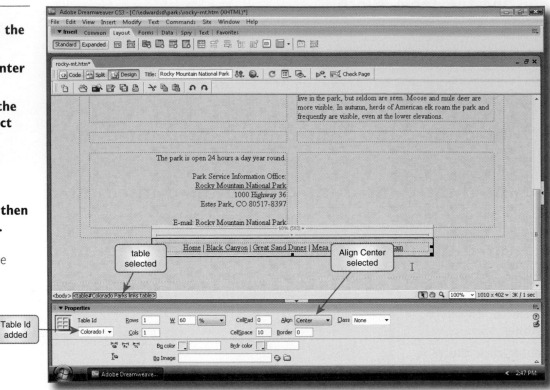

FIGURE 3-39

3

• **Click anywhere in the Document window to deselect the table.**

Next, you add absolute, e-mail, and relative links to the Rocky Mountain National Park page. The following steps show how to add the links. The relative links you added for the other three parks — Black Canyon, Great Sand Dunes, and Mesa Verde — are not active at this point. You will add pages for these three parks later in this chapter. As discussed previously, the Black Canyon and Great Sand Dunes parks are contained on one Web page. When you add the relative link for the Great Sand Dunes park, you also will add a link and a named anchor. When the Great Sand Dunes link is clicked, the portion of the Web page containing the Great Sand Dunes section is displayed. As discussed in Chapter 2, a **named anchor** is a link to a specific place within a document.

To Add Links to the Rocky Mountain National Park Page

1 Select the first instance of **Rocky Mountain National Park** located in the first table in row 3, column 1.

2 Type `http://www.nps.gov/romo/` in the Link box. Press ENTER to create an absolute link.

3 Select the second instance of **Rocky Mountain National Park**, located in the first table in row 3, column 1.

4 Click Insert on the menu bar and then click Email Link. When the Email Link dialog box is displayed, click the Email Link Text text box, and then type `romo@parks.gov` as the e-mail address. Click the OK button.

5 Select Home in the second table. Type `index.htm` in the Link box and press ENTER to create the relative link.

6 Select Black Canyon in the second table. Type `blca.htm` in the Link box and press ENTER to create the relative link.

7 Select Great Sand Dunes in the second table. Type `blca.htm#sand_dunes` in the Link box and press ENTER to create the relative link to the named anchor.

8 Select Mesa Verde in the second table. Type `meve.htm` in the Link box and press ENTER to create the relative link.

9 Select Rocky Mountain in the second table. Type `rocky-mt.htm` in the Link box and press ENTER to create the relative link.

10 Click the Save button on the Standard toolbar.

11 Press the F12 key to view the Web page. Scroll down to view the links, as shown in Figure 3-40.

12 Click the Home link to display the index.htm page and test each of the links. Then click the Browser Back button.

13 Close the browser and return to the Dreamweaver window.

The links are added to the Web page (Figure 3-40). The links for Black Canyon, Great Sand Dunes, and Mesa Verde National Parks are not active at this point. You will add these pages later in this chapter.

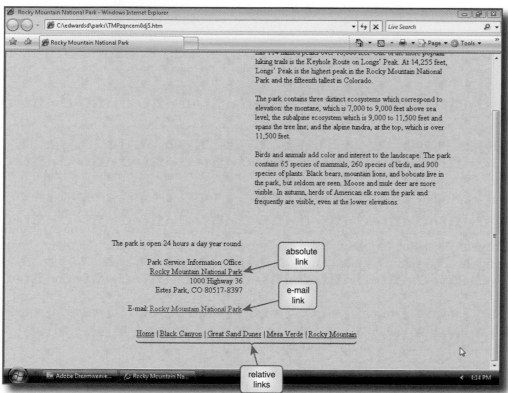

FIGURE 3-40

Editing and Modifying Table Structure

Thus far, you have created two tables and made adjustments in Dreamweaver for the Rocky Mountain National Park Web page. For various reasons, as you create and develop Web sites, you will need to edit and modify a table, change the dimensions of a table, add rows and columns, or delete the table and start over. The following section describes how to accomplish editing, modifying, and deleting table elements within the structure.

DELETE A ROW OR COLUMN Select a row or column and then press the DELETE key. You also can delete a row or column by clicking a cell within the row or column, right-clicking to display the context menu, pointing to Table, and then clicking Delete Row or Delete Column on the Table submenu.

INSERT A ROW OR COLUMN To insert a row or column, click in a cell. Right-click to display the context menu, point to Table, and then click Insert Row or Insert Column on the Table submenu. To insert more than one row or column and to control the row or column insertion point, click in a cell, right-click to display the context menu, point to Table, and then click Insert Rows or Columns on the Table submenu to display the Insert Rows or Columns dialog box (Figure 3-41). Make your selections and then click the OK button. To add a row automatically, press the TAB key in the last cell of a table.

FIGURE 3-41

MERGE AND SPLIT CELLS By merging and splitting cells, you can set alignments that are more complex than straight rows and columns. To merge two or more cells, select the cells and then click Merge Cells in the Property inspector. The selected cells must be contiguous and in the shape of a line or a rectangle. You can merge any number of adjacent cells as long as the entire selection is a line or a rectangle. To split a cell, click the cell and then click Split Cells in the Property inspector to display the Split Cell dialog box (Figure 3-42 on the next page). In the Split Cell dialog box, specify how to split the cell and then click the OK button. You can split a cell into any number of rows or columns, regardless of whether it was merged previously. When you split a cell into two rows, the other cells in the same row as the split cell are not split. The same is true if a cell is split into two or more columns — the other cells in the same column are not split. To select a cell quickly, click in the cell and then click the <td> tag on the tag selector.

FIGURE 3-42

RESIZE A TABLE, COLUMNS, AND ROWS You can resize an entire table or resize individual rows and columns. To resize the table, select the table and change the W (width) in the Property inspector. A second method is to select the table and then drag one of the table selection handles. When you resize an entire table, all of the cells in the table change size proportionately. If you have assigned explicit widths or heights to a cell or cells within the table, resizing the table changes the visual size of the cells in the Document window but does not change the specified widths and heights of the cells. To resize a column or row, select the column or row and change the properties in the Property inspector. A second method to resize a column is to select the column and then drag the right border of the column. To resize a row, select the row and then drag the lower border of the row.

DELETE A TABLE You easily can delete a table. Select the table tag in the tag selector and then press the DELETE key. All table content is deleted along with the table.

Merging Cells and Adding Images

The concept of merging cells probably is familiar to you if you have worked with spreadsheets or word processing tables. In HTML, however, merging cells is a complicated process. Dreamweaver makes this easy by hiding some complex HTML table restructuring code behind an easy-to-use interface in the Property inspector. Dreamweaver also makes it easy to add images to a table. When you add and then select an image in a table cell, the Property inspector displays the same properties as were displayed when you added and selected an image in the Document window in Chapter 2. When the image in the cell is not selected, the Property inspector displays the same properties as it does for any cell. These properties were described earlier in this chapter.

You will merge two cells (rows 1 and 2, column 1) and add three images to the Rocky Mountain National Park page. The first and second images go into the merged cells, and the third image goes in row 3, column 2. The steps on the next page show how to merge two cells.

To Merge Two Cells

1

• **If necessary, scroll up and then click row 1, column 1 in the first table.**

• **Drag to select the cells in rows 1 and 2 in column 1.**

The two cells are selected (Figure 3-43).

FIGURE 3-43

2

• **Click the Merge Cells button.**

The two cells are merged (Figure 3-44).

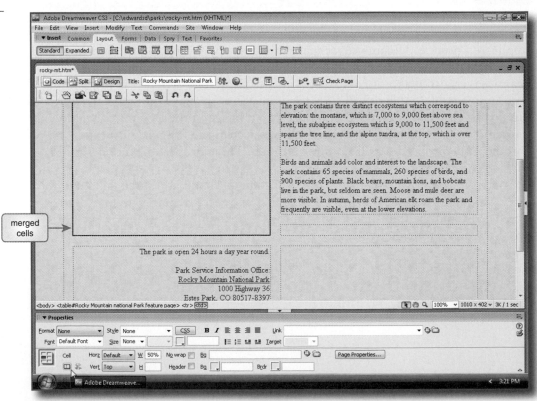

FIGURE 3-44

Recall from Chapter 2 that when you inserted an image, the default Image Tag Accessibility Attributes dialog box was displayed. In this box, you can add Alternate text or create a link to a text file with a long description. For images in this chapter and the other chapters in this book, instructions are to add alternate text. The Property inspector for images contains an Alternate text option. Therefore, you will disable the Image Tag Accessibility Attributes dialog box and add the Alternate text through the Property inspector.

To Disable the Image Tag Accessibility Attributes Dialog Box

1 **Click Edit on the menu bar and then click Preferences.**

2 **Click Accessibility in the Category list.**

3 **Click the check boxes to deselect Form objects, Frames, Media, and Images and then click the OK button.**

Next, you add three images to the table. You then align the three images and modify the size of one of the images. The following steps illustrate how to display the images in the Assets panel and then add, align, and modify images in a table displayed in Standard and Expanded modes.

To Add Images to a Standard Mode Table

1

• **Click the panel groups expander arrow and then click the Assets tab in the panel groups.**

• **If necessary, click the Images button and the Site option button.**

• **Scroll to the top of the table and then click the cell in row 1, column 1.**

• **Press the ENTER key.**

• **Drag the keyhole_longs_peak.gif image from the Assets panel to the insertion point in the merged cell. If necessary, click the Refresh Site List button to view the images.**

FIGURE 3-45

The keyhole_longs_peak.gif image is inserted in the cell and selected (Figure 3-45). The Property inspector for images is displayed.

2

• **Click the Expanded Tables mode button and then click to the right of the keyhole_longs_peak.gif image. If a Getting Started in Expanded Tables Mode dialog box is displayed, read the information and click the OK button. The dialog box may not appear if the Don't show me this message again check box was checked previously.**

• **Press the ENTER key.**

The table expands and the insertion point is displayed below the keyhole_longs_peak.gif image (Figure 3-46). The alberta_falls.gif image will be inserted at the location of the insertion point.

FIGURE 3-46

3

• **Drag the alberta_falls.gif image to the insertion point and then, if necessary, scroll down to view the image.**

The alberta_falls.gif image is displayed below the keyhole_longs_peak.gif image and is selected (Figure 3-47).

FIGURE 3-47

4

• **Scroll up and click the keyhole_longs_ peak.gif image to select it.**

The keyhole_longs_ peak.gif image is selected (Figure 3-48). The Property inspector displays image properties.

FIGURE 3-48

5

• **Click the Image text box in the Property inspector and type** Keyhole_Longs_Peak **as the image ID.**

• **Click the Alt box, type** Keyhole Longs Peak **as the Alt text, and then press the ENTER key.**

The specified properties are applied to the keyhole_longs_peak.gif image (Figure 3-49).

FIGURE 3-49

6

• **Scroll down and then click the alberta_falls.gif image to select it.**

• **Click the Image text box in the Property inspector and then type** Alberta_Falls **as the image ID.**

• **Press the TAB key and then type** 300 **in the W box.**

• **Press the TAB key to move to the H box and then type** 220 **as the new value.**

• **Click the Alt box, type** Alberta Falls **as the Alt text, and then press the ENTER key.**

• **Click the Align Center button.**

FIGURE 3-50

The specified properties are applied to the alberta_falls.gif image and the image is resized and centered in the cell (Figure 3-50).

7

• **Scroll down and to the right. Click row 3, column 2.**

The insertion point is displayed in the cell (Figure 3-51). The elk.gif image will be inserted at the location of the insertion point.

FIGURE 3-51

8

• **Drag the elk.gif image from the Assets panel to the insertion point in row 3, column 2.**

• **Verify that the elk.gif image is selected, click the Image text box, and type** Elk. **Click the Alt box, type** Rocky Mountain Elk **as the Alt text, and then press the ENTER key.**

• **Click the Align box arrow and select Top.**

• **Click the Align Center button.**

The elk.gif image is centered in the cell and is selected (Figure 3-52). The Alt text is entered and Top is selected in the Align box.

FIGURE 3-52

9

• **Scroll up. Click the cell in row 2, column 2 and then drag to select this cell and the cell in row 3, column 2.**

The two cells are selected (Figure 3-53).

FIGURE 3-53

10

 Click the Merge Cells button.

The two cells are merged and the image moves up (Figure 3-54).

FIGURE 3-54

11

• **Scroll up and select all of the text in row 1, column 2.**

• **Click the Size arrow and select 18.**

• **Click the Vert box arrow and select Middle.**

The size is applied to the text and style2 is created. The text is centered vertically in the cell (Figure 3-55).

FIGURE 3-55

• **Scroll down and select the text in row 2, column 1.**

• **Click the Style arrow and select style2.**

• **Click anywhere in the document to deselect the text.**

Style2 is applied to the text (Figure 3-56).

FIGURE 3-56

• **Click the Standard button.**

• **Click the Save button.**

• **Press the F12 key to view the page in your browser.**

• **The Rocky Mountain National Park page is displayed in the browser (Figure 3-57).**

• **Close the browser window.**

Dreamweaver is displayed.

FIGURE 3-57

Creating the Black Canyon/Great Sand Dunes National Park Web Page

To create the Black Canyon/Great Sand Dunes Web page, you open a new Document window. You start by applying the background image. This is the same background image you used for the Colorado Parks Web site in Chapters 1 and 2. The following steps illustrate how to open a new Document window and apply a background image.

To Open a New Document Window and Add a Background Image to the Black Canyon/Great Sand Dunes Web Page

1 Click File on the menu bar and then click New. If necessary, click Blank Page and then click HTML in the Page Type List.

2 Click the Create button.

3 Click the Save button on the Standard toolbar and then type blca as the file name. Save the Web page in the parks folder.

4 Click Modify on the menu bar and then click Page Properties.

5 Click the Browse button to the right of the Background image box.

6 If necessary, navigate to the parks\images folder.

7 Click parksbg.gif and then click the OK button in the Select Image Source dialog box.

8 Click the OK button in the Page Properties dialog box. If a warning dialog box displays, click OK. Collapse the Panel groups.

The background is added. The path and file name (\edwardsd\parks\blca.htm) appear on the Dreamweaver title bar (Figure 3-58). Your name will be displayed instead of edwardsd.

FIGURE 3-58

Next, you insert and center a six-row, two-column table. You create the Black Canyon section by adding text and two images. Next, you create the Great Sand Dunes section by adding text and two images and adding a named anchor. You modify image placement and create a text style. You also add absolute links and e-mail addresses for the two parks. Then you copy and paste the Links table from the Rocky Mountain Park page to the Black Canyon/Great Sand Dunes page.

The next step is to insert and center a table and to add a title to the table, as shown in the following steps.

To Insert and Center a Table

1 Click the Table button on the Layout Insert bar.

2 In the Table dialog box, change the settings as follows: Rows 6, Columns 2, Table width 90 Percent, Border thickness 4, Cell padding 10, and Cell spacing 2.

3 Click the Summary text box and then type `Black Canyon/Great Sand Dunes National Parks feature page` **as the Summary text.**

4 Click the OK button to insert the table.

5 Title the page Black Canyon/Great Sand Dunes.

6 Click the Table ID text box in the Property inspector and then type `Black Canyon/Great Sand Dunes National Parks feature page` **as the table ID.**

7 Click the Align box arrow and then click Center.

8 Click the Save button on the Standard toolbar.

The centered table is added to the Web page (Figure 3-59). The Web page is saved in the parks folder.

FIGURE 3-59

An understanding of HTML and how it relates to a table and to parts of a table provides you with the ability to use code to select a table and table components and to modify a table. Merging and varying the span of columns (as you did in the Rocky Mountain National Park page) and merging and varying the span of rows is helpful for grouping information, adding emphasis, or deleting empty cells. When you merge two cells in a row, you are spanning a column. Continuing with the <table> example on page DW 224 and spanning the two cells in row 1, the HTML tags would be <td colspan="2">First cellSecond cell</td>. When you merge two cells in a column, you are spanning a row. The attribute ROWSPAN would replace COLSPAN in the above example. Understanding COLSPAN and ROWSPAN will help you determine when and if two columns or two rows have been merged.

For the Rocky Mountain National Park page, you entered a heading outside the table and links to the other pages in a second table. For the Black Canyon/Great Sand Dunes page, you merge the cells in row 1 and then merge the cells in row 4. You enter a heading in row 1 and row 4. The following steps illustrate how to merge the cells in rows 1 and 4.

To Merge Cells in Row 1 and Row 4

1 Click row 1, column 1 and then drag to select all of row 1.

2 Click the Merge Cells button in the Property inspector.

3 Click row 4, column 1 and then drag to select all of row 4.

4 Click the Merge Cells button in the Property inspector.

The cells in row 1 are merged into one column, and the cells in row 4 also are merged into one column (Figure 3-60).

FIGURE 3-60

Next, you add and center a heading in row 1 of the table. The steps on the next page show how to add and center the heading in row 1.

To Add a Heading to Row 1

1

• **Click row 1 and then click the Align Center button in the Property inspector.**

The insertion point is aligned in the middle of the row (Figure 3-61).

FIGURE 3-61

2

• **Type** Black Canyon of the Gunnison National Park **and then use the Format pop-up menu to apply Heading 1.**

• **Select the heading.**

• **Click the Color Hexadecimal box and type** #336633.

• **Click to the right of the heading.**

The text is centered in row 1, and Heading 1 and color are applied to the text. In the Style box, style1 is created (Figure 3-62).

FIGURE 3-62

3

• **Click row 4 and then click the Align Center button in the Property inspector.**

• **Type** Great Sand Dunes National Park Preserve.

• **Apply Heading 1 and style1 to the text in row 4.**

The text is centered in row 4, and Heading 1 and color are applied to the text. (Figure 3-63).

FIGURE 3-63

Splitting and Merging Cells

Tables in a traditional sense generally are thought of as having an internal **symmetry**; that is, cells of the same size form neatly arranged columns and rows. On a Web page, however, by varying the size of a cell, you can use tables to create an asymmetrical arrangement. This design option allows for more visual variation on a Web page. In a three-column table, for example, you could specify the width of the first column as 20 percent and that of the second and third columns as 40 percent each. Depending on the number of columns, hundreds of percentage variations can be applied. In the Black Canyon/Great Sand Dunes page, you adjust the width for columns 1 and 2 and then change the vertical alignment to Top within both columns. The steps on the next page show how to adjust the width and change the vertical spacing.

> *More About*
>
> ### Column Width
>
> In addition to using the Property inspector to change the width or height of a column, you also can change cell widths and heights directly in the HTML code.

To Adjust the Column Width

1

• **Click row 2, column 1.**

The insertion point is located in row 2, column 1 (Figure 3-64).

FIGURE 3-64

2

• **Click the W box in the Property inspector.**

• **Type** 60% **and then press the ENTER key.**

• **Click row 2, column 2.**

• **Click the W box in the Property inspector.**

• **Type** 40% **and then press the ENTER key.**

Column 1 is increased in size to reflect the new percentage. and column 2 is decreased in size to reflect the new percentage (Figure 3-65).

FIGURE 3-65

3

• **Select row 2, columns 1 and 2.**

• **Click the Vert box arrow in the Property inspector and then select Top from the Vert pop-up menu.**

Top is selected in the Vert box (Figure 3-66). No noticeable differences are displayed in the table. Any image or text in these cells, however, will align to the top.

FIGURE 3-66

Now you add text to the table. Table 3-4 contains the text for the Black Canyon/Great Sand Dunes Web page. After you type the text, you format it using style2. When applying a style to text, it is not necessary to select the paragraph. Just click anywhere within the paragraph and then apply the style.

Table 3-4	Black Canyon/Great Sand Dunes Web Page Text
SECTION	**TEXT FOR BLACK CANYON/GREAT SAND DUNES WEB PAGE**
Part 1	The Black Canyon of the Gunnison National Park contains 2,000 foot narrow canyon walls, which drop almost vertically to the Gunnison River. Two camp-grounds are located in the park – one on the south rim and one on the north rim. The visitor's center is located on South Rim Drive and provides a video theater with two orientation programs.
Part 2	Located in the southwest section of Colorado, some of the park's more popu-lar recreational activities are camping, backpacking, bird and wildlife viewing, fishing, and rafting. In the winter months, visitors enjoy cross-country skiing and snowshoeing. The park is open year round, but access to the south rim is limited in the winter.
Part 3	Park Service Information Office:\ Black Canyon of the Gunnison National Park\ Park Headquarters\ 102 Elk Creek\ Gunnison, CO 81230-8397\<ENTER> E-mail: Black Canyon of the Gunnison

(continued)

SECTION	TEXT FOR BLACK CANYON/GREAT SAND DUNES WEB PAGE
Part 4	One of the nation's newest national parks, Great Sand Dunes was upgraded from a national monument and preserve in the year 2000. Located at the foot of the Sangre de Cristo mountain range, the dunes appear to stretch to infinity. The dunes cover approximately 39 square miles and are the tallest in North America – over 750 feet. The park is open all year, 24 hours a day.\<ENTER\> Park Service Information Office:\<br\> Great Sand Dunes National Park\<br\> Park Headquarters\<br\> 11999 Highway 150\<br\> Mosca, CO 81146\<ENTER\> E-mail: Great Sand Dunes

Table 3-4 Black Canyon/Great Sand Dunes Web Page Text (continued)

More About

Inserting Images into a Table

In Adobe Dreamweaver CS3, you can work in Design view or Code view to insert images in a document.

To Add and Format Text for the Black Canyon/Great Sand Dunes Web Page

1

- **Click row 2, column 2.**

- **Type the text of Part 1 as shown in Table 3-4 on the previous page.**

The text is entered as shown in Figure 3-67.

FIGURE 3-67

2

• **Click row 3, column 1.**

• **Type the text of Part 2 as shown in Table 3-4 on page DW 257.**

The text is entered as shown in Figure 3-68.

FIGURE 3-68

3

• **Click row 3, column 2.**

• **Type the text of Part 3 as shown in Table 3-4.**

• **Press the ENTER key and insert line breaks as indicated in Table 3-4.**

The text is entered as shown in Figure 3-69.

FIGURE 3-69

4

• **Click row 5, column 2.**

• **Type the text of Part 4 as shown in Table 3-4 on page DW 258.**

• **Press the ENTER key and insert line breaks as indicated in Table 3-4.**

The text is entered as shown in Figure 3-70.

FIGURE 3-70

5

• **Select the text in row 2, column 2.**

• **Click the Size box arrow and select 18 to create style2.**

• **Click anywhere in the row to deselect the text.**

Style2 is applied to the text (Figure 3-71).

FIGURE 3-71

6

• **Apply style2 to the rest of the text in the table.**

• **Select the text in row 3, column 2 and right align.**

Style2 is applied to the rest of the text and the text in row 3, column 2 is aligned to the right (Figure 3-72).

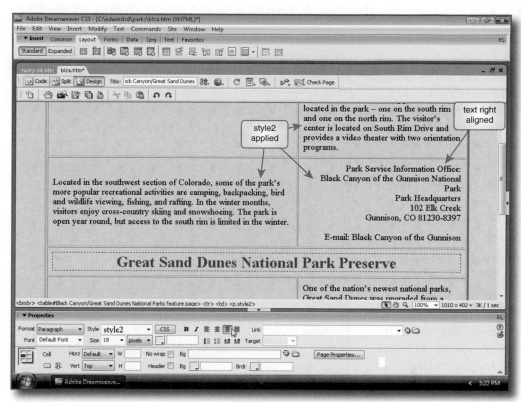

FIGURE 3-72

The next step is to add the images to the Web page. You add and align four images and resize two of the images.

Adobe
Dreamweaver CS3

To Add Images to the Black Canyon/Great Sand Dunes Web Page

1

• Click the panel groups expander arrow to display the panel groups. If necessary, click the Assets tab.

• Click row 2, column 1.

• Drag the black_canyon01.jpg image to the insertion point in row 2, column 1.

• Click the Image text box and then type canyon01 as the image ID.

• Change the width in the W box to 425 and the height in the H box to 215.

• Click the Alt box and then type Black Canyon view as the Alt text. Press the ENTER key.

• Click the Align Center button.

FIGURE 3-73

The black_canyon01.jpg image is displayed in row 2, column 1, and the selected image is resized and centered (Figure 3-73).

2

• **If necessary, scroll down and click to the left of Park Service Information Office: in row 3, column 2.**

• **Drag the black_canyon02 image to the insertion point.**

• **Click the Image text box and then type** canyon02 **as the image ID.**

• **Change the W to 200.**

• **Click the Align Right button.**

• **Click the Align box arrow and select Left.**

• **Click the Alt text box and then type** Black Canyon view 2 **as the Alt text.**

• **Press the ENTER key.**

FIGURE 3-74

The black_canyon02 image is displayed in row 3, column 2. The selected image is resized and aligned to the left (Figure 3-74).

3

- **Click row 5, column 1.**

- **Drag the sand_dunes_ 01 image to the insertion point.**

- **Click the image text box and then type** sand_dunes01 **as the image ID.**

- **Press the TAB key and type** 435 **as the new value in the W box.**

- **Press the TAB key and type** 300 **as the new value in the H box.**

- **Click the Align Center button.**

- **Type** Sand Dunes view **as the Alt text and then press the ENTER key.**

The image is inserted into the cell, resized, and centered (Figure 3-75).

FIGURE 3-75

4 ───────────

- **Click to the left of the first word in the first paragraph in row 5, column 2 (to the left of the word "One").**

- **Drag the sand_ dunes_02 image to the insertion point.**

- **Click the Files panel expander arrow to collapse the panel groups.**

- **Click the Image text box and then type** sand_dunes02 **as the image ID.**

- **Press the TAB key and type** 170 **as the new value in the W box.**

- **Press the TAB key and type** 105 **as the new value in the H box.**

- **Click the V Space box and type** 12.

- **Click the Align box arrow and then click Right.**

- **Type** Elk at Sand Dune **as the Alt text and then press the ENTER key.**

- **Click the Border box, type** 1, **and then press the ENTER key.**

- **Click the Save button.**

FIGURE 3-76

The image is inserted into the cell, resized, and aligned right. A one-pixel border frames the image (Figure 3-76).

Adding a Table Border and a Table Border Color

The purpose of most tables in a Web page is to provide a structure for the positioning of text and images. When a table is created within Dreamweaver, therefore, the default border is 0 (zero), or no visible border. The **Border** command specifies the width, in pixels, of the line that frames the table and its various parts. Adding a border to a table transforms the table into a graphical element itself. Depending on the content, a border can become a visual cue for the reader by separating content. For the Black Canyon/Great Sand Dunes page, a border is applied to the full table. You cannot apply a border to an individual cell unless the table consists of only one cell.

When you created the table for the Black Canyon/Great Sand Dunes Web page, you specified a border size of 4. By default, borders are gray, but the border color can be changed. Using the color picker, you can apply a color of your choice. You can apply a border color to a single cell or to a range of cells.

Background images and background color work the same for a table as they do for a Web page. The image or color, however, is contained within the table and does not affect the rest of the page. Background color and images can be applied to a single cell or to a range of cells. The following steps illustrate how to add color to the table border and a background color to the merged cells. The border color is the same color you applied to the titles of the two parks.

To Add Border Color and Cell Background Color

1

• **Scroll to the top of the page.**

• **Click <table#Black Canyon/Great Sand Dunes National Parks feature page> in the tag selector and then click the Border color hexadecimal color box.**

• **Type** #336633 **and then press the ENTER key.**

The border color is applied to the table (Figure 3-77).

FIGURE 3-77

2

• If necessary, scroll up. Click anywhere in row 1.

• Click the Bg hexadecimal color box, type #669966, and then press the ENTER key.

• Scroll down and click anywhere in row 4.

• Click the Bg hexadecimal color box, type #669966, and then press the ENTER key.

The background color is applied to rows 1 and 4 (Figure 3-78).

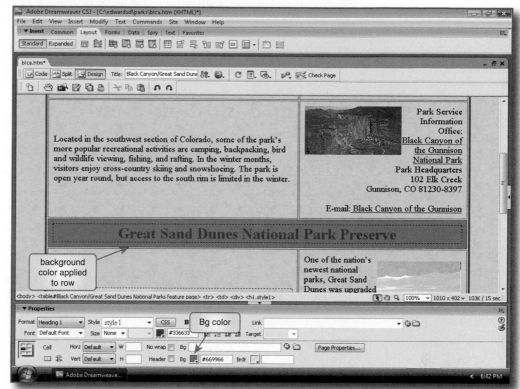

FIGURE 3-78

Your last tasks for the Black Canyon/Great Sand Dunes page are to add links, check spelling, copy the relative links you created in the rocky-mt page, and then save the page. The following steps illustrate how to spell check; add the absolute, relative, and e-mail links to the Black Canyon/Great Sand Dunes page; and then save the Web page.

To Add a Named Anchor and Links to and Spell Check the Black Canyon/Great Sand Dunes Page

1 Scroll down and select the first instance of Black Canyon of the Gunnison National Park in the address in row 3, column 2. Type http://www.nps.gov/blca/ in the Link box and then press the ENTER key.

2 Select the second instance of Black Canyon of the Gunnison. Click Insert on the menu bar and then click Email Link. Type blca@parks.gov in the E-mail text box. Click the OK button in the Email Link dialog box.

3 Scroll down and select the first instance of Great Sand Dunes in the address in row 5, column 2. Type http://www.nps.gov/grsa/ in the Link box and then press the ENTER key.

4 Select Great Sand Dunes. Click Insert on the menu bar and then click Email Link. Type grsa@parks.gov in the Email text box. Click the OK button in the Email Link dialog box.

5 Click the rocky-mt.htm tab.

6 Scroll down and then select the links in the Links table.

7 Press CTRL+C to copy the links.

8 Click the blca.htm tab, select row 6, merge the cells, and then click the merged cell.

9 Press CTRL+V to paste the links.

10 If necessary, select the links and then click the Align Center button. Click anywhere in the document to deselect the links.

11 Click Text on the menu bar and then click the Check Spelling command. Check the spelling and make any necessary corrections.

12 Click to the right of the Great Sand Dunes National Park Preserve heading. Click Insert on the menu bar and then click Named Anchor.

13 Type sand_dunes in the Named Anchor dialog box and then click the OK button.

14 Click the Save button on the Document toolbar.

15 Press the F12 key to view the Web page in your browser, as shown in Figure 3-79. If necessary, save any changes. Close the browser.

In the browser, the Black Canyon/Great Sand Dunes page is displayed (Figure 3-79).

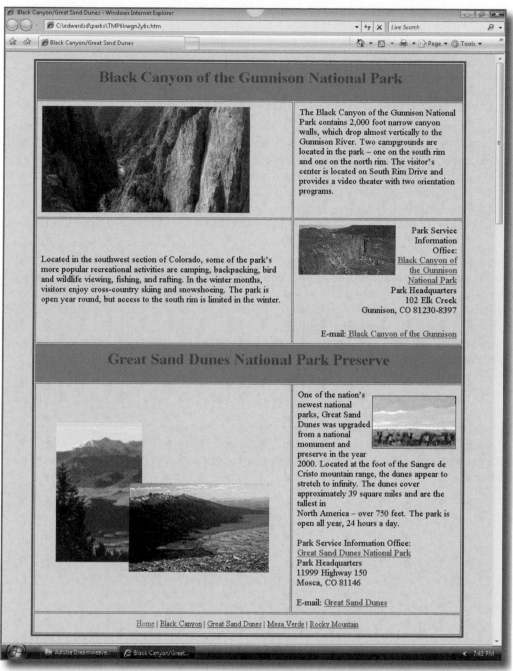

FIGURE 3-79

Layout Mode

Tables created in Standard mode are useful for creating Web pages that are simple in format or contain tabular data. A second option for creating tables in Dreamweaver is the Layout mode. If you have used a desktop publishing program such as Microsoft Publisher, you will find that Dreamweaver's layout mode operates under a similar process. You can draw and place boxes anywhere on the page.

Layout mode provides more flexibility than Standard mode. Comparable to a desktop publishing program, you draw your own tables and cells in Layout mode. When using **Layout mode**, you are creating the framework for the entire table. The layout can be as simple or as complex as you want.

Layout mode is a tool unique to Dreamweaver. Terms such as Layout mode and layout cell do not exist in HTML. When you draw a **layout table**, Dreamweaver creates an HTML table. When you draw a **layout cell**, Dreamweaver creates a tag (<td>) in the table. The <td> tag is a container for the content rendered inside one cell of a table element. When a cell is drawn in a layout table, it stays within the row-and-column grid as it does in Standard mode. Cells cannot overlap, but they can span rows and columns. When you draw cells of different widths and different heights, Dreamweaver creates additional cells in the HTML table to fill in the empty spots.

You can use Layout mode to modify the structure of an existing page created in Standard mode. Layout mode, however, provides the greatest advantage when you are designing the page from the start. As you draw the table and/or cells in Layout mode, Dreamweaver creates the code. If you draw a layout cell first, a layout table is inserted automatically to serve as a container for the layout cell. A layout cell cannot exist outside of a layout table. You can create your page using one layout table with several layout cells contained within the table or you can have multiple layout tables. For uncomplicated pages, use one layout table. For a more complicated layout, use multiple tables. Using multiple layout tables isolates parts of your layout so one section does not affect another. For example, the cell size within a table can affect the other cells in the same row and column. Multiple tables eliminate this problem, especially for pages with numerous elements.

When you draw a table in Layout mode, Dreamweaver outlines the table in green and cells in blue. A tab labeled Layout Table displays at the top of each table. Clicking the tab selects the table. When you complete your page design for the Mesa Verde National Park, it will look similar to the page shown in Figure 3-80. However, because this a freeform type of activity, most likely your page will have some variations.

The steps beginning on the next page show how to add a new page, add a background image, and prepare the work area of the page. This page contains one layout table and 10 layout cells.

Q: Can I change the color of the table outline when in layout mode?

A: Yes — click Edit, select Preferences, and then select the Layout Mode category. Click the Table Outline Color box and then select a color of your choice.

Q: Does Dreamweaver support nested layout tables?

A: Yes — you can draw a layout table inside another layout table.

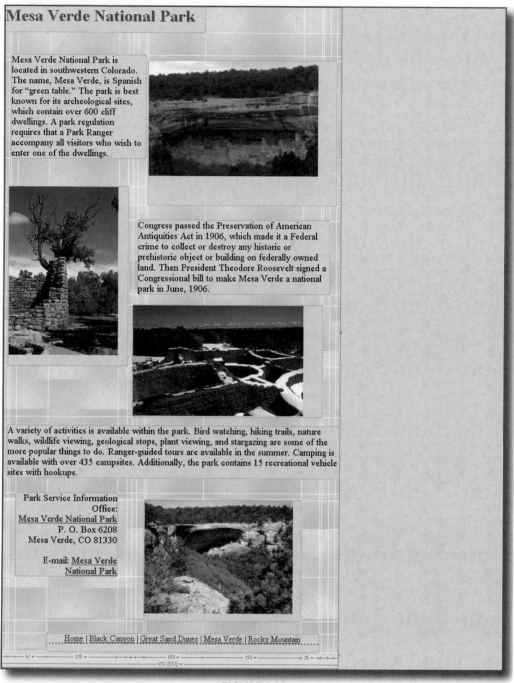

FIGURE 3-80

To Add a New Page and Add a Background Image to the Mesa Verde National Park Web Page

1. Click File on the menu bar and then click New. If necessary, click Blank Page. If necessary, click HTML in the Page Type list.

2. Click the Create button.

3. Click the Save button on the Standard toolbar and save the Web page in the parks folder. Type `meve` as the file name.

More About

The Grid Feature

Dreamweaver's grid feature is a visual guide that allows for precise positioning. Options include changing the grid square size and specifying that table and cell edges snap to the grid edges. To turn on the grid, click View on the menu bar, point to Grid, and then click Show Grid on the Grid submenu.

4 Click Modify on the menu bar and then click Page Properties.

5 Click the Browse button to the right of the Background image box.

6 If necessary, navigate to the parks\images folder.

7 Click parksbg.gif and then click the OK button in the Select Image Source dialog box.

8 Click the OK button in the Page Properties dialog box. If an Adobe alert dialog box appears, click OK.

9 Type Mesa Verde National Park as the title.

10 If necessary, click the expander button in the panel groups to hide the panels.

11 Click the Save button.

FIGURE 3-81

Using Visual Guides

Dreamweaver provides three types of visual guides — rulers, tracing image, and grid — to help you design documents and to project how the page will appear in a browser.

RULERS Provide a visual cue for positioning and resizing layers or tables

TRACING IMAGE Are used as the page background to duplicate a design

GRID Provides precise positioning and resizing of layer

You can use the rulers to help approximate cell width and height and cell location within a table, or you can use the pixel measurements that display in the right corner of the status bar. For this chapter, you use the rulers as a visual guide. Then, if necessary, you can make final adjustments to the cells and table using the settings in the Property inspector. The following step illustrates how to display the rulers in the Document window.

To Display the Rulers

1

• **Click View on the menu bar, point to Rulers, and then click Show on the Rulers submenu.**

• **Click the Property inspector expander arrow.**

The rulers are displayed at the top and left margins of the Document window (Figure 3-82). The rulers' measurements are in pixels. The lower pane of the Property inspector is collapsed.

FIGURE 3-82

Creating a Layout Table for the Mesa Verde National Park Web Page

You begin creating the Mesa Verde National Park page by drawing a table. In the table, you create ten cells: one cell to hold the heading, four cells to hold text content, four cells to hold images, and one cell to contain links to the home page and the national park pages.

Your next task is to draw the layout table. This table has an approximate width of 650 pixels and an approximate height of 1100 pixels. The following steps on the next page illustrate how to create the layout table. Figure 3-80 on page DW 271 provides a visual guide for cell locations. Most likely, however, because this a freeform type of table, your cell locations will contain some variations.

To Create the Layout Table

1

• **Click View on the menu bar, point to Table Mode, and then click Layout Mode on the submenu.**

The Draw Layout Table and Draw Layout Cell buttons, located on the Layout tab, become accessible. Expanded mode is displayed above the Ruler. If the Draw Layout Table and Draw Layout Cell buttons are not accessible, press ALT+F6.

FIGURE 3-83

2

• **Click the Draw Layout Table button.**

• **Position the mouse pointer at the upper-left corner of the Document window.**

The mouse pointer changes to a crosshair or plus sign (+), which indicates that you can draw a table (Figure 3-84).

FIGURE 3-84

3

• **Use the rulers and pixel measurements in the right corner of the status bar as a guide and drag to draw a table with a width of approximately 650 pixels and a height of approximately 1100 pixels. Use the Rulers to help guide you with the width and height.**

• **If necessary, make any adjustments in the Property inspector Width and Height boxes.**

The table is added to the Document window and is outlined in green. The Property inspector changes to reflect the table in Layout mode (Figure 3-85). The Layout Table tab is displayed at the top of the table. If you are one or two pixels from the left margin, that is acceptable. You will center the table later.

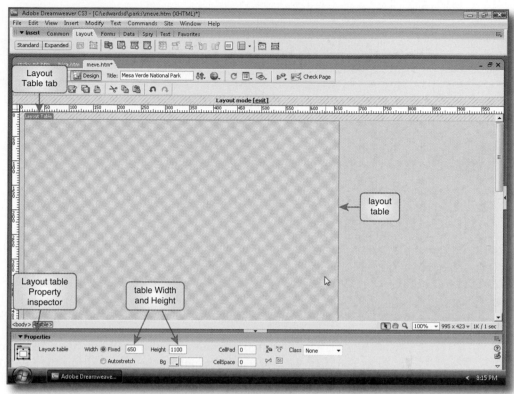

FIGURE 3-85

Layout Table and Layout Cell Properties

When a layout table is selected, the Property inspector displays properties related to the layout table. Some properties, such as width and height, background color, cell padding, and cell spacing, are the same as those for a table in Standard mode. The following describes the properties unique to the table in Layout mode (Figure 3-86 on the next page).

FIXED Sets the table to a fixed width.

AUTOSTRETCH The rightmost column of the table stretches to fill the browser window width. The column header area for an autostretch column displays a wavy line instead of a number. If the layout includes an autostretch column, the layout always fills the entire width of the browser window.

FIGURE 3-86

If the table is not the correct width or height or needs other modifications, adjustments can be made through the Width, Height, and other properties of the Property inspector.

For maximum flexibility, you should draw each cell as you are ready to add content to the cell. This method leaves blank space in the table, making it easier to move or resize cells. Occasionally, the value you enter will cause a cell to overlap another cell or cells. If this happens, a Dreamweaver alert dialog box is displayed. Read the information and then click OK. Dreamweaver will adjust the cell size to a valid value.

The first step is to add a cell that will contain the table heading. Once the cell is added, you type and format the heading within the layout cell. The heading is aligned to the left at the top of the table. The following steps illustrate how to add a layout cell and to enter and format a left-aligned heading.

To Add a Layout Cell and Heading

1

• **Click the Draw Layout Cell button on the Layout bar.**

The layout table area is selected (Figure 3-87).

FIGURE 3-87

Click the upper-left corner of the layout table and drag to draw a cell with an approximate width of 425 and an approximate height of 50.

• **Click the cell outline or the <td> in the tag selector to select the cell and make any necessary width and height adjustments in the Property inspector Width and Height boxes.**

A layout cell is created in the upper-left corner of the layout table. The cell is displayed in the table with a blue outline (Figure 3-88). The handles on the borders indicate that the cell is selected. This is the first cell.

FIGURE 3-88

Click the cell and type Mesa Verde National Park **as the heading.**

• **Apply Heading 1 to the text.**

• **If necessary, select the text. Click the hexadecimal color text box, type** #336633, **and then press the ENTER key.**

The heading is inserted into the cell, and Heading 1 and style1 are applied to the text (Figure 3-89). Text properties are displayed in the Property inspector.

FIGURE 3-89

Adding Content and Images to the Cells

In the previous steps, you added content to a layout cell. Adding text content and images to layout cells is similar to adding content and images to cells in a Standard mode table. The only place content can be inserted in a layout table is in a layout cell. When Dreamweaver creates a layout cell, it automatically assigns a vertical alignment of Top. You have the same options as you did in Standard mode to change the alignment to Middle, Bottom, or Baseline. When you insert an image into a layout cell, all the properties in the Property inspector that were available for images in Standard mode also are available in Layout mode. If you need to move a layout cell, click the outline of the cell to select it. Hold down the mouse button and drag the cell to a new location. To move the cell in small increments, select the cell and then press the UP, DOWN, LEFT, or RIGHT ARROW keys.

Next, you draw a layout cell directly below the heading cell. This cell will hold text. You enter the text into the layout cells just as you entered it in the cells in the Standard mode table. Table 3-5 contains the text for the Mesa Verde National Park Web page. If necessary, refer to Figure 3-80 on page DW 271 for a visual guide on the layout cell's placement.

Table 3-5 Mesa Verde National Park Web Page Text	
SECTION	TEXT FOR MESA VERDE NATIONAL PARK WEB PAGE
Part 1	Mesa Verde National Park is located in southwestern Colorado. The name, Mesa Verde, is Spanish for "green table." The park is best known for its archeological sites, which contain over 600 cliff dwellings. A park regulation requires that a Park Ranger accompany all visitors who wish to enter one of the dwellings.
Part 2	Congress passed the Preservation of American Antiquities Act in 1906, which made it a Federal crime to collect or destroy any historic or prehistoric object or building on federally owned land. Then President Theodore Roosevelt signed a Congressional bill to make Mesa Verde a national park in June, 1906.
Part 3	A variety of activities is available within the park. Bird watching, hiking trails, nature walks, wildlife viewing, geological stops, plant viewing, and stargazing are some of the more popular things to do. Ranger-guided tours are available in the summer. Camping is available with over 435 campsites. Additionally, the park contains 15 recreational vehicle sites with hookups.
Part 4	Park Service Information Office: Mesa Verde National Park P. O. Box 6208 Mesa Verde, CO 81330<ENTER> E-mail: Mesa Verde National Park<ENTER>

To Create and Add Text to a Layout Cell for the Mesa Verde National Park Web Page

1

• **Click the Draw Layout Cell button.**

• **Click about 50 pixels to the right of and below the first cell, and then draw a cell with an approximate width of 250 and an approximate height of 150, as shown in Figure 3-90.**

• **Click the cell to select it and make any necessary width and height adjustments in the Property inspector Width and Height boxes.**

• **If necessary, select and drag the cell or use the keyboard arrow keys for placement.**

The second cell is added to the table and is selected (Figure 3-90). This cell will contain text.

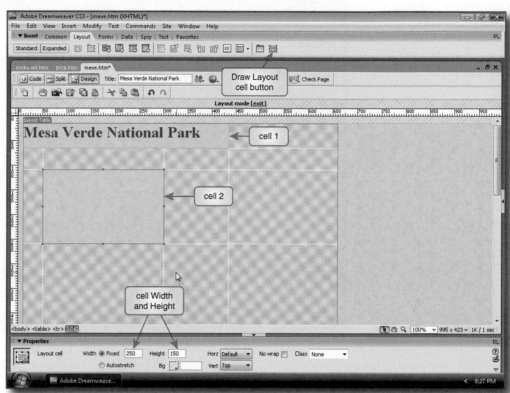

FIGURE 3-90

2

• **Click the cell and type the text of Part 1 as shown in Table 3-5 on page DW 278.**

The text is entered into the second cell (Figure 3-91).

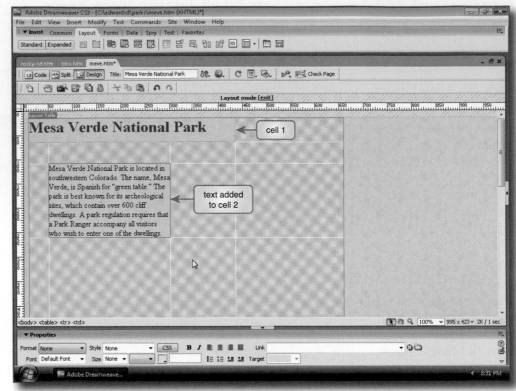

FIGURE 3-91

The third cell you draw will contain an image. You draw this cell to the right of the second cell. You add images to the layout cells just as you added images to the cells in the Standard mode table — by dragging the image from the Assets panel to the cell. The following steps show how to draw the third cell and insert an image into the cell.

To Add an Image to a Layout Cell

1

• **Click the Draw Layout Cell button and then draw a cell to the right of the second cell and about 65 pixels below the first cell, with an approximate width of 310 and an approximate height of 225, as shown in Figure 3-92.**

• **Click the cell outline to select it and make any necessary width and height adjustments in the Property inspector Width and Height boxes.**

• **If necessary, scroll to view the entire cell.**

• **Click the panel groups expander button and then, if necessary, click the Assets tab.**

FIGURE 3-92

The third cell is added to the table and is selected, and the Assets panel is displayed (Figure 3-92). This third cell will contain an image.

2

• If necessary, click the cell you have just drawn and then drag the cliff_palace.jpg file from the Assets panel to the insertion point.

• Click the Image text box in the Property inspector and then type cliff_palace as the image ID.

• Click the Alt text box and type Cliff palace as the alt text. Press the ENTER key.

The image is selected and displayed in the third cell, and the Alt text and image ID are displayed in the Property inspector (Figure 3-93).

FIGURE 3-93

3

• If necessary, scroll down and to the left, and then click the Draw Layout Cell button.

• Click approximately 50 pixels below the second cell and about 20 pixels to the right of the table border.

• Draw a cell with a width of approximately 220 and a height of approximately 320, as shown in Figure 3-94.

• Click the outline of the cell to select it and make any necessary width and height adjustments in the Property inspector Width and Height boxes.

The fourth cell is added to the table and is selected (Figure 3-94). The cell will contain an image.

FIGURE 3-94

4

• **If necessary, click the cell and then drag the cedar_tree_tower.gif image from the Assets panel to the cell.**

• **Click the Image text box and type** tree_tower **as the image ID. Press the ENTER key.**

• **Click the Alt text box in the Property inspector and type** Cedar tree tower **as the Alt text. Press the ENTER key.**

The image is selected and displayed in the fourth cell, and the Alt text and image ID are displayed in the Property inspector (Figure 3-95).

• **Click anywhere on the page to deselect the image.**

FIGURE 3-95

So far, you have added four cells to the layout table — one containing the heading, one containing text, and two containing images. Now you add five more cells. Two of the cells will contain images and three will contain text.

To Add Five Cells to the Mesa Verde National Park Web Page

• **Click the Draw Layout Cell button.**

• **Click approximately 20 pixels below the third cell and 25 pixels to the left, and draw a cell with a width of approximately 340 and a height of approximately 120.**

• **If necessary, click the outline of the cell to select it and make any necessary width and height adjustments in the Property inspector Width and Height boxes.**

• **Click the cell and type the text of Part 2 as shown in Table 3-5 on page DW 278.**

The fifth cell is added to the table. The cell contains text (Figure 3-96).

FIGURE 3-96

2

• **Scroll down. Click the Draw Layout Cell button.**

• **Click about 20 pixels below and about 10 pixels to the left of the fifth cell, and draw a cell with a width of approximately 330 and a height of approximately 215.**

• **If necessary, click the cell outline to select it and then make any necessary width and height adjustments in the Property inspector Width and Height boxes.**

• **Drag the winter_view.jpg image to the insertion point.**

• **Click the Image text box and type**

FIGURE 3-97

winter_view **as the image ID. Click the Alt text box in the Property inspector and then type** Mesa Verde winter view **as the Alt text.**

• **Click anywhere on the page to deselect the image.**

• **Click the Save button on the Standard toolbar.**

The sixth cell is added to the table and contains the winter_view.jpg image (Figure 3-97).

3

• **If necessary, scroll down. Click the Draw Layout Cell button.**

• **Click at the left margin about 20 pixels below the sixth cell.**

• **Drag to the right to create a cell with an approximate width of 650 and an approximate height of 85.**

• **Click the cell outline to select it and make any necessary width and height adjustments in the Property inspector Width and Height boxes.**

• **Click the cell and then type the text of Part 3 as shown in Table 3-5 on page DW 278.**

FIGURE 3-98

The seventh cell is inserted, and the text is displayed (Figure 3-98).

4

• **If necessary, scroll down. Click the Draw Layout Cell button and draw the eighth cell about 20 pixels below the seventh cell, with an approximate width of 210 and an approximate height of 145.**

• **Select the cell and make any necessary adjustments to the width and height in the Property inspector.**

• **Click cell 8 and type the text of Part 4 as shown in Table 3-5 into the cell.**

• **Align the text to the right.**

• **Click anywhere in the document to deselect the text.**

FIGURE 3-99

The eighth cell is inserted, and the text is displayed right-aligned in the cell (Figure 3-99).

5

• **Click the Draw Layout Cell button and draw the ninth cell to the right of the eighth cell and about 10 pixels lower than cell 8, with an approximate width of 270 and an approximate height of 180.**

• **Select the cell and make any necessary adjustments to the width and height in the Property inspector.**

• **If necessary, click cell 9 and then drag the step_house.jpg image to the ninth cell.**

• **Type** step_house **as the image ID and** Mesa Verde step house **as the Alt text. Press the ENTER key.**

FIGURE 3-100

The ninth cell is inserted, and the step_house.jpg image is displayed (Figure 3-100).

6

• Scroll down and then click the Draw Layout Cell button.

• Draw the tenth cell about 20 pixels below cell 9 and about 100 pixels from the left border, with an approximate width of 525 and an approximate height of 35.

• Select the cell and make any necessary adjustments to the width and height in the Property inspector.

• Click the rocky-mt.htm tab, scroll down to the Links table. Select and copy the links text.

• Click the meve.htm tab.

• Click cell 10 and then paste the links text into the cell.

• Click the Align Center button.

• Select the cell, click the Horz box arrow, and then click Center.

• Click the Save button.

The text for the links is displayed centered in cell 10, and the page is saved (Figure 3-101).

FIGURE 3-101

Next, you format the text, adding the same style that you did for the previous two National Park pages.

To Create and Apply Style2 to Text

1

- **Scroll up and select the text in cell 2.**
- **Click the Size box arrow and select 18 to create style2.**
- **Select the text in cells 5, 7, and 8 one at a time and apply style2.**

The text is formatted with style2 (Figure 3-102).

FIGURE 3-102

Next, you add absolute and e-mail links to the Mesa Verde National Park page. The following step on the next page shows how to add the links.

To Add Absolute and E-Mail Links

1

• **Select the first instance of Mesa Verde National Park in cell 8. Type** http://www.nps.gov/meve/ **in the Link box and then press the** ENTER **key.**

• **Select the second instance of Mesa Verde National Park. Click Insert on the menu bar and then click Email Link. When the Email Link dialog box is displayed, type** mese@parks.gov **as the e-mail address. Click the OK button.**

The links are added, as shown in Figure 3-103.

FIGURE 3-103

Centering the Table in Standard Mode

Layout mode does not provide all the features that are provided for a table in Standard mode. For example, you cannot select a number of rows or select a number of columns when creating Web pages in Layout mode, and you cannot center a table when in Layout mode. To access these features requires that the table be displayed in Standard mode. Your next task is to center the table. The following steps illustrate how to display the Web page in Standard mode, center the table, and turn off the rulers.

To Center a Table Created in Layout Mode

1

• **Click the Standard mode button on the Layout Insert bar. Click any cell in the table and then click the <table> tag in the tag selector.**

The table is displayed in Standard mode and is selected (Figure 3-104).

FIGURE 3-104

2

• **Click the Table Id text box and type** mesa_verde **for the Table Id.**

• **Click the Align box arrow in the Property inspector and then click Center.**

• **Click the Save button on the Standard toolbar.**

The table is selected and centered in the Document window (Figure 3-105).

FIGURE 3-105

• Press the F12 key to view the page in your browser.

The Web page is displayed centered in the browser (Figure 3-106). If the table has excessive extra space at the end of the page, adjust the H number in the Property inspector.

4

• Close the browser.

• Click View on the menu bar, point to Rulers, and then click the Show command to deselect it.

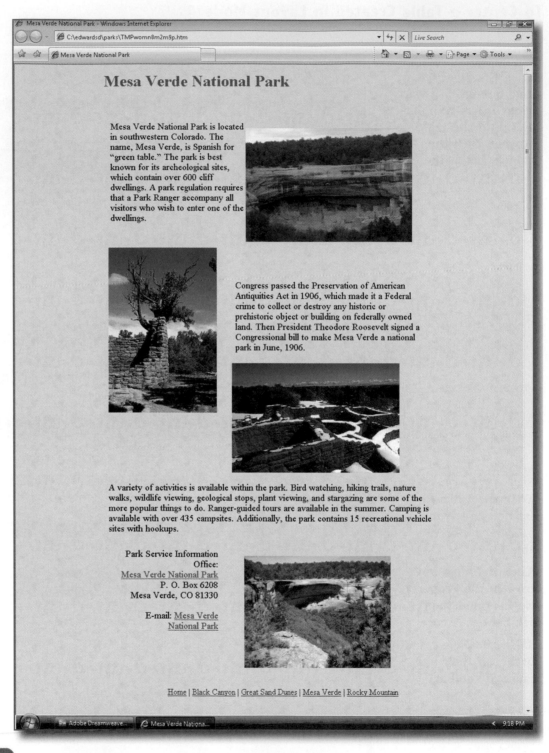

FIGURE 3-106

More About

Layout Tables

For more information about Dreamweaver CS3 layout tables, visit the Dreamweaver CS3 More About Web page (scsite.com/dwcs3/more.htm) and then click Dreamweaver CS3 Layout Tables.

The Web site has expanded to include pages with information on the four National Parks located in Colorado. To integrate the pages within the Web site, you add links from the natl_parks.htm page. The following steps show how to add the links.

To Add Links to the National Parks Web Page

1

• **Click File on the menu bar, select Open, and then open the natl_parks.htm page in the parks folder.**

• **If necessary, expand the panel groups and then select the Files tab.**

The natl_parks.htm page is displayed (Figure 3-107).

FIGURE 3-107

2

• **Select the Rocky Mountain National Park heading and then drag** rocky-mt.htm **from the Files panel to the Link box.**

• **Select the Black Canyon of the Gunnison National Park heading and then drag** blca.htm **from the Files panel to the Link box.**

• **Select the Mesa Verde National Park heading and then drag** meve.htm **from the Files panel to the Link box.**

• **Select the Great Sand Dunes National Park and Preserve heading and then type** blca.htm#sand_dunes **for the link to the Web page and to the named anchor. Press the ENTER key and then click anywhere in the document.**

FIGURE 3-108

The links are added to the four parks (Figure 3-108).

3

• **Press the F12 key to view the page in your browser. Test each link and then close the browser.**

• **Save the natl_parks.htm page and then close the page.**

• **Close the other three pages — rocky-mt.htm, blca.htm, and meve.htm. Save these pages if necessary.**

Head Content

HTML files consist of two main sections: the head section and the body section. The head section is one of the more important sections of a Web page. A standard HTML page contains a <head> tag and a <body> tag. Contained within the head section is site and page information. With the exception of the title, the information contained in the head is not displayed in the browser. Some of the information contained in the head is accessed by the browser, and other information is accessed by other programs such as search engines and server software.

Head Content Elements

Dreamweaver makes it easy to add content to the head section through the Insert menu. To access these commands, point to HTML, and then point to the submenu of the command you want to select.

META A <meta> tag contains information about the current document. This information is used by servers, browsers, and search engines. HTML documents can have as many <meta> tags as needed. Each item uses a different set of tags.

KEYWORDS Keywords are a list of words that someone would type into a search engine search field.

DESCRIPTION The description contains a sentence or two that can be used in a search engine's results page.

REFRESH The <refresh> tag is processed by the browser to reload the page or load a new page after a specified amount of time has elapsed.

BASE The base tag sets the base URL to provide an absolute link and/or a link target that the browser can use to resolve link conflicts.

LINK The link element defines a relationship between the current document and another file. This is not the same as a link in the Document window.

Keywords, descriptions, and refresh settings are special-use cases of the meta tag. The following steps show how to add keywords and a description to the index.htm page.

> ### More About
>
> ### Head Content
>
> Meta tags are information inserted into the head content area of Web pages. The meta description tag allows you to influence the description of a page in the search engines that support the tag. For more information about meta tags, visit the Dreamweaver CS3 More About Web page (scsite.com/dwcs3/more.htm) and then click Dreamweaver CS3 Meta Tags.

To Add Keywords and a Description

1

• **Open the index.htm file.**

• **Click Insert on the menu bar, point to HTML, point to Head Tags on the HTML submenu, and then point to Keywords on the Head Tags submenu (Figure 3-109).**

The Head Tags submenu is displayed (Figure 3-109).

FIGURE 3-109

2

• **Click the Keywords command.**

• **Type** parks, Colorado, national parks, state parks **in the Keywords text box.**

The Keywords dialog box is displayed. Keywords are added to the Keywords dialog box (Figure 3-110). When a search engine begins a search for any of the keywords, the Web site address will be displayed in the browser search results.

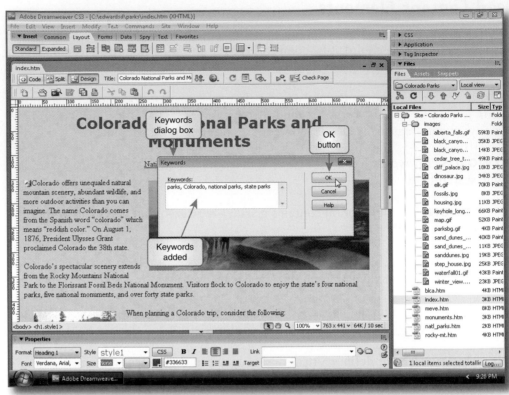

FIGURE 3-110

3

• **Click the OK button.**

• **Click Insert on the menu bar, point to HTML, point to Head Tags on the HTML submenu, and then click Description on the Head Tags submenu. Type** A Web site featuring Colorado state and national parks **in the Description text box.**

The Description dialog box is displayed as shown in Figure 3-111, with a description added.

FIGURE 3-111

4

- **Click the OK button and then click the Code button on the Document toolbar.**

The keywords and description that you entered are displayed in Code view (Figure 3-112).

5

- **Click the Design button on the Document toolbar and then click the Save button on the Standard toolbar.**

The Web page is saved.

FIGURE 3-112

Other Ways

1. Click Code button on Document toolbar, type keywords code in code window
2. Click Insert on the menu bar, click HTML, click the Head drop-down arrow, and then click Description or Keywords in Head menu

Publishing a Web Site

In Chapter 1 you defined a local site, and in Chapters 1, 2, and 3 you added Web pages to the local site. This local site resides on your computer's hard disk, a network drive, or possibly a USB drive or a Zip disk. You can view the organization of all files and folders in your site through the Files panel.

To prepare a Web site and make it available for others to view requires that you publish your site by putting it on a Web server for public access. A Web server is an Internet- or intranet-connected computer that delivers, or *serves up*, Web pages. You upload files to a folder on a server and download files to a folder in the Files panel on your computer. Generally, when Web site designers publish to a folder on a Web site, they do so by using a file transfer (FTP) program such as WS_FTP, Cute FTP, or Windows Web Folders. Dreamweaver, however, includes built-in support that enables you to connect and transfer your local site to a Web server without requiring an additional program. To publish to a Web server requires that you have access to a Web server.

Publishing and maintaining your site using Dreamweaver involves the following steps:

1. Using the Site Definition Wizard to enter the FTP information
2. Specifying the Web server to which you want to publish your Web site
3. Connecting to the Web server and uploading the files
4. Synchronizing the local and remote sites

Your school or company may have a server that you can use to upload your Web site. Free Web hosting services such as those provided by Angelfire, Tripod, or Geo-Cities are other options. These services, as well as many other hosting services, also offer low-cost Web hosting from approximately $3.95 to $9.95 a month. The FreeSite.com Web site contains a list of free and inexpensive hosting services, and FreeWebspace.net provides a PowerSearch form for free and low-cost hosting.

Table 3-6 contains a list of Web hosting services. Appendix C contains step-by-step instructions on publishing a Web site to a remote folder.

Table 3-6   Web Site Hosting Services

NAME	WEB SITE	COST
Angelfire®	angelfire.lycos.com	Free (ad-supported); starting at $4.95 monthly ad-free
Yahoo! GeoCities	geocities.yahoo.com	Free (ad-supported); starting at $4.95 monthly ad-free
Tripod®	tripod.lycos.com	Free (ad-supported); starting at $4.95 monthly ad-free
The FreeSite.com	thefreesite.com/Free_Web_Space	A list of free and inexpensive hosting sites
FreeWebspace.net	freewebspace.net	A searchable guide for free Web space

For an updated list of Web site hosting services, visit the Adobe Dreamweaver CS3 Web page (scsite.com/dwcs3) and then click Web Hosting. If required by your instructor, publish the Colorado Parks Web site to a remote server by following the steps in Appendix C.

With your work completed, you are ready to quit Dreamweaver.

Quitting Dreamweaver

After you add pages to your Web site and add the head content, Chapter 3 is complete. The following step illustrates how to close the Web site, quit Dreamweaver CS3, and return control to Windows.

More About

Publishing Your Colorado Parks Web Site

Appendix C contains step-by-step instructions on publishing the Colorado Parks Web site.

To Close the Web Site and Quit Dreamweaver

1 **Click the Close button on the right corner of the Dreamweaver title bar.**

The Dreamweaver window, the Document window, and the Colorado Parks Web site all close. If you have unsaved changes, Dreamweaver will prompt you to save the changes. Clicking the Yes button in the Dreamweaver dialog box saves the changes.

Chapter Summary

Chapter 3 introduced you to tables and to Web page design using tables. You created three Web pages, using the Standard mode for two pages and the Layout mode for the third page. You merged and split cells and learned how to add text and images to the tables. Next, you added a border color and cell background color. Finally, you added head content to one of the Web pages.

What You Should Know

Having completed this chapter, you should be able to perform the tasks below. The tasks are listed in the same order they were presented in the chapter. For a list of the buttons, menus, toolbars, and commands introduced in this chapter, see the Quick Reference Summary at the back of this book and refer to the Page Number column.

1. Copy Data Files to the Parks Web Site (DW 208)
2. Start Dreamweaver and Open the Colorado Parks Web Site (DW 209)
3. Open a New Document Window (DW 210)
4. Add a Background Image to the Rocky Mountain National Park Web Page (DW 211)
5. Insert and Format the Heading (DW 212)
6. Display the Insert Bar and Select the Layout Category (DW 214)
7. Insert a Table Using Standard Mode (DW 218)
8. Select and Center a Table (DW 227)
9. Change Vertical Alignment from Middle to Top (DW 229)
10. Specify Column Width (DW 230)
11. Add a Table ID to the Rocky Mountain National Park Feature Table (DW 231)
12. Add Rocky Mountain National Park Text (DW 232)
13. Add a Second Table to the Rocky Mountain National Park Web Page (DW 234)
14. Adjust the Table Width, Center the Text, and Add the Table ID (DW 237)
15. Add Links to the Rocky Mountain National Park Page (DW 238)
16. Merge Two Cells (DW 242)
17. Disable the Image Tag Accessibility Attributes Dialog Box (DW 243)
18. Add Images to a Standard Mode Table (DW 243)
19. Open a New Document Window and Add a Background Image to the Black Canyon/Great Sand Dunes Web Page (DW 250)
20. Insert and Center a Table (DW 251)
21. Merge Cells in Row 1 and Row 4 (DW 253)
22. Add a Heading to Row 1 (DW 254)
23. Adjust the Column Width (DW 256)
24. Add and Format Text for the Black Canyon/Great Sand Dunes Web Page (DW 258)
25. Add Images to the Black Canyon/Great Sand Dunes Web Page (DW 262)
26. Add Border Color and Cell Background Color (DW 266)
27. Add a Named Anchor and Links to and Spell Check the Black Canyon/Great Sand Dunes Page (DW 267)
28. Add a New Page and Add a Background Image to the Mesa Verde National Park Web Page (DW 271)
29. Display the Rulers (DW 273)
30. Create the Layout Table (DW 274)
31. Add a Layout Cell and Heading (DW 276)
32. Create and Add Text to a Layout Cell for the Mesa Verde National Park Web Page (DW 279)
33. Add an Image to a Layout Cell (DW 281)
34. To Create and Apply Style2 to Text (DW 289)
35. Add Five Cells to the Mesa Verde National Park Web Page (DW 284)
36. Add Absolute and E-Mail Links (DW 290)
37. Center a Table Created in Layout Mode (DW 291)
38. Add Links to the National Parks Web Page (DW 293)
39. Add Keywords and a Description (DW 295)
40. Close the Web Site and Quit Dreamweaver (DW 298)

Learn It Online

Instructions: To complete the Learn It Online exercises, start your browser, click the Address bar, and then enter the Web address scsite.com/dwcs3/learn. When the Dreamweaver CS3 Learn It Online page is displayed, follow the instructions in the exercises below. Each exercise has instructions for printing your results, either for your own records or for submission to your instructor.

1 Chapter Reinforcement TF, MC, and SA

Below Dreamweaver Chapter 3, click the Chapter Reinforcement link. Print the quiz by clicking Print on the File menu for each page. Answer each question.

2 Flash Cards

Below Dreamweaver Chapter 3, click the Flash Cards link and read the instructions. Type 20 (or a number specified by your instructor) in the Number of playing cards text box, type your name in the Enter your Name text box, and then click the Flip Card button. When the flash card is displayed, read the question and then click the ANSWER box arrow to select an answer. Flip through Flash Cards. If your score is 15 (75%) correct or greater, click Print on the File menu to print your results. If your score is less than 15 (75%) correct, then redo this exercise by clicking the Replay button.

3 Practice Test

Below Dreamweaver Chapter 3, click the Practice Test link. Answer each question, enter your first and last name at the bottom of the page, and then click the Grade Test button. When the graded practice test is displayed on your screen, click Print on the File menu to print a hard copy. Continue to take practice tests until you score 80% or better.

4 Who Wants To Be a Computer Genius?

Below Dreamweaver Chapter 3, click the Computer Genius link. Read the instructions, enter your first and last name at the bottom of the page, and then click the PLAY button. When your score is displayed, click the PRINT RESULTS link to print a hard copy.

5 Wheel of Terms

Below Dreamweaver Chapter 3, click the Wheel of Terms link. Read the instructions, and then enter your first and last name and your school name. Click the PLAY button. When your score is displayed, right-click the score and then click Print on the shortcut menu to print a hard copy.

6 Crossword Puzzle Challenge

Below Dreamweaver Chapter 3, click the Crossword Puzzle Challenge link. Read the instructions, and then enter your first and last name. Click the SUBMIT button. Work the crossword puzzle. When you are finished, click the Submit button. When the crossword puzzle is redisplayed, click the Print Puzzle button to print a hard copy.

7 Tips and Tricks

Below Dreamweaver Chapter 3, click the Tips and Tricks link. Click a topic that pertains to Chapter 3. Right-click the information and then click Print on the shortcut menu. Construct a brief example of what the information relates to in Dreamweaver to confirm that you understand how to use the tip or trick.

8 Newsgroups

Below Dreamweaver Chapter 3, click the Newsgroups link. Click a topic that pertains to Chapter 3. Print three comments.

9 Expanding Your Horizons

Below Dreamweaver Chapter 3, click the Expanding Your Horizons link. Click a topic that pertains to Chapter 3. Print the information. Construct a brief example of what the information relates to in Dreamweaver to confirm that you understand the contents of the article.

10 Search Sleuth

Below Dreamweaver Chapter 3, click the Search Sleuth link. To search for a term that pertains to this chapter, select a term below the Chapter 3 title and then use the Google search engine at google.com (or any major search engine) to display and print two Web pages that present information on the term.

Apply Your Knowledge

1 Modifying the Bryan's Lawn Service Web Site

Instructions: Start Dreamweaver. See the inside back cover of this book for instructions for downloading the Data Files or see your instructor for information on accessing the files in this book.

The Bryan's Lawn Service Web site currently contains four pages. You will add a fifth page with a table created using Standard mode. The new Web page will include a seven-row, three-column centered table with a list of services, how often the services are scheduled, and the price of each service. You merge one of the rows and then add and center an image in the row. A border color is applied to the entire table, and the first row has a background color applied. Keywords and a description are added. You then add a link to the home page, save the page, and upload the Web site to a Web server. The new page added to the Web site is shown in Figure 3-113. Software and hardware settings determine how a Web page is displayed in a browser. Your Web page may appear different from the one shown in Figure 3-113.

Appendix C contains instructions for uploading your local site to a remote site.

FIGURE 3-113

1. Use the Windows Computer tool to copy the fertilizing.gif image from the DataFiles folder to your /lawn/images folder.
2. Select Lawn Service from the Site pop-up menu in the Files panel. Click File on the menu bar and then click New. If necessary, click Blank Page and then click the Create button. Save the page as prices.htm.
3. Use the Page Properties dialog box to apply the lawnbg.jpg image to the new page.

(continued)

Apply Your Knowledge

Modifying the Bryan's Lawn Service Web Site *(continued)*

4. If necessary, display the Insert bar. Click the upper-left corner of the Document window. Type Services Price Chart and then apply Heading 1 to the text. Center the text. Change the font to Arial, Helvetica, sans-serif. If necessary, deselect the title, press the ENTER key, and then click the Layout category on the Insert bar. If necessary, click the Standard mode button and then click the Table button in the Layout category. Type the following data in the Table dialog box: 7 for Rows, 3 for Columns, 70 for Table width, 3 for border thickness, 5 for Cell padding, and 2 for Cell spacing. If necessary, select percent in the drop-down box to the right of the Table width text box.
5. Type the text as shown in Table 3-7. Press the TAB key to move from cell to cell.

Table 3-7 Bryan's Lawn Services Price Chart

SERVICES	SCHEDULE	YEARLY PRICE
Mowing/trimming	Weekly	$1,170
Pruning	Monthly	$500
Fertilizing	Quarterly	$450
Irrigation	As needed	Price varies with size of lawn
Weed and insect control	As needed	Price varies with size of lawn

6. Click anywhere in row 1 and then click the <tr> tag in the tag selector to select row 1. Apply Heading 2 and center the heading. Change the font to Arial, Helvetica, sans-serif. Click the Background Color box in the Property inspector and apply background color #009900.
7. Click anywhere in row 7 in the table and then click the <tr> tag in the tag selector to select row 7. Click the Merge Cells using spans button and then click the Align Center button in the Property inspector. If necessary, display the Assets panel. With the insertion point in the middle of the merged row 7, drag the fertilizing.gif image to the insertion point and then type Fertilizing as the Alt text.
8. Click the <table> tag in the tag selector and then apply border color #009900. Center the table.
9. Position the insertion point outside the table by clicking to the right of the table. Press the ENTER key. Type Home and then create a relative link to the index.htm file.
10. Click Insert on the menu bar, point to HTML, point to Head Tags, and then click the Keywords command. When the Keywords dialog box is displayed, type lawn service, price schedule, your name in the Keywords text box, and then click the OK button. Click Insert on the menu bar, point to HTML, point to Head Tags, and then click the Description command. When the Description dialog box is displayed, type Bryan's Lawn Service price schedule in the Description text box and then click the OK button.
11. Title the page Bryan's Lawn Service - Prices. Check spelling. Save the Web page.
12. Open the index.htm page and then scroll to the end of the page. Click at the end of the sentence that reads, "Our mission is to be the premier..." and then press the ENTER key. Type Check our Prices. If necessary, click the Bold button in the Property inspector to remove the bold formatting. Create a link from the words Check our Prices to the prices.htm page. Save the index.htm Web page.
13. Submit the assignment as requested by your instructor. Close the Lawn Service Web site. Close Dreamweaver.

In the Lab

1 Adding a Page with a Table to the CandleLight Web Site

Problem: Publicity from the Web site has generated several requests for examples of Tracy Coady's candles. Tracy has asked you to add a page to the site that shows some of her creations and the price of each candle. The Web page will have a link to the home page and will be named products. The new page is shown in Figure 3-114. Appendix C contains instructions for uploading your local site to a remote site.

FIGURE 3-114

Instructions: Perform the following tasks:

1. Use the Windows Computer tool to copy the six images (candle3.gif through candle8.gif) from the DataFiles folder to your /candle/images folder.
2. Start Dreamweaver. Select CandleLight from the Files pop-up menu in the Files panel. Click File on the menu bar and then click New. If necessary, click Blank Page and then click the Create button. Save the page as products.htm.
3. Use the Page Properties dialog box to add the candlebg.jpg image. Title the page CandleLight Specialty Candles.
4. Click the upper-left corner of the page and then press the ENTER key.
5. If necessary, click the Insert bar's Layout category, click the Standard mode button, and then click the Table button. Type the following data in the Table dialog box: 6 for Rows, 3 for Columns, 80 for Table width, 3 for Border thickness, 3 for Cell padding, and 3 for Cell spacing. Select percent in the drop-down box to the right of the Table width text box.

(continued)

Adding a Page with a Table to the CandleLight Web Site *(continued)*

6. Merge the three cells in row 1 into one cell. Click the Align Center button in the Property inspector and then type `CandleLight Specialty Candles` as the heading. Apply Heading 1 to the text heading. Change the font to Georgia, Times New Roman, Times, serif. Change the Text Color to #990000.

7. Click row 2, column 1 and then drag to select all cells in rows 2 through 6. Click the Align Center button, click the Vert box arrow, and then select Middle. Set the width to 33%. Repeat this step for rows 2 through 6 in both column 2 and column 3.

8. Display the Assets panel. Click row 2, column 1 and drag candle3.gif to the insertion point. If the Image Tag Accessibility Attributes dialog box displays, click the Cancel button. Repeat this step, dragging candle4.gif to row 2, column 2, and candle5.gif to row 2, column 3.

9. Type the following information in row 3: `$7.25` in column 1, `$7.25` in column 2, and `$4.50` in column 3.

10. Merge the three cells in row 4.

11. Click column 1, row 5 and drag candle6.gif to the insertion point. Repeat this step, dragging candle7.gif to column 2, row 5, and candle8.gif to column 3, row 5.

12. Type the following information in row 6: `$7.00` in column 1, `$4.50` in column 2, and `$3.75` in column 3.

13. Select the table by clicking <table> in the tag inspector. Use the Property inspector to center-align the table.

14. Click outside of the table to the right and then press the ENTER key. Type `Home` and create a link from the products.htm page to the index.htm page. Save the products.htm page.

15. Open the index.htm page and click to the right of the Company history link. Press the ENTER key. Type `Products` and then create a link to the products.htm page. Save the index.htm page.

16. View your page in your browser. Verify that your link works. Submit the assignment as requested by your instructor. Close your browser. Close Dreamweaver.

2 Adding a Table Page to the Credit Web Site

Problem: The Credit Protection Web site has become very popular. Linda Reyes receives numerous e-mail messages requesting that the Web site be expanded. Several messages have included a request to provide some hints and tips about how to save money. Linda asks you to create a new page for the Web site so she can share some of this information. Figure 3-115a shows the table layout, and Figure 3-115b shows the Web page. Appendix C contains instructions for uploading your local site to a remote site.

In the Lab

Tips and Hints
Saving Money

Checking

Automobiles

1. Select a model that combines a low purchase price with low financing, maintenance, and repair costs.
2. Comparison shop -- call at least five dealerships.

1. Select a checking account with a low or no minimum balance requirement.
2. Request a list of all fees.
3. Use direct deposit.

Credit Cards

1. Pay off the entire bill each month.
2. Switch to a credit card with a low Annual Percentage Rate (APR).
3. Get rid of all credit cards except one or two.

Home | Questions | Theft

(a) Table Layout
FIGURE 3-115

(continued)

Adding a Table Page to the Credit Web Site *(continued)*

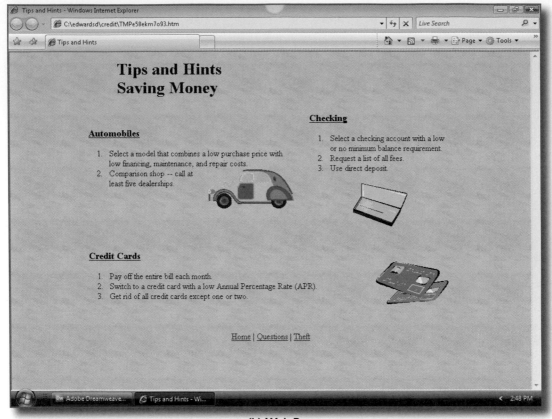

(b) Web Page

FIGURE 3-115

Instructions: Perform the following tasks:

1. Use the Windows Computer tool to copy the three images (car.gif, check.gif, and credit_card.gif) from the DataFiles folder to your /credit/images folder. Start Dreamweaver. Select Credit Protection from the Site pop-up menu in the Files panel.

2. Add a new Web page and name it saving.htm. Add the creditbg.jpg background image. Title the page Tips and Hints.

3. If necessary, display the rulers. Press ALT+F6 to activate the Draw Layout Table button.

4. Click the Draw Layout Table button on the Layout tab and then create a table with a fixed width of approximately 700 pixels and a height of approximately 550 pixels.

5. Use Figure 3-115a on the previous page as a guide and draw the five layout cells. Use the information in Table 3-8 for the widths and heights.

In the Lab

NUMBER	CELL NAME	W	H	IMAGE ALT TEXT	IMAGE NAME	CELL TEXT
	Table 3-8 Credit Protection Cell Layout Guide					
1	Heading	340	75	None	None	Tips and Hints Saving Money
2	Automobiles	365	185	Car	car.gif	1. Select a model that combines a low purchase price with low financing, maintenance, and repair costs. 2. Comparison shop — call at least five dealerships.
3	Checking	306	232	Checking Account	check.gif	1. Select a checking account with a low or no minimum balance requirement. 2. Request a list of all fees. 3. Use direct deposit.
4	Credit Cards	700	115	Credit Cards	credit_card.gif	1. Pay off the entire bill each month. 2. Switch to a credit card with a low Annual Percentage Rate (APR). 3. Get rid of all credit cards except one or two.
5	Links	700	40	None	None	Home | Questions | Theft

6. Use Table 3-8 as a reference and type the text into each of the layout cells. Apply Heading 1 to the text in the first cell. Apply Heading 3 to the headings in cells 2 through 4 and then underline the headings.

7. Insert the images into the cells. Refer to the invisible element marker in Figure 3-115a as the insertion point for the images in cells 2 and 4. For cell 3, press the ENTER key twice after item 3 and then click the Align Center button in the Property inspector. Drag the check.gif image to the insertion point. Use the Property inspector to select Right from the Align drop-down menu for the car.gif and credit_card.gif images.

8. Add the appropriate relative links to cell 5, using Table 3-9 as a guide.

Table 3-9 Links for Cell 5	
TEXT	LINK
Home	index.htm
Questions	questions.htm
Theft	theft.htm

9. Click the Standard mode button on the Layout tab, select the table, and then center the table.

(continued)

In the Lab

Adding a Table Page to the Credit Web Site *(continued)*

10. Click the Head button in the Common category of the Insert bar. Click the Keywords button in the pop-up menu and then type credit, money, tips, checking, saving, your name in the Keywords dialog box. Open the Description dialog box and then type Tips and hints on how to save money. Save the Web page.

11. Open the index.htm page and click to the right of the last bulleted item. Press the ENTER key twice. Type Tips and Hints on Saving and create a link from this text to the saving.htm page. Save the index.htm page.

12. View the Web site in your browser and verify that your links work. Close the browser. Submit the assignment as requested by your instructor.

3 Adding a Table Page to the Lexington, NC Web Site

Problem: In his job as a member of the Lexington marketing group, Jerry Smith has been exploring the city's services. On a recent tour, Jerry discovered that the city contains an outstanding police department. He would like to feature the Lexington Police Department on the Web site and has requested that you add a new page to the Lexington, NC Web site. You elect to use a layout table to create this page. The Web page is displayed in Figure 3-116. Appendix C contains instructions for uploading your local site to a remote site.

FIGURE 3-116

Instructions: Perform the following tasks:

1. Use the Windows Computer tool to copy the four images (police1.jpg through police4.jpg) from the DataFiles folder to your /city/images folder. Start Dreamweaver. Select Lexington, NC from the Site pop-up menu in the Files panel.

2. Add a new page and then save the page with the file name police.htm. Add the background image you added in Chapter 1. Add the citybg.gif background image. Title the page Lexington, NC - Police Department.

3. If necessary, display the rulers. Press ALT+F6 to activate the Draw Layout Table button.

4. Create a layout table with a fixed width of approximately 650 pixels and a height of approximately 675 pixels.

5. Use Figure 3-116 as a guide and draw the 10 layout cells. Use the information in Table 3-10 for the widths, heights, and file names.

Table 3-10 Lexington, NC Cell Layout Guide

NUMBER	CELL TYPE	W	H	IMAGE ALT TEXT	FILE NAME	CELL TEXT
1	Heading	650	85	None	None	City of Lexington Police Department
2	Image	256	192	Police Department	police1.jpg	None
3	Text	256	30	None	None	Lexington PD Headquarters
4	Image	256	192	Tribute Statue	police2.jpg	None
5	Text	256	30	None	None	Tribute Statue
6	Image	256	192	Pile of Pigs	police3.jpg	None
7	Text	256	30	None	None	Pile of Pigs Display
8	Image	256	192	Cruisers	police4.jpg	None
9	Text	256	30	None	None	Lexington Police Department Cruisers
10	Text	650	30	None	None	Home

6. Type the text into each of the layout cells as indicated in Table 3-10. Apply Heading 1 to the first line of text in the first cell and Heading 2 to the second line of text.

7. Insert the images into the cells. Refer to Table 3-10 for the image file names.

8. Click the Standard mode button on the Layout category, select the table, and then center the table. Create a relative link to the index.htm Web page using the text in cell 10.

9. Add Lexington, North Carolina, police, safety, and your name as keywords. Type A tribute to the Lexington Police Department as the description. Save the police.htm page.

10. Open the index.htm page. Click to the right of the Recipes link and then press the SPACEBAR. Add a vertical line, press the SPACEBAR, and then type Police Department. Create a link from the Police Department text to the police.htm page.

11. View the Web site in your browser. Close the browser. Submit the assignment as requested by your instructor.

Cases and Places

The difficulty of these case studies varies:
■ are the least difficult and ■■ are the most difficult. The last exercise is a group exercise.

1 ■ The sports Web site has become very popular. Several of your friends have suggested that you add a statistics page. You agree that this is a good idea. Create the new page. Using the Internet or other resources, find statistics about your selected sport. Add a background image to the page and use Standard mode to insert a table that contains your statistical information. Add an appropriate heading to the table and an appropriate title for the page. Create a link to the home page. Save the page in your sports Web site. For a selection of images and backgrounds, visit the Dreamweaver CS3 Media Web page (scsite.com/dwcs3/media) and then click Media below Chapter 3.

2 ■ Modify your hobby Web site. Expand the topic and add an additional page that includes a table created in Standard mode. The table should contain a minimum of three rows and three columns, and a 2-pixel border. Include information in the table about your hobby. Include a minimum of two images in the table. Merge one of the rows or one of the columns and add a border color. Add a background image to the page and give your page a title. Create a link to the home page. Save the page in your hobby Web site. For a selection of images and backgrounds, visit the Dreamweaver CS3 Media Web page (scsite.com/dwcs3/media) and then click Media below Chapter 3.

3 ■■ Modify your favorite type of music Web site by adding a new page. The new page should contain a table with four rows and three columns created in Standard mode. Merge one of the rows and add a background color to the row. Add at least two images to your table. Center the images in the cell. View your Web pages in your browser. Give your page a title and save the page in your music subfolder. Appendix C contains instructions for uploading your local site to a remote site. For a selection of images and backgrounds, visit the Dreamweaver CS3 Media Web page (scsite.com/dwcs3/media) and then click Media below Chapter 3.

Cases and Places

4 ■■ Your campaign for office is going well. You want to add a new page to the Web site to include pictures and text listing some of your outstanding achievements. Apply a color scheme and a background image to the page. Draw a layout table with a minimum of four layout cells. Include your picture in one of the cells. Add an appropriate title, keywords, and a description to the page. Center the table. Save the page in the office subfolder and then view the page in your browser. Appendix C contains instructions for uploading your local site to a remote site. For a selection of images and backgrounds, visit the Dreamweaver CS3 Media Web page (scsite.com/dwcs3/media) and then click Media below Chapter 3.

5 ■■ **Working Together** The students at your school are requesting more information about the student trips. To accommodate the request, the members of your team decide to add another page to the Web site. Each team member is responsible for researching possible destinations and developing content for the selected destination. Add a heading to the new page and format it appropriately. Draw a layout table with a minimum of six layout cells. Each member adds at least one image and text content to a cell. One member formats the page — including the text and images. Add a title, keywords, meta tags, and a description. Save the page and view it in your browser. Appendix C contains instructions for uploading your local site to a remote site. For a selection of images and backgrounds, visit the Dreamweaver CS3 Media Web page (scsite.com/dwcs3/media) and then click Media below Chapter 3.

Appendix A

 Dreamweaver Help

Dreamweaver Help

This appendix shows you how to use the many components of Dreamweaver Help. At any time while you are using Dreamweaver, you can interact with its Help system and display information on any Dreamweaver topic. It is a complete reference manual at your fingertips.

The Using Dreamweaver CS3 Help system is viewed through your browser. The system contains comprehensive HTML-based information about all Dreamweaver features, including the following:

- A table of contents in which the information is organized by subject.
- An alphabetical index that points to important terms and links to related topics.
- A search tool that allows you to find any character string in all topic text.

Other Help features include context-sensitive help, information on Dreamweaver extensions, help on using ColdFusion, and online reference manuals, including an HTML reference manual. For additional tutorials and online movies, you can access the Adobe Dreamweaver resources Web site at http://www. adobe.com/support/documentation/en/dreamweaver/.

The Dreamweaver Help Menu

One of the more commonly used methods to access Dreamweaver's Help features is through the Help menu and function keys. Dreamweaver's Help menu provides an easy system to access the available Help options (Figure A-1 on the next page). Table A-1 on the next page summarizes the commands available through the Help menu.

FIGURE A-1

Table A-1 Summary of Commands on the Help Menu	
COMMAND ON HELP MENU	FUNCTION
Dreamweaver Help	This command accesses the Adobe Help Viewer for Dreamweaver CS3.
Help Resources Online	This command accesses the Dreamweaver Help files online; these are the same files accessed through the Dreamweaver Help command.
Extending Dreamweaver	The Extending Dreamweaver command opens the Extending Dreamweaver CS3 Help files.
Dreamweaver API Reference	The Dreamweaver API Reference command opens the Dreamweaver API Reference Help files.
What's New in Dreamweaver CS3	This command is a direct link to the What's New in Dreamweaver CS3 section located in the Dreamweaver Help files.
Spry Framework Help	The Spry framework for Ajax is a JavaScript library, which provides the Web site developer with an option to incorporate XML data and other kinds of effects.
ColdFusion Help	The ColdFusion Help command displays the ColdFusion Documentation window. ColdFusion is a Web application server that lets you create applications that interact with databases.

Table A-1 Summary of Commands on the Help Menu (*continued*)

COMMAND ON HELP MENU	FUNCTION
Reference	The Reference command opens the Reference panel, which displays below the document windows. The Reference panel contains the complete text from several reference manuals, including references on HTML, Cascading Style Sheets, JavaScript, and other Web-related features.
Dreamweaver Exchange	This command links to the Adobe Exchange Web site, where you can download for free and/or purchase a variety of Dreamweaver add-on features.
Manage Extensions	The Extensions command displays the Adobe Extension Manager window where you can install, enable, and disable extensions. An extension is an add-on piece of software or a plug-in that enhances Dreamweaver's capabilities. Extensions provide the Dreamweaver developer with the capability to customize how Dreamweaver looks and works.
Dreamweaver Support Center	The Dreamweaver Support Center provides access to the online Adobe Dreamweaver support.
Dreamweaver Developer Center	The Developer Center offers search options and developer assistance.
Adobe Online Forums	The Adobe Online Forums command provides access to the Adobe Online Forums Web page. The forums provide a place for developers of all experience levels to share ideas and techniques.
Adobe Training	This online site provides information and links related to training and certification.
Registration	This Web site displays your registration information and provides a print option.
Download e-License	Download electronic license from Adobe Web site.
Return e-License	Return electronic license to Adobe.
Updates	This command provides an option for online updating of software.
About Dreamweaver	The About Dreamweaver command opens a window that provides copyright information and the product license number.

Navigating the Dreamweaver CS3 Help System

The Dreamweaver Help command accesses Dreamweaver's primary Help system and provides comprehensive information about all Dreamweaver features. Three options are available: Contents, Index, and Search. Additionally, the Browse list box provides Help access to other Adobe products.

Using the Contents Sheet

The **Contents** sheet is useful for displaying Help when you know the general category of the topic in question, but not the specifics. You click a plus icon to expand a Help category and display a list of specific topics. You then can click a topic to open a page related to that topic. The following example shows how to use the Contents sheet to obtain information on how to spell check a Web page.

To Obtain Help Using the Contents Sheet

1

• **Open Dreamweaver, if necessary.**

• **Click Help on the menu bar and then click Dreamweaver Help.**

• **Dreamweaver displays the Adobe Help Viewer for Dreamweaver CS3.**

• **If necessary, double-click the title bar to maximize the window.**

The Adobe Help Viewer for Dreamweaver CS3 is displayed (Figure A-2). Three options are available: Contents, Index, and Search.

FIGURE A-2

2

• **Click the plus sign to the left of Workspace, and then click the word Workspace.**

The plus sign changes to a minus sign and the Workspace help is opened. The help information is displayed in the right pane (Figure A-3). Additional links are displayed below the selected topic. Links to these topics also are displayed in the right pane.

FIGURE A-3

3

• **Click the plus sign to the left of Using toolbars, inspectors, context menus, and panels, and then click the Display toolbars link.**

The information on the subtopic is displayed in the right pane (Figure A-4).

FIGURE A-4

Once the information on the subtopic is displayed, you can read it, you can click a link contained within the subtopic, or you can click the Print button on the toolbar to obtain a printed copy. Other commands on the toolbar are Back, Forward, About Adobe Help Viewer, Browse, and Search. The Back and Forward buttons move you back or forward to previously accessed screens. The About Adobe Help Viewer provides basic information about the Help Viewer program, the Browse button provides links to other references, and the Search text box can be used to search all of Help. To view related topics, click the Previous or Next buttons in the displayed window.

Using the Index Sheet

The second sheet in the Using Dreamweaver window is the Index sheet. Use the Index sheet to display Help when you know the keyword or the first few letters of the keyword. The next steps show how to use the Index sheet to obtain help on cropping images.

To Use the Index Sheet

1

• **Click the Index link.**

The Index sheet is displayed (Figure A-5).

FIGURE A-5

2

• **Click the letter I and then click the plus sign to the left of images.**

Images topics and subtopics are displayed (Figure A-6).

FIGURE A-6

3

• **Click the cropping plus sign and then click Crop an image.**

Information about cropping an image is displayed in the right pane (Figure A-7).

FIGURE A-7

Using the Search Feature

Using the Search feature allows you to find any character string, anywhere in the text of the Help system. The next steps show how to use the Search feature to obtain help about cropping images.

To Use the Search Feature

1

• **Click the Search text box.**

• **Type** cropping **in the Search text box and then press the ENTER key.**

The Search results display a list of six topics containing references to cropping (Figure A-8). All of these topics contain the word cropping somewhere within the document.

FIGURE A-8

2

- **Click option number 3, which is Edit images in Dreamweaver.**

The Help screen for Edit images in Dreamweaver is displayed in the right pane. (Figure A-9).

3

- **Close the Help window.**

You return to Dreamweaver.

FIGURE A-9

Context-Sensitive Help

Using **context-sensitive help**, you can open a relevant Help topic in panels, inspectors, and most dialog boxes. To view these Help features, you click a Help button in a dialog box, choose Help on the Options pop-up menu in a panel group, or click the question mark icon in an inspector.

Using the Question Mark Icon to Display Help

Many of the panels and inspectors within Dreamweaver contain a question mark icon. Clicking this icon displays context-sensitive help. Assume for the following example that you want to know about tables. The following steps show how to use the question mark icon to view context-sensitive help through the Property inspector. In this example, the default Property inspector for text is displayed.

To Display Context-Sensitive Help on Text

1

• Point to the question
mark icon in the
Property inspector
(Figure A-10).

FIGURE A-10

2

• Click the question
mark icon.

*The Adobe Help Viewer for
Dreamweaver CS3 is
displayed, and information
pertaining to Setting text
properties in the Property
inspector is displayed in the
right pane (Figure A-11).*

3

• Close the Adobe Help
Viewer for Dreamweaver
CS3 and return to
Dreamweaver.

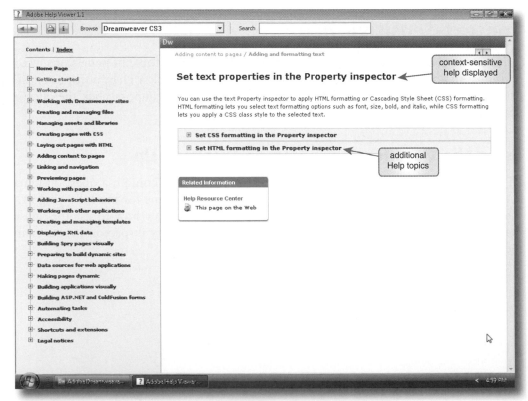

FIGURE A-11

Using the Options Menu to Display Help

Panels and dialog boxes also contain context-sensitive help. The following steps show how to display context-sensitive help for the Files panel. In this example, the Files panel is open and displayed within the Dreamweaver window.

To Use the Options Menu to Display Context-Sensitive Help for the Files Panel

1

• **Click the Options button on the Files title bar and then point to Help on the Options pop-up menu.**

The Options pop-up menu is displayed (Figure A-12).

FIGURE A-12

2

• **Click the Help command.**

The Adobe Help Viewer for Dreamweaver CS3 is displayed, and information pertaining to using the Files panel is displayed in the right pane (Figure A-13).

3

• **Close the Adobe Help Viewer for Dreamweaver CS3 and return to Dreamweaver.**

FIGURE A-13

Using the Reference Panel

The Reference panel is another valuable Dreamweaver resource. This panel provides you with a quick reference tool for HTML tags, JavaScript objects, Cascading Style Sheets, and other Dreamweaver features. The next example shows how to access the Reference panel, review the various options, and select and display information on the <body> tag.

To Use the Reference Panel

1

• **Click Window on the menu bar and then point to Reference (Figure A-14).**

FIGURE A-14

2

• **Click Reference, and then, if necessary, click O'REILLY HTML Reference in the Book pop-up menu.**

The Reference panel in the Code panel group displays tag information (Figure A-15).

FIGURE A-15

3

• **Click the Tag button arrow and then point to BODY in the tag list.**

BODY is highlighted in the tag list (Figure A-16).

FIGURE A-16

4

• **Click BODY.**

Information on the <body> tag is displayed (Figure A-17).

FIGURE A-17

5

• **Click the Book button arrow and review the list of available reference books.**

A list of 13 reference books is displayed (Figure A-18). These are complete books and can be accessed in the same way the HTML reference book was accessed.

6

• **Close Dreamweaver.**

• **If the Adobe Dreamweaver dialog box to save changes is displayed, click the No button.**

FIGURE A-18

Online Help Support

Dreamweaver also provides several support Web sites, including online forums and links to third-party online forums. Examples of these online forums and discussion groups are as follows:

- Dreamweaver — For Dreamweaver users developing Web sites.
- Dreamweaver Application Development — For Dreamweaver users creating dynamic Web sites.
- Dreamweaver Extensibility — For Dreamweaver users interested in extending the functionality of Dreamweaver.
- Dynamic HTML — This group discusses questions and issues regarding Dynamic HTML.
- General Information — This group discusses general information regarding Adobe products that does not pertain to the other online forums.

For a selection of Help links, visit the Dreamweaver CS3 Web page (scsite.com/dreamweavercs3) and then click Appendix Help.

Apply Your Knowledge

1 Viewing the Dreamweaver Help Resources Online

Instructions: Start Dreamweaver. Perform the following tasks using the Dreamweaver Help Resources Online command.

1. Click Help on the menu bar and then click Help Resources Online.
2. Click PDF below the Using Dreamweaver link to display the Adobe Dreamweaver CS3 User Guide.
3. Click the plus sign to the left of Chapter 3: Working with Dreamweaver Sites, click the plus sign to the left of Setting up a Dreamweaver site, and then click the About Dreamweaver sites link.
4. Use a word-processing program to write a short overview of what you learned.
5. Submit your assignment in the format specified by your instructor.

2 Using the Help Index

Instructions: Start Dreamweaver. Perform the following tasks using the Index sheet in the Dreamweaver CS3 Help system.

1. Press the F1 key to display the Adobe Help Viewer for Dreamweaver CS3.
2. Click Index, click the letter L, and then click the plus sign to the left of links.
3. Next, click the plus sign to the left of checking, click Find broken, external, and orphaned links, and then read this information.
4. Use a word-processing program to write a short overview of what you learned.
5. Submit your assignment in the format specified by your instructor.

3 Using Context-Sensitive Help

Instructions: Start Dreamweaver. Perform the following tasks using context-sensitive help in the Assets panel.

1. Click the Assets tab in the Files panel group. Verify that the Images icon is selected.
2. Click the Options button and then click Help on the Options pop-up menu.
3. Read the information in the right pane about the Assets panel.
4. Use your word-processing program to prepare a report on how to set up a favorite list of assets.
5. Submit your assignment in the format specified by your instructor.

Appendix B

Dreamweaver and Accessibility

Dreamweaver and Accessibility

Tim Berners-Lee, World Wide Web Consortium (W3C) founder and inventor of the World Wide Web, indicates that the power of the Web is in its universality. He says that access by everyone, regardless of disability, is an essential aspect of the Web. In 1997, the W3C launched the **Web Accessibility Initiative** and made a commitment to lead the Web to its full potential. The initiative includes promoting a high degree of usability for people with disabilities. The United States government established a second initiative addressing accessibility and the Web through Section 508 of the Federal Rehabilitation Act.

Dreamweaver includes features that assist you in creating accessible content. Designing accessible content requires that you understand accessibility requirements and make subjective decisions as you create a Web site. Dreamweaver supports three accessibility options: screen readers, keyboard navigation, and operating system accessibility features.

Using Screen Readers with Dreamweaver

Screen readers assist the blind and vision-impaired by reading text that is displayed on the screen through a speaker or headphones. The screen reader starts at the top-left corner of the page and reads the page content. If the Web site developer uses accessibility tags or attributes during the creation of the Web site, the screen reader also recites this information and reads nontextual information such as button labels and image descriptions. Dreamweaver makes it easy to add text equivalents for graphical elements and to add HTML elements to tables and forms through the accessibility dialog boxes. Dreamweaver supports two screen readers: JAWS and Window Eyes.

Activating the Accessibility Dialog Boxes

To create accessible pages in Dreamweaver, you associate information, such as labels and descriptions, with your page objects. After you have created this association, the screen reader can recite the label and description information.

You create the association by activating and attaching the accessibility dialog boxes to objects on your page. These dialog boxes appear when you insert an object for which you have activated the corresponding Accessibility dialog box. You activate the Accessibility dialog boxes through the Preferences dialog box. You can activate Accessibility dialog boxes for form objects, frames, images, and media. Accessibility for tables is accomplished by adding Summary text to the Table dialog box and adding image Ids and Alt text through the Property inspector. The steps on the following pages use the Colorado Parks index page as an example to show how to display the Preferences dialog box and activate the Image Accessibility dialog box.

To Activate the Images Accessibility Dialog Box

1

• **Start Dreamweaver and, if necessary, open the Colorado Parks site.**

• **Double-click index.htm in the Files panel to open the index.htm page.**

• **Click Edit on the menu bar and then point to Preferences (Figure B-1).**

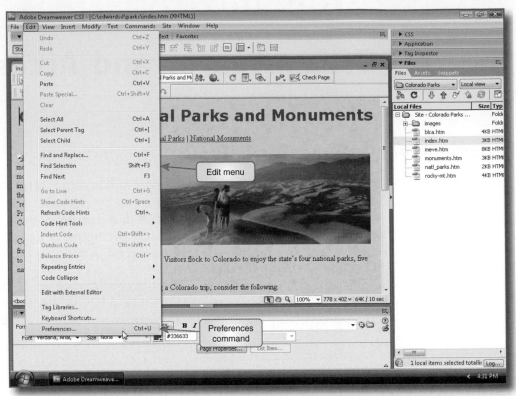

FIGURE B-1

2

• **Click Preferences.**

The Preferences dialog box is displayed (Figure B-2).

FIGURE B-2

3

- Click Accessibility in the Category list, click the Images check box in the Accessibility area to select it, deselect the other check boxes, if necessary, and then point to the OK button.

The Accessibility category is highlighted, and the Images check box is selected (Figure B-3). The Accessibility area includes four different options for which you can activate Accessibility dialog boxes: Form objects, Frames, Media, and Images.

FIGURE B-3

4

- Click the OK button.

The Preferences dialog box closes, and the Dreamweaver Document window is displayed. No change is apparent in the Document window, but the Image Tag Accessibility Attributes dialog box has been activated.

Inserting Accessible Images

Selecting Images in the Accessibility category activates the Image Tag Accessibility Attributes dialog box. Thus, any time you insert an image into a Web page, this dialog box will be displayed. This dialog box contains two text boxes: Alternate Text and Long Description. The screen reader reads the information you enter in both text boxes. You should limit your Alternate Text entry to about 50 characters. For longer descriptions, provide a link in the Long Description text box to a file that gives more information about the image. It is not required that you enter data into both text boxes. The steps on the next page show how to use the Image Tag Accessibility Attributes dialog box when inserting an image.

To Insert Accessible Images

1

• **Position the insertion point where you want to insert the image.**

• **Click Insert on the menu bar and then point to Image (Figure B-4).**

FIGURE B-4

2

• **Click Image. If necessary, open the images folder and then click a file name.**

• **Point to the OK button.**

The Select Image Source dialog box is displayed (Figure B-5).

FIGURE B-5

3

- **Click the OK button.**

The Image Tag Accessibility Attributes dialog box is displayed. The insertion point is blinking in the Alternate text text box (Figure B-6). To display the Image Tag Accessibility Attributes dialog box, you must insert the image by using the Insert menu or by clicking the Image button on the Common tab of the Insert bar. Dragging an image from the Assets panel to the Document window does not activate the Image Tag Accessibility Attributes dialog box if the Accessibility feature is not selected.

FIGURE B-6

4

- **Type a brief description of the image in the Alternate text text box.**

- **Click the folder icon to display the Select File dialog box. Locate and then click the description file name. Click the OK button in the Select File dialog box.**

- **Point to the OK button.**

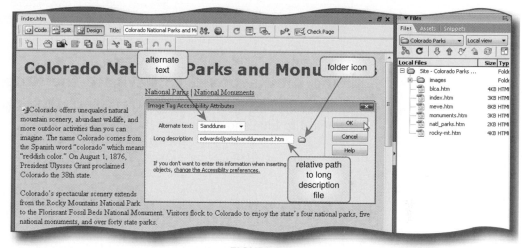

FIGURE B-7

The image description is displayed in the Alternate text text box, and the long description file location is displayed in the Long description text box (Figure B-7).

5

- **Click the OK button in the Image Tag Accessibility Attributes dialog box.**

No changes are displayed in the Document window. When the page is displayed in the browser, however, the screen reader recites the information you entered in the Image Tag Accessibility Attributes Alternate text text box. If you included a link to a file with additional information in the Long description text box, the screen reader accesses the file and recites the text contained within the file.

6

- **Close Dreamweaver. Do not save the changes to the Web page.**

Navigating Dreamweaver with the Keyboard

Keyboard navigation is a core aspect of accessibility. This feature also is of particular importance to users who have repetitive strain injuries (RSIs) or other disabilities, and to those users who would prefer to use the keyboard instead of a mouse. You can use the keyboard to navigate the following elements in Dreamweaver: floating panels, the Property inspector, dialog boxes, frames, and tables.

Using the Keyboard to Navigate Panels

When you are working in Dreamweaver, several panels may be open at one time. A dotted outline around the panel title bar indicates that the panel is selected (Figure B-8). Press CTRL+ALT+SHIFT+TAB to move to the previous panel. If necessary, expand the selected panel by pressing the SPACEBAR. Pressing the SPACEBAR again collapses the panel. Use the arrow keys to scroll the panel. Press the SPACEBAR to make a selection.

FIGURE B-8

Using the Keyboard to Navigate the Property Inspector

The following steps use the Colorado Parks index page to show how to use the keyboard to hide and display the Property inspector.

To Use the Keyboard to Hide and Display the Property Inspector

1

• **Start Dreamweaver and, if necessary, open the Colorado Parks site. Double-click index.htm in the Files panel to open the index.htm file, and then click in paragraph 1. Press CTRL+F3 to hide the Property inspector and then CTRL+F3 to redisplay the Property inspector.**

The Property inspector is redisplayed and Paragraph is selected. (Figure B-9).

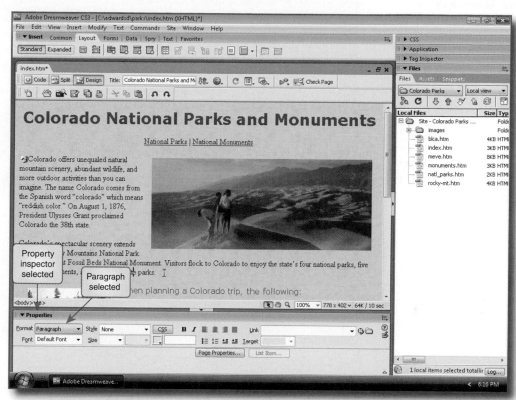

FIGURE B-9

2

• **Press the TAB key three times to move to the Style box.**

None is highlighted in the Style box (Figure B-10).

FIGURE B-10

3

• Use the keyboard DOWN ARROW key to select style1 and then press the ENTER key.

Style1 is selected and applied to the text (Figure B-11).

4

• Close Dreamweaver. Do not save any of the changes.

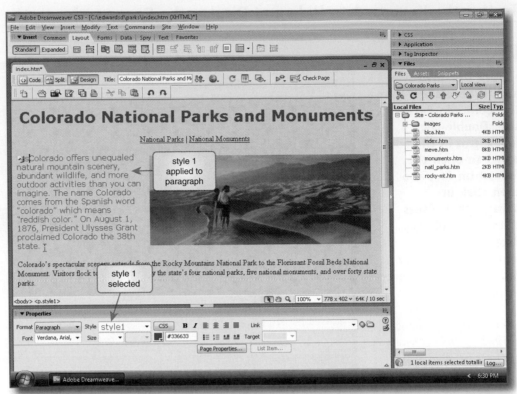

FIGURE B-11

Operating System Accessibility Features

The third method of accessibility support in Dreamweaver is through the Windows operating system's high contrast setting. **High contrast** changes the desktop color themes for individuals who have vision impairment. The color schemes make the screen easier to view by heightening screen contrast with alternative color combinations. Some of the schemes also change font sizes.

You activate this option through the Windows Control Panel. The high contrast setting affects Dreamweaver in two ways:

- The dialog boxes and panels use system color settings.
- Code view syntax color is turned off.

Design view, however, continues to use the background and text colors you set in the Page Properties dialog box. The pages you design, therefore, continue to render colors as they will display in a browser. The following steps show how to turn on high contrast and how to change the current high contrast settings.

To Turn On High Contrast

1

• **In Windows Vista, click the Start button on the taskbar and then click Control Panel on the Start menu.**

The Control Panel Home window is displayed (Figure B-12).

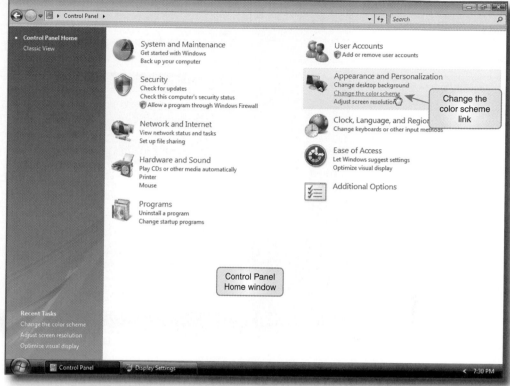

FIGURE B-12

2

• **Click Change the color scheme.**

The Appearance Settings dialog box is displayed. (Figure B-13).

FIGURE B-13

3

• **Click High
Contrast #2.**

*The Appearance Settings
dialog box is displayed
(Figure B-14).*

FIGURE B-14

4

• **Click the Cancel button to close the Appearance and Settings dialog box.**

*The settings return to their original values. To retain these settings on your computer would require
that you click the OK button.*

5

• **Close the Control Panel.**

The Control Panel closes, and the Windows Vista desktop is displayed.

Appendix C

Publishing to a Web Server

Publishing to a Remote Site

With Dreamweaver, Web designers usually define a local site and then do the majority of their designing using the local site. You defined a local site in Chapter 1. In creating the projects in this book, you have added Web pages to the local site, which resides on your computer's hard disk, a network drive, USB drive, or possibly a Zip disk. To prepare a Web site and make it available for others to view requires that you publish your site by uploading it to a Web server for public access. A Web server is an Internet- or intranet-connected computer that delivers the Web pages to online visitors. Dreamweaver includes built-in support that enables you to connect and transfer your local site to a Web server. Publishing to a Web server requires that you have access to a Web server. Your instructor will provide you with the location, user name, and password information for the Web server on which you will publish your site.

After you establish access to a Web server, you will need a remote site folder. The remote folder will reside on the Web server and will contain your Web site files. Generally, the remote folder is defined by the Web server administrator or your instructor. The name of your local root folder in this example is your last name and first initial. Most likely, the name of your remote folder also will be your last name and first initial. You upload your local site to the remote folder on the Web server. The remote site connection information must be defined in Dreamweaver through the Site Definition Wizard. You display the Site Definition Wizard and then enter the remote site information. Dreamweaver provides five different protocols for connecting to a remote site. These methods are as follows:

- **FTP** (File Transfer Protocol): This protocol is used on the Internet for sending and receiving files. It is the most widely used method for uploading and downloading pages to and from a Web server.
- **Local/Network:** This option is used when the Web server is located on a local area network (LAN) or a company or school intranet. Files on LANs generally are available for internal viewing only.
- **SourceSafe Database, RDS (Remote Development Services), and WebDAV:** These three protocols are systems that permit users to edit and manage files collaboratively on remote Web servers.

You most likely will use the FTP option to upload your Web site to a remote server.

Defining a Remote Site

You define the remote site by changing some of the settings in the Site Definition dialog box. To allow you to create a remote site using FTP, your instructor will supply you with the following information:

- **FTP host:** the Web address for the remote host of your Web server.
- **Host directory:** the directory name and path on the server where your remote site will be located.
- **Login:** your user name.
- **Password:** the FTP password to authenticate and access your account.

Assume for the following example on the next page that you are defining a remote site for the Colorado Parks Web site.

To Define a Remote Site

1

• **If necessary, open Dreamweaver.**

• **Click Site on the menu bar and then click Manage Sites.**

• **Click Colorado Parks in the Manage Sites dialog box.**

The Manage Sites dialog box is displayed, and Colorado Parks is selected (Figure C-1).

FIGURE C-1

2

• **Click the Edit button and then click the Advanced tab.**

The Site Definition dialog box is displayed, and Local Info is selected in the Category column (Figure C-2).

FIGURE C-2

3

• **Click the Remote Info category.**

• **Click the Access button arrow in the Remote Info pane and point to FTP.**

Remote Info is selected in the Category column, and FTP is highlighted in the pop-up menu. (Figure C-3).

FIGURE C-3

4

• **Click FTP.**

• **Click each of the following boxes in the Site Definition for Colorado Parks dialog box, and fill in the information as provided by your instructor: FTP host, Host directory, Login, and Password.**

Information for the author, Dolores Wells, is displayed in Figure C-4. Your screen will contain the information provided by your instructor.

FIGURE C-4

5

• Click the Test button to test the connection. If the Windows Security Alert dialog box is displayed, click the Unblock button.

• If your connection is not successful, review your text box entries and make any necessary corrections. If all entries are correct, check with your instructor.

Dreamweaver tests the connection and responds with an Adobe Dreamweaver CS3 dialog box (Figure C-5).

FIGURE C-5

6

• Click the OK button in the Adobe Dreamweaver CS3 dialog box and then click the OK button in the Site Definition for Colorado Parks dialog box to return to the Dreamweaver workspace. If an Adobe Dreamweaver CS3 dialog box is displayed, click the OK button. Click the Done button to close the Manage Sites dialog box.

• If necessary, use the Files panel to open the Colorado Parks site and double-click the index.htm file to display the index.htm Web page.

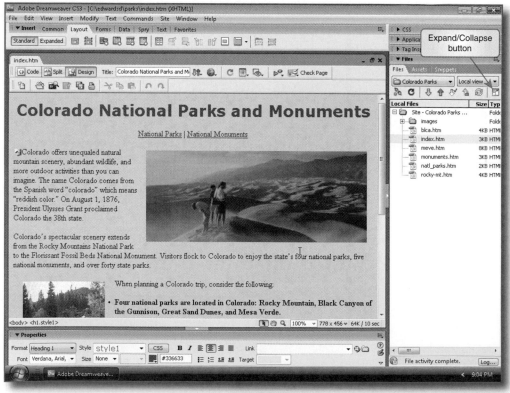

FIGURE C-6

The Colorado National Parks and Monuments page is displayed (Figure C-6).

Connecting to a Remote Site

Now that you have completed the remote site information and tested your connection, you can interact with the remote server. The remote site folder on the Web server for your Web site must be established before a connection can be made. This folder, called the **remote site root**, generally is created by the Web server administrator or your instructor. This book uses the last name and the first initial (edwardsd) for the name of the remote site folder. Naming conventions other than your last name and first initial may be used on the Web server to which you are connecting. Your instructor will supply you with this information. If all information is correct, connecting to the remote site is done easily through the Files panel. The following steps illustrate how to connect to the remote site and display your remote site folder.

To Connect to a Remote Site

1

• **Click the Files panel Expand/Collapse button.**

The Site panel expands to show both a right and left pane (Figure C-7). The right pane contains the local site. The left pane contains information for accessing your remote files by clicking the Connects to remote host button.

FIGURE C-7

2

• **Verify that the root folder is selected. Click the Connects to remote host button.**

The connection is made, and the parks root folder is displayed (Figure C-8). The Connects to remote host/Disconnects from remote host button is a toggle button; it changes to indicate that the connection has been made. The root folder on the remote site must be created by your instructor or Web server administrator before a connection can be made.

FIGURE C-8

Uploading Files to a Remote Server

Your next step will be to upload your files to the remote server. **Uploading** is the process of transferring your files from your computer to the remote server. **Downloading** is the process of transferring files from the remote server to your computer. Dreamweaver uses the term **put** for uploading and **get** for downloading.

To Upload Files to a Remote Server

1

• **Click the Put File(s) button. Point to the OK button.**

The Adobe Dreamweaver CS3 dialog box is displayed to verify that you want to upload the entire site (Figure C-9).

FIGURE C-9

2

• **Click the OK button.**

As the files begin to upload, a Status dialog box is displayed with the progress information. The files are uploaded to the server (Figure C-10). The files may be displayed in a different order from that on the local site. The display order on the server is determined by the settings on that computer.

FIGURE C-10

3

• **Close Dreamweaver.**

Remote Site Maintenance and Site Synchronization

Now that your Web site is on a Web server, you will want to continue to maintain the site. When you are connected to the remote site, you can apply many of the same commands to a folder or file on the remote site as you do to a folder or file on the local site. You can create and delete folders; cut, copy, delete, duplicate, paste, and rename files; and so on. These commands are available through the context menu.

To mirror the local site on the remote site, Dreamweaver provides a synchronization feature. Synchronizing is the process of transferring files between the local and remote sites so both sites have an identical set of the most recent files. You can select to synchronize the entire Web site or select only specific files. You also can specify

Direction. Within Direction, you have three options: upload the newer files from the local site to the remote site (put); download newer files from the remote site to the local site (get); or upload and download files to and from the remote and local sites. Once you specify a direction, Dreamweaver automatically synchronizes files. If the files are already in sync, Dreamweaver lets you know that no synchronization is necessary. To access the Synchronize command, you first connect to the remote server and then select Synchronize on the Site menu (Figure C-11).

To save the verification information to a local file, click the Save Log button at the completion of the synchronization process. Another feature within Dreamweaver allows you to verify which files are newer on the local site or the remote site. These options are available through the Files panel Edit menu by selecting Select Newer Local or Select Newer Remote.

FIGURE C-11

Apply Your Knowledge

1 Defining and Uploading the Bryan's Lawn Service Web Site to a Remote Server

Instructions: Perform the following steps to define and upload the Bryan's Lawn Service Web site to a remote server.

1. If necessary, open Dreamweaver. Click Site on the menu bar, click Manage Sites, and then click Lawn Service. Click the Edit button. When the Site Definition dialog box is displayed, click the Advanced tab and then click Remote Info. Fill in the information as provided by your instructor, and then test the connection. Click the OK button to close the Site Definition dialog box, and then click the Done button to close the Manage Sites dialog box.

2. Click the Expand/Collapse button on the Files panel toolbar and then click the Connects to remote host button. Click the local file root folder and then click the Put File(s) button on the Site panel toolbar to upload your Web site. Click the OK button in response to the Are you sure you wish to put the entire site? dialog box. Review your files to verify that they were uploaded. The files on the remote server may be displayed in a different order from those on the local site.

3. Click the Disconnects from remote host button on the Files panel toolbar. Click the Expand/Collapse button on the Files panel toolbar to display the local site and the Document window.

4. Close Dreamweaver.

2 Defining and Uploading the CandleLight Web Site to a Remote Server

Instructions: Perform the following steps to define and upload the CandleLight Web site to a remote server.

1. If necessary, open Dreamweaver. Click Site on the menu bar, click Manage Sites, and then click CandleLight. Click the Edit button to display the Site Definition dialog box. Click the Advanced tab and then click Remote Info. Fill in the information as provided by your instructor, and then test the connection. Click the OK button to close the Site Definition dialog box, and then click the Done button to close the Manage Sites dialog box.

2. Click the Expand/Collapse button on the Files panel toolbar and then click the Connects to remote host button. Click the local file root folder and then click the Put File(s) button on the Files panel toolbar to upload your Web site. Click the OK button in response to the Are you sure you wish to put the entire site? dialog box. Review your files to verify that they were uploaded. The files on the remote server may display in a different order from those on the local site.

3. Click the Disconnects from remote host button. Click the Expand/Collapse button on the Files panel toolbar to display the local site and the Document window. Close Dreamweaver.

Apply Your Knowledge

3 Defining and Uploading the Credit Protection Web Site to a Remote Server

Instructions: Perform the following steps to define and upload the Credit Protection Web site to a remote server.

1. If necessary, open Dreamweaver. Click Site on the menu bar, click Manage Sites, and then click Credit Protection. Click the Edit button. Click the Advanced tab and then click Remote Info. Fill in the information as provided by your instructor, and then test the connection. Click the OK button to close the Site Definition dialog box, and then click the Done button to close the Manage Sites dialog box.

2. Click the Expand/Collapse button on the Files panel toolbar and then click the Connects to remote host button. Click the local file root folder and then click the Put File(s) button on the Files panel toolbar to upload your Web site. Click the OK button in response to the Are you sure you wish to put the entire site? dialog box. Upload your files to the remote site. Review your files to verify that they were uploaded. The files on the remote server may display in a different order from those on the local site.

3. Disconnect from the site. Click the Expand/Collapse button on the Files panel toolbar to display the local site and the Document window. Close Dreamweaver.

4 Defining and Uploading the Lexington, NC Web Site to a Remote Server

Instructions: Perform the following steps to define and upload the Lexington, NC Web site to a remote server.

1. If necessary, open Dreamweaver. Click Site on the menu bar, click Manage Sites, and then click Lexington, NC. Click the Edit button. Click the Advanced tab and then click Remote Info. Fill in the information as provided by your instructor, and then test the connection. Click the OK button to close the Site Definition dialog box, and then click the Done button to close the Manage Sites dialog box.

2. Connect to the remote site and then click the local file root folder. Upload your files to the remote site. Disconnect from the site. Click the Expand/Collapse button on the Files panel toolbar to display the local site and the Document window. Close Dreamweaver.

FILE MENU

Action	Shortcut
New	Ctrl+N
Open	Ctrl+O
Browse in Bridge	Ctrl+Alt+O
Open in Frame	Ctrl+Shift+O
Close	Ctrl+W
Close All	Ctrl+Shift+W
Save	Ctrl+S
Save As	Ctrl+Shift+S
Print Code	Ctrl+P
Preview in Browser Submenu	
Firefox	Ctrl+F12
IExplore	F12
Device Central	Ctrl+Alt+F12
Check Page Submenu	
Links	Shift+F8
Validate Submenu	
Markup	Shift+F6

EDIT MENU

Action	Shortcut
Undo	Ctrl+Z or Alt+BkSp
Redo	Ctrl+Y or Ctrl+Shift+Z
Cut	Ctrl+X or Shift+Del
Copy	Ctrl+C or Ctrl+Ins
Paste Special	Ctrl+Shift+V
Paste	Ctrl+V
Select All	Ctrl+A
Select Parent Tag	Ctrl+[
Select Child	Ctrl+]
Find and Replace	Ctrl+F
Find Selection	Shift+F3
Find Next	F3
Go to Line	Ctrl+G
Show Code Hints	Ctrl+Space
Refresh Code Hints	Ctrl+.
Indent Code	Ctrl+Shift+>
Outdent Code	Ctrl+Shift+<
Balance Braces	Ctrl+'
Code Collapse Submenu	
Collapse Selection	Ctrl+Shift+C
Collapse Outside Selection	Ctrl+Alt+C
Expand Selection	Ctrl+Shift+E

Action	Shortcut
Collapse Full Tag	Ctrl+Shift+J
Collapse Outside Full Tag	Ctrl+Alt+J
Expand All	Ctrl+Alt+E
Preferences	Ctrl+U

VIEW MENU

Action	Shortcut
Zoom In	Ctrl+=
Zoom Out	Ctrl+-
Magnification Submenu	
50%	Ctrl+Alt+5
100%	Ctrl+Alt+1
200%	Ctrl+Alt+2
300%	Ctrl+Alt+3
400%	Ctrl+Alt+4
800%	Ctrl+Alt+8
1600%	Ctrl+Alt+6
Fit Selection	Ctrl+Alt+0
Fit All	Ctrl+Shift+0
Fit Width	Ctrl+Alt+Shift+0
Switch Views	Ctrl+`
Refresh Design View	F5
Head Content	Ctrl+Shift+H
Table Mode Submenu	
Expanded Tables Mode	F6
Layout Mode	Alt+F6
Visual Aids Submenu	
Hide All	Ctrl+Shift+I
Rulers Submenu	
Show	Ctrl+Alt+R
Grid Submenu	
Show Grid	Ctrl+Alt+G
Snap To Grid	Ctrl+Alt+Shift+G
Guides Submenu	
Show Guides	Ctrl+;
Lock Guides	Ctrl+Alt+;
Snap To Guides	Ctrl+Shift+;
Guides Snap To Elements	Ctrl+Shift+/
Plugins Submenu	
Play	Ctrl+Alt+P
Stop	Ctrl+Alt+X
Play All	Ctrl+Alt+Shift+P
Stop All	Ctrl+Alt+Shift+X
Show/Hide Panels	F4

INSERT MENU

Action	Shortcut
Tag	Ctrl+E
Image	Ctrl+Alt+I
Media Submenu	
Flash	Ctrl+Alt+F
Table	Ctrl+Alt+T
Named Anchor	Ctrl+Alt+A
HTML Submenu	
Special Characters Submenu	
Line Break	Shift+Return
Non-Breaking Space	Ctrl+Shift+Space
Template Objects Submenu	
Editable Region	Ctrl+Alt+V

MODIFY MENU

Action	Shortcut
Page Properties	Ctrl+J
CSS Styles	Shift+F11
Quick Tag Editor	Ctrl+T
Make Link	Ctrl+L
Remove Link	Ctrl+Shift+L
Table Submenu	
Select Table	Ctrl+A
Merge Cells	Ctrl+Alt+M
Split Cell	Ctrl+Alt+S
Insert Row	Ctrl+M
Insert Column	Ctrl+Shift+A
Delete Row	Ctrl+Shift+M
Delete Column	Ctrl+Shift+-
Increase Column Span	Ctrl+Shift+]
Decrease Column Span	Ctrl+Shift+[
Arrange Submenu	
Align Left	Ctrl+Shift+1
Align Right	Ctrl+Shift+3
Align Top	Ctrl+Shift+4
Align Bottom	Ctrl+Shift+6
Make Same Width	Ctrl+Shift+7
Make Same Height	Ctrl+Shift+9
Timeline Submenu	
Add Object to Timeline	Ctrl+Alt+Shift+T

TEXT MENU

Action	Shortcut
Indent	Ctrl+Alt+]
Outdent	Ctrl+Alt+[
Paragraph Format Submenu	
None	Ctrl+0
Paragraph	Ctrl+Shift+P
Heading 1	Ctrl+1
Heading 2	Ctrl+2
Heading 3	Ctrl+3
Heading 4	Ctrl+4
Heading 5	Ctrl+5
Heading 6	Ctrl+6
Align Submenu	
Left	Ctrl+Alt+Shift+L
Center	Ctrl+Alt+Shift+C
Right	Ctrl+Alt+Shift+R
Justify	Ctrl+Alt+Shift+J
Style Submenu	
Bold	Ctrl+B
Italic	Ctrl+I
Check Spelling	Shift+F7

COMMANDS MENU

Action	Shortcut
Start Recording	Ctrl+Shift+X

SITE MENU

Action	Shortcut
Get	Ctrl+Shift+D
Check Out	Ctrl+Alt+Shift+D
Put	Ctrl+Shift+U
Check In	Ctrl+Alt+Shift+U
Check Links Sitewide	Ctrl+F8

WINDOW MENU

Action	Shortcut
Insert	Ctrl+F2
Properties	Ctrl+F3
CSS Styles	Shift+F11
AP Elements	F2
Databases	Ctrl+Shift+F10
Bindings	Ctrl+F10
Server Behaviors	Ctrl+F9
Components	Ctrl+F7
Files	F8
Assets	F11

Action	Shortcut
Snippets	Shift+F9
Tag Inspector	F9
Behaviors	Shift+F4
Results	F7
Reference	Shift+F1
History	Shift+F10
Frames	Shift+F2
Code Inspector	F10
Timelines	Alt+F9
Show/Hide Panels	F4

HELP MENU

Action	Shortcut
Dreamweaver Help	F1
ColdFusion Help	Ctrl+F1
Reference	Shift+F1

PAGE VIEWS

To toggle the display of	Shortcut
Layout mode	Control+F6
Expanded Tables mode	F6
Live Data mode	Control+R
Live Data	Control+Shift+R
Switch between Design and Code views	Control+`
Head content	Control+Shift+H
Server debug	Control+Shift+G
Refresh Design view	F5
Switch to next document	Control+Tab
Switch to previous document	Control+Shift+Tab
Close window	Control+F4

VIEWING PAGE ELEMENTS

To toggle the display of	Shortcut
Visual aids	Control+Shift+I
Rulers	Control+Alt+R
Guides	Control+;
Lock guides	Control+Alt+;
Snap to guides	Control+Shift+;
Guides snap to elements	Control+Shift+/
Grid	Control+Alt+G
Snap to grid	Control+Alt+Shift+G
Page properties	Control+J

EDITING TEXT

Action	Shortcut
Create a new paragraph	Enter
Insert a line break 	Shift+Enter
Insert a nonbreaking space	Control+Shift+Spacebar
Move text or object to another place in the page	Drag selected item to new location
Copy text or object to another place in the page	Control-drag selected item to new location
Select a word	Double-click
Go to next word	Control+Right
Go to previous word	Control+Left
Go to previous paragraph	Control+Up
Go to next paragraph	Control+Down
Select until next word	Control+Shift+Right
Select from previous word	Control+Shift+Left
Select until next paragraph	Control+Shift+Down
Select from previous paragraph	Control+Shift+Up
Open and close the Property inspector	Control+F3
Check spelling	Shift+F7

FORMATTING TEXT

Action	Shortcut
Indent	Control+Alt+]
Outdent	Control+Alt+[
Format > None	Control+0 (zero)
Paragraph Format	Control+Shift+P
Apply Headings 1 through 6 to a paragraph	Control+1 through 6
Align > Left	Control+Alt+Shift+L
Align > Center	Control+Alt+Shift+C
Align > Right	Control+Alt+Shift+R
Align > Justify	Control+Alt+Shift+J
Make selected text bold	Control+B
Make selected text italic	Control+I

Note: Some text formatting shortcuts have no effect when working in the code editors.

FINDING AND REPLACING TEXT

Action	Shortcut
Find	Control+F
Find next/Find again	F3
Find selection	Shift+F3

CODE EDITING

Action	Shortcut
Switch to Design view	Control+`
Print code	Control+P
Validate markup	Shift+F6
Edit tag	Shift+F5
Open Quick Tag	Editor Control+T
Open Snippets panel	Shift+F9
Show code hints	Control+Spacebar
Insert tag	Control+E
Surround with #	Control+Shift+3
Select parent tag	Control+[
Balance braces	Control+'
Select all	Control+A
Bold	Control+B
Italic	Control+I
Copy	Control+C
Find and replace	Control+F
Find selection	Shift+F3
Find next	F3
Paste	Control+V
Paste Special	n/a
Cut	Control+X
Redo	Control+Y
Undo	Control+Z
Delete word left	Control+Backspace
Delete word right	Control+Delete
Go to line	Control+G
Select line up	Shift+Up
Select line down	Shift+Down
Character select left	Shift+Left
Character select right	Shift+Right
Move to page up	Page Up
Move to page down	Page Down
Select to page up	Shift+Page Up
Select to page down	Shift+Page Down
Move word left	Control+Left
Move word right	Control+Right
Select word left	Control+Shift+Left
Select word right	Control+Shift+Right

Action	Shortcut
Move to start of line	Home
Move to end of line	End
Select to start of line	Shift+Home
Select to end of line	Shift+End
Move to top of code	Control+Home
Move to end of code	Control+End
Select to top of code	Control+Shift+Home
Select to end of code	Control+Shift+End
Collapse selection	Control+Shift+C
Collapse outside selection	Control+Alt+C
Expand selection	Control+Shift+E
Collapse full tag	Control+Shift+J
Collapse outside full tag	Control+Alt+J
Expand All	Control+Alt+E

WORKING IN TABLES

Action	Shortcut
Select table (with insertion point inside the table)	Control+A (+A, +A)
Move to the next cell	Tab
Move to the previous cell	Shift+Tab
Insert a row (before current)	Control+M
Add a row at end of table	Tab in the last cell
Delete the current row	Control+Shift+M
Insert a column	Control+Shift+A
Delete a column	Control+Shift+ - (hyphen)
Merge selected table cells	Control+Alt+M
Split table cell	Control+Alt+S
Increase column span	Control+Shift+]
Decrease column span	Control+Shift+[

Note: Some table shortcuts do not work in Layout view.

WORKING IN FRAMES

Action	Shortcut
Select a frame	Alt-click in frame
Select next frame or frameset	Alt+Right Arrow
Select previous frame or frameset	Alt+Left Arrow
Select parent frameset	Alt+Up Arrow

Action	Shortcut
Select first child frame or frameset	Alt+Down Arrow
Add a new frame to frameset	Alt-drag frame border
Add a new frame to frameset using push method	Alt+Control-drag frame border

WORKING WITH TEMPLATES

Action	Shortcut
Create new editable region	Control+Alt+V

WORKING WITH AP ELEMENTS

Action	Shortcut
Select an element	Control+Shift-click
Select and move element	Shift+Control-drag
Add or remove element from selection	Shift-click element border
Move selected element by pixels	Arrow keys
Move selected element by snapping increment	Shift+arrow keys
Resize selected element by pixels	Control+arrow keys
Resize selected element by snapping increment	Control+Shift+arrow keys
Align element left	Control+Shift+1
Align element right	Control+Shift+3
Align element top	Control+Shift+4
Align element bottom	Control+Shift+6
Make same width	Control+Shift+7
Make same height	Control+Shift+9

WORKING WITH THE TIMELINE

Action	Shortcut
Display Timeline	Alt+F9
Add object to Timeline	Control+Alt+Shift+T

WORKING WITH IMAGES

Action	Shortcut
Change image source attribute	Double-click image
Edit image in external editor	Control-double-click image

ZOOMING

Action	Shortcut
Zoom in	Control+=
Zoom out	Control+-
Magnify 50%	Control+Alt+5
Magnify 100%	Control+Alt+1
Magnify 200%	Control+Alt+2
Fit selection	Control+Alt+0
Fit all	Control+Shift+0
Fit width	Control+Shift+Alt+0
Switch to Zoom mode from Regular mode	Shift+Control+Alt+Z
Switch to Regular mode from Zoom mode	V+0
Switch to Hand mode from Regular mode	Shift+Control+Alt+H
Switch to Hand mode from Zoom mode	H+Spacebar

MANAGING HYPERLINKS

Action	Shortcut
Check links	Shift+F8
Create hyperlink (select text)	Control+L
Remove hyperlink	Control+Shift+L
Drag and drop to create a hyperlink from a document	Select the text, image, or object, then Shift-drag the selection to a file in the Files panel
Drag and drop to create a hyperlink using the Property inspector	Select the text, image, or object, then drag the point-to-file icon in Property inspector to a file in the Files panel
Open the linked-to document in Dreamweaver	Control-double-click link
Check links in the entire site	Control+F8

TARGETING AND PREVIEWING IN BROWSERS

Action	Shortcut
Preview in primary browser	F12
Preview in secondary browser	Shift+F12 or Control+F12

DEBUGGING IN BROWSERS

Action	Shortcut
Debug in primary browser	Alt+F12
Debug in secondary browser	Control+Alt+F12

SITE MANAGEMENT AND FTP

Action	Shortcut
Refresh	F5
Create new file	Control+Shift+N
Create new folder	Control+Alt+Shift+N
Delete file	Delete
Copy file	Control+C
Cut file	Control+X
Paste file	Control+V
Duplicate file	Control+D
Rename file	F2
Get selected files or folders from remote FTP site	Control+Shift+D or drag files from Remote to Local pane in Files panel
Put selected files or folders to remote FTP site	Control+Shift+U or drag files from Local to Remote pane in Files panel
Check out	Control+Alt+Shift+D
Check in	Control+Alt+Shift+U
View site map	Alt+F8
Cancel FTP	Escape

SITE MAP

Action	Shortcut
View site files	F8
View as root	Control+Shift+R
Link to existing file	Control+Shift+K
Change link	Control+L
Remove link	Control+Shift+L
Show/Hide link	Control+Shift+Y
Show page titles	Control+Shift+T

PLAYING PLUGINS

Action	Shortcut
Play plugin	Control+Alt+P
Stop plugin	Control+Alt+X
Play all plugins	Control+Alt+Shift+P
Stop all plugins	Control+Alt+Shift+X

INSERTING OBJECTS

Action	Shortcut
Any object (image, Shockwave movie, and so on)	Drag file from the Explorer or Files panel to the Document window
Image	Control+Alt+I
Table	Control+Alt+T
Flash	Control+Alt+F
Shockwave	Control+Alt+D
Named anchor	Control+Alt+A

OPENING AND CLOSING PANELS

Action	Shortcut
Insert bar	Control+F2
Properties	Control+F3
CSS Styles	Shift+F11
Behaviors	Shift+F4
Tag Inspector	F9
Snippets	Shift+F9
Reference	Shift+F1
Databases	Control+Shift+F10
Bindings	Control+F10
Server Behaviors	Control+F9
Components	Control+F7
Files	F8
Assets	F11
Results	F7
Code inspector	F10
Frames	Shift+F2
History	Shift+F10
AP Elements	F2
Timeline	Alt+F9
Show/Hide panels	F4

Index